Henrik Ibsen
Plays: Five

Brand, Emperor and Galilean

These two mighty plays, along with the equally ambitious *Peer Gynt* and *The Pretenders*, form a great epic quartet that stands at the fulcrum of Ibsen's career. They mark the end of a spate of largely forgotten romantic comedies and historical tragedies and seem to clear the ground for the twelve great prose plays which occupied the last decades of his life.

Though never intended for performance, *Brand* has been successfully staged in Britain several times. *Emperor and Galilean*, consisting of two linked five-act plays, has been broadcast in Britain but not yet staged.

Michael Meyer's translations have won praise for their accuracy and liveliness on both stage and page. They have been performed extensively in the theatre and on radio and television. 'Where previous translators have adopted either a stiffly Victorian style, or one so modern as to destroy the illusion that we were seeing a period play, Mr Meyer has found a form of speech common both to the period in which the plays were written and to the present.' (*The Times*.) 'Meyer's translations of Ibsen are a major fact in one's general sense of post-war drama. Their vital pace, their unforced insistence on the poetic centre of Ibsen's genius, have beaten academic versions from the field.' (George Steiner, *New Statesman*.)

Michael Meyer is also Ibsen's biographer and a leading authority on his work. This edition includes Meyer's illuminating introductions to each play, as well as a chronology of Ibsen's life and writings.

Also by Henrik Ibsen
in the Methuen World Classics series
translated and introduced by Michael Meyer

PLAYS: ONE
Ghosts, The Wild Duck, The Master Builder

PLAYS: TWO
A Doll's House, An Enemy of the People, Hedda Gabler

PLAYS: THREE
Rosmersholm, Little Eyolf, The Lady from the Sea

PLAYS: FOUR
John Gabriel Borkman, The Pillars of Society,
When We Dead Awaken

PLAYS: SIX
Peer Gynt, The Pretenders

Available in Methuen Student Editions

A Doll's House
Ghosts

HENRIK IBSEN

Plays : Five

Brand

Emperor and Galilean

Translated and introduced by
Michael Meyer

Methuen Drama

METHUEN WORLD CLASSICS

This collection first published in Great Britain in paperback
in 1986 by Methuen London Ltd
Reissued with a new cover design 1994
by Methuen Drama
an imprint of Reed Consumer Books Ltd
Michelin House, 81 Fulham Road, London SW3 6RB
and Auckland, Melbourne, Singapore and Toronto

Brand was first published in Great Britain in 1960 by Rupert
Hart-Davis Ltd, and subsequently by Methuen and Co Ltd.,
in 1967. Reprinted 1973, 1978 and 1981 by Eyre
Methuen Ltd. Reprinted by Methuen London Ltd, in 1982.
Copyright © Michael Meyer 1960. Introduction copyright ©
Michael Meyer 1960.

Emperor and Galilean was first published in this translation in
this edition. Copyright © Michael Meyer 1986. Introduction
Copyright © Michael Meyer 1986.

Ibsen, Henrik
   Plays, five.—(World dramatists)
   1. Norwegian drama—Translations into English
   2. English Drama—Translations from Norwegian
   I. Title   II. Series
   839.8′226   PT8854

   ISBN 0 413 60490 X

The front cover shows a detail from *Manfred on the Jungfrau* (1837)
by John Martin, reproduced by courtesy of Birmingham
Museums and Art Gallery

Printed in Great Britain by
Cox & Wyman Ltd, Reading, Berkshire

Contents

Henrik Johan Ibsen: A Chronology

1828   Born at Skien in south-east Norway on 20 March, the second child of Knud Ibsen, a merchant, and his wife Marichen, *née* Altenburg.

1834-5   Father becomes ruined. The family moves to Venstoep, a few miles outside Skien.

1844   Ibsen (aged fifteen) becomes assistant to an apothecary at Grimstad, a tiny seaport further down the coast. Stays there for six years in great poverty.

1846   Has an illegitimate son with a servant-girl, Else Sofie Jensdatter.

1849   Writes his first play, *Catiline* (in verse).

1850   Leaves Grimstad to become a student in Christiania (now Oslo). Writes second play, *The Warrior's Barrow*.

1851   Is invited to join Ole Bull's newly formed National Theatre at Bergen. Does so, and stays six years, writing, directing, designing costumes and keeping the accounts.

1852   Visits Copenhagen and Dresden to learn about the theatre. Writes *St John's Eve*, a romantic comedy in verse and prose.

1853   *St John's Eve* acted at Bergen. Failure.

1854   Writes *Lady Inger of Oestraat*, an historical tragedy in prose.

1855   *Lady Inger of Oestraat* acted at Bergen. Failure. Writes *The Feast at Solhaug*, another romantic verse-and-prose comedy.

1856   *The Feast at Solhaug* acted at Bergen. Small success. Meets Suzannah Thoresen. Writes *Olaf Liljekrans*, a third verse-and-prose comedy.

1857   *Olaf Liljekrans* acted at Bergen. Failure. Leaves Bergen to become artistic manager of the Christiania Norwegian Theatre. Writes *The Vikings at Helgeland*, an historical prose tragedy.

1858   Marries Suzannah Thoresen. *The Vikings at Helgeland* staged. Small success.

1859   Their only child, Sigurd, born.

1860-1 Years of poverty and despair. Unable to write.

1862   Writes *Love's Comedy*, a modern verse satire, his first play for five years. It is rejected by his own theatre, which goes bankrupt.

1863   Ibsen gets part-time job as literary adviser to the Danish-controlled Christiania Theatre. Extremely poor. Applies unsuccessfully to Government for financial support. Resorts to moneylenders. Writes *The Pretenders*, another historical prose tragedy. Is granted a travel stipend by the Government; this is augmented by a collection raised by Bjoernson and other friends.

1864   *The Pretenders* staged in Christiania. A success. He leaves Norway and settles in Rome. Remains resident abroad for the next twenty-seven years. Begins *Emperor and Galilean*.

1865   Writes *Brand*, in verse (as a play for reading, not acting), in Rome and Ariccia.

1866   *Brand* published. Immense success; Ibsen becomes famous throughout Scandinavia (but it is not acted for nineteen years).

1867   Writes *Peer Gynt*, in verse (also to be read, not acted), in Rome, Ischia and Sorrento. It, too, is a great success; but is not staged for seven years.

1868   Moves from Rome and settles in Dresden.

1869   Attends opening of Suez Canal as Norwegian delegate. Completes *The League of Youth*, a modern prose comedy.

1871   Revises his shorter poems and issues them in a volume. His farewell to verse; for the rest of his life he publishes exclusively in prose.

1873   Completes (after nine years) *Emperor and Galilean*, his last historical play. Begins to be known in Germany and England.

1874   Returns briefly to Norway for first time in ten years. The students hold a torchlight procession in his honour.

1875   Leaves Dresden after seven years and settles in Munich. Begins *The Pillars of Society*, the first of his twelve great modern prose dramas.

1876   *Peer Gynt* staged for first time. *The Vikings at Helgeland* is performed in Munich, the first of his plays to be staged outside Scandinavia.

1877   Completes *The Pillars of Society*. This makes him famous in Germany, where it is widely acted.

1878   Returns to Italy for a year.

1879   Writes *A Doll's House* in Rome and Amalfi. It causes an immediate sensation, though a decade elapses before it makes Ibsen internationally famous. Returns for a year to Munich.

1880   Resettles in Italy for a further five years. First performance of an Ibsen play in England (*The Pillars of Society* for a single matinée in London).

1881   Writes *Ghosts* in Rome and Sorrento. Violently attacked; all theatres reject it, and bookshops return it to the publisher.

1882   Writes *An Enemy of the People* in Rome. Cordially received. *Ghosts* receives its first performance (in Chicago).

1884   Writes *The Wild Duck* in Rome and Gossensass. It, and all his subsequent plays, were regarded as obscure and were greeted with varying degrees of bewilderment.

1885   Revisits Norway again, for the first time since 1874. Leaves Rome and resettles in Munich.

1886   Writes *Rosmersholm* in Munich.

1888   Writes *The Lady from the Sea* in Munich.

1889   Meets and becomes infatuated with the eighteen-year-old Emilie Bardach in Gossensass. Does not see her again, but the experience shadows the remainder of his writing. Janet Achurch acts Nora in London, the first major English-speaking production of Ibsen.

1890   Writes *Hedda Gabler* in Munich.

1891   Returns to settle permanently in Norway.

1892   Writes *The Master Builder* in Christiania.

1894   Writes *Little Eyolf* in Christiania.

1896   Writes *John Gabriel Borkman* in Christiania.

1899   Writes *When We Dead Awaken* in Christiania.

1901   First stroke. Partly paralysed.

1903   Second stroke. Left largely helpless.

1906   Dies in Christiania on 23 May, aged seventy-eight.

Brand

Introduction

In 1863 Ibsen's fortunes were at their lowest ebb. He had written nine plays, six of them historical. Of these the first, *Catiline*, had never been performed; *The Warrior's Barrow*, *St John's Eve*, *Lady Inger of Oestraat* and *Olaf Liljekrans* had appeared, all with disastrous results; only two, *The Feast at Solhaug* and *The Vikings at Helgeland*, had achieved any recognition at all, and that very limited. Worst of all, his most recent play, *Love's Comedy*, had been rejected, and the Norwegian Theatre of Christiania, where he had for seven years been artistic director, had gone bankrupt. Thus, at the age of thirty-five, he found himself virtually penniless, dependent on a tiny university grant and an even tinier salary which he received from the Danish Theatre of Christiania as literary adviser. With a wife and small son to support, he had to resort to moneylenders. Moreover, the Norwegian Parliament had rejected his application for a poet's stipend, while granting the applications of his fellow-poets Bjoernson and Vinje.

Fortunately, just when he must have been very close to despair, he achieved his first real success, with *The Pretenders*. First staged on 17 January 1864, it was presented eight times in less than two months – 'a success', says Professor Halvdan Koht, 'unique for a play as long and serious as this in a town as small as the Christiania of those days. . . . Now for the first time he rested in a full and free confidence in his own ability to write, and in his calling as a poet.'

At this juncture another piece of good fortune came his way, for he received the news that an order in council had allotted him 400 specie-dollars (about £100) for foreign travel. This was, in fact, much too small a sum to enable him to undertake the long journey southwards on which he had set his heart, but Bjoernson helped him to scrape together a little more, and when the ice broke in the spring of 1864 Ibsen set off towards Rome.

The war between Denmark and Germany over Schleswig-Holstein had just broken out, and the refusal of Norway and Sweden to help her Scandinavian neighbour angered Ibsen. While he was in Copenhagen that April, on the way to Rome, news arrived of the fall of Dybboel to German troops; and next month, when he reached Berlin, he saw the Danish cannons captured at Dybboel being led in triumph through the streets of the capital, while Germans lining the route spat at them. 'It was for me', Ibsen wrote, 'a sign that, some day, history would spit in the eyes of Sweden and Norway for their part in this affair.' Later, looking back on this period, he wrote: 'It was now that *Brand* began to grow inside me like a foetus.'

He reached Rome in the middle of June. A few days later the Scandinavian community there held a small farewell party before breaking up to go to the country and so escape the summer heat. Ibsen attended this party, and his friend Lorenz Dietrichson has described the scene. 'It was the first evening for some while that Ibsen had spent among Scandinavians, and he began to speak of the painful and disturbing impressions of recent events in the war which he had received on his journey. Gradually and almost imperceptibly, his talk took on the character of an improvised speech; all the bitterness which had for so long been stored up within him, all the fiery indignation and passion for the Scandinavian cause which he had bottled up for so long, found an outlet. His voice began to ring, and in the evening dusk one saw only his burning eyes. When he had finished, no one cried Bravo or raised his glass, but I think we all felt that that evening the Marseillaise of the North had rung out into the Roman night air.'

Writing to his mother-in-law, Magdalene Thoresen, Ibsen angrily described how Danes in Rome were attending Sunday service in the German church, and sat silent in their pews while the German pastor prayed for victory for the Prussian arms in their righteous cause.

After a fortnight in Rome, Ibsen moved out to the small hill town of Genzano, and stayed there for two months. Lorenz Dietrichson was living there with his family, and it was during a conversation with Dietrichson that Ibsen first conceived the idea of writing a tragedy about the Emperor Julian – the play that, slowly and with many interruptions, developed over the next nine years into *Emperor and Galilean*. It was in Genzano, too, that he began to write an epic poem. Shortly after he returned to Rome in the autumn, he mentioned in a letter that 'for some time I have been working on a big poem', optimistically adding that he hoped to have both that and the play about Julian ready by the following spring or summer. This poem was called *Brand*.

Ibsen based it on a Danish poem written some twenty years previously, Frederik Paludan-Müller's *Adam Homo*. Paludan-Müller's chief character was an everyday man who shunned ideals and compromised incessantly with the world and with himself. Ibsen intended his chief character to be the exact opposite of *Adam Homo* – a man who shunned compromise.

Then, in September, a young Norwegian named Christopher Bruun arrived in Rome.

He was a theologian, but was hesitating to take Holy Orders because he felt that life and the teaching of the Norwegian State Church were incompatible. Like Ibsen, he had been angered by the German attack on Denmark but, unlike Ibsen, he had volunteered as a soldier, and had fought with the Danes at the battle of Dybboel. Ibsen got to know Bruun at once – he had already seen a good deal of Bruun's mother and sister at Genzano. They discussed the war, and Bruun asked Ibsen why, if he felt so strongly, he had not volunteered himself. 'We poets have other tasks to perform,' Ibsen replied; but a doubt remained in his mind. He wondered whether he had been right to compromise; and with this doubt was linked

another. Was he right to believe so inflexibly in his calling as
a writer and thus, in all probability, condemn his wife and
child to continued poverty so that he might follow this calling?

Ibsen had already decided to make the chief character of
his long poem a discontented priest, and had at first based him
on his own memories of a revivalist named G. A. Lammers,
who had converted Ibsen's parents and brothers in Skien
during the eighteen-fifties. Bruun's personality now began to
intrude into the character of Brand, and his ideas into the
subject-matter of the poem. Ibsen struggled painfully with it
throughout the autumn, winter, spring and summer, while at
the same time doing historical research for *Emperor and Galilean*. At length, in July 1865, at Ariccia, a small town south of
Rome, he threw aside the poem, of which he had completed
some two hundred stanzas, and decided to rewrite it as a poetic
drama.

At first this, too, progressed slowly and with difficulty. Ibsen
has described how the turning-point came. In a letter to
Bjoernson, dated 12 September 1865, he wrote:

'I did not know where to turn. Then, one day, I went into
St Peter's – I had gone into Rome on some business – and
suddenly everything I wanted to say appeared to me in a strong
and clear light. I have thrown overboard the work with which
I had been torturing myself for a year without getting anywhere, and in the middle of July I started on something new
which has been making such progress as no other work of
mine has ever done. . . . It is a dramatic poem, of serious
content; contemporary subject-matter – five acts in rhymed
verse (but no *Love's Comedy*). The fourth act is almost finished,
and I feel I shall be able to complete the fifth in a week. I
work both morning and afternoon, which I have never been
able to do before. It is blessedly peaceful out here; no one I
know. I read nothing but the Bible.'

Ibsen finished the dramatic version of *Brand* in three months.
The fifth act (about a third of the play) took longer than the

week he had predicted, but he managed it in a little under five weeks, and by mid-October the play was ready to be posted to his Danish publisher, Hegel of Gyldendal's. Hegel could not get it out in time for Christmas, as Ibsen had hoped, and it was not until 15 March 1866 that *Brand* appeared on the bookstalls. It created an immediate and widespread sensation throughout Scandinavia, where the movement toward liberalism and individualism was just reaching its climax. *Brand* stated sharply and vividly the necessity of following one's private conscience and 'being oneself' and it ran quickly through three editions. A fourth was in the press by the end of the year. Georg Brandes has described the effect which *Brand* had on the Scandinavia of the time:

'It was a book which left no reader cold. Every receptive and unblunted mind felt, on closing the book, a penetrating, nay, an overwhelming impression of having stood face to face with a great and indignant genius, before whose piercing glance weakness felt itself compelled to cast down its eyes. What made the impression less definite, namely, the fact that this mastermind was not quite clear and transparent, rendered it, on the other hand, all the more fascinating.'

And August Strindberg, who was seventeen when *Brand* appeared, later called it 'the voice of a Savonarola'.

The influence of Paludan-Müller's *Adam Homo* on *Brand* has already been noted. Another important literary influence may (though some dispute it) have been the Danish philosopher Kierkegaard. Georg Brandes, writing the year after *Brand* appeared, observed: 'It actually seems as if Ibsen had aspired to the honour of being called Kierkegaard's poet'; and it has been suggested that it was Kierkegaard's *Either-Or* which gave Ibsen the idea of 'All or Nothing'. A more probable influence, in my opinion, is Kierkegaard's *Fear and Trembling*, which dwells continually on the legend of Abraham and Isaac. 'No one was as great as Abraham, and who is capable of understanding him?'; the sentence might well serve to sum up *Brand*. There are other sentences in *Fear and Trembling* which apply to *Brand*: 'There was the man who was great through his strength, and the man who was great through his wisdom, and the man who was great through his hope, and the man who was great through his love; but Abraham was greater than any of these, great through the power whose strength is weakness, great through the wisdom whose secret is foolishness, great through the hope whose expression is madness, great through the love which is hatred of oneself.' And elsewhere there is a reference to 'that vast passion which disdains the fury of the elements and the powers of creation in order to battle with God'. Moreover *Fear and Trembling* contains a long section on the legend of Agnes and the Triton, and I think it possible that Ibsen, consciously or unconsciously, may have taken his heroine's name from this passage. He based the character of Agnes largely on Bruun's sister, Thea; and Bruun was an ardent disciple of Kierkegaard.

A journey which Ibsen had made through the Norwegian countryside in 1862 to gather folk-lore also left its mark on the play. Many of the descriptions of natural scenery in *Brand* stem from this journey – for example, the steep descent from the Sogn mountains, and the dangers of life in a fjordside village with its storms and landslips.

Although the character of Brand was based partly on that of the revivalist, G. A. Lammers, and partly on that of Christopher Bruun, Ibsen also, by his own admission, put a good deal of himself into the part: 'Brand,' he once said, 'is myself in my best moments.' He later wrote to Georg Brandes that he could, in fact, as easily have made Brand a sculptor or a politician, or even Galileo – 'except that then of course he would have to have held strongly to his beliefs, and not pretended that the earth stood still'. I suspect that Ejnar, the painter, represented Ibsen's idea of himself in his worst moments; Ibsen was an accomplished painter and in his youth had seriously considered following art instead of literature as a profession.

A great deal has been written about the symbolism of *Brand*, and the different significances that might be attached to the hawk, the Ice Church, and so forth. Dr Arne Duve, in his stimulating book *Symbolikken i Henrik Ibsens Skuespill*, suggests that the hawk represents the life of the emotions, i.e. love, and that it is Brand's fear of the powers of life and light that makes him, in the fifth act, dismiss the hawk contemptuously as 'the spirit of compromise'. The Ice Church, Dr Duve thinks, represents the opposite of the hawk, i.e. the negation of love. Gerd, like Brand, fears and distrusts love (like him, she is the daughter of a loveless marriage), and Brand's negation of love finally leads him, too, to the terrible citadel of the Ice Church; what Ibsen, thirty years later in *John Gabriel Borkman*, was to term 'the coldness of the heart'. The Ice Church finally killed Brand, just as the coldness of the heart killed John Gabriel Borkman. On the other hand, Michael Elliott, who directed the brilliant and acclaimed 1959 production at Hammersmith, believed that the hawk represents nothing as specific as love, but rather in a general way, 'whatever one rejects', just as Room 101 in George Orwell's *1984* contained 'the worst thing in the world', whatever that might be. I agree with this theory, and believe that the Ice Church stands for the false citadel which each of us builds in his own imagination as a refuge from his particular hawk.

Ibsen never intended *Brand* for the stage; he wrote it, as he wrote *Peer Gynt* eighteen months later, simply to be read. His years as a dramatist and a theatre director had made him bitterly aware of the technical limitations of the theatre and its audiences. Consequently he chose a form in which he need make no concessions to these limitations. He wrote scenes which demand, among other things, a storm at sea and an avalanche; and his final version was, like *Peer Gynt*, more than twice the length of an average play.

Despite *Brand*'s success with the reading public, nineteen years passed before anyone attempted to stage it. At length, on 24 March 1885, Ludvig Josephson presented it at Nya Teatern in Stockholm. August Lindberg has described the first night. 'It lasted for six and a half hours, until 12.30 a.m. Such ladies as survived to the end lay dozing on their escorts' shoulders, with their corsets and bodices unbuttoned.' In spite of its length, however, the play proved a success, and during the next two decades *Brand* was performed in almost every European country which boasted a serious theatre, except England. Lugné-Poe produced it at his Théâtre de L'Oeuvre in Paris in 1895, and it was staged in several towns in Germany around the turn of the century. Strangely enough, it was not produced in Norway until 1904, but it has since been revived there on a number of occasions, and remains one of Ibsen's most admired and most quoted plays in his own country. It was especially successful in Russia in the early years of this century; it was introduced into the repertory of the Moscow Arts Theatre in 1907, and caused excitement by its outspoken criticisms of society. The Russians introduced it to America when they visited New York in 1912; and in 1928 the Pitoëffs scored a success with it in Paris, in a production which used ultra-simple décor.

England, as usual, had to wait longer than most other countries before seeing the play, although Edmund Gosse had written about it at considerable length as early as January 1873 (in a long article in the *Fortnightly Review* entitled 'Ibsen, the Norwegian Satirist'), and at least three separate translations into English had been made before the end of the century. In June 1893 the fourth act was presented as a curtain-raiser to *The Master Builder* for two matinées and two evening performances, during a three-weeks Ibsen season at the Opera Comique in London; Bernard Gould[1] played Brand, Elizabeth

---

[1] Alias Bernard Partridge, the well-known artist.

Robins Agnes, and Frances Ivor the Gipsy Woman. On 29 November 1911 the Ibsen Club staged the fourth act (with the last act of *A Doll's House*) at the Ibsen Rehearsal Studio in London, but the play was not presented in a complete form until 10 November 1912, when the Irish actor, W. G. Fay, produced it in William Wilson's prose translation at the Royal Court Theatre for a single performance under the auspices of the Play Actors. *The Times*, after deploring the omission of the scene between Brand and his mother, and that in which Brand decides to give up his first mission and settle down in the fjordside village, went on:

'Mr W. G. Fay, the producer, had done his work well. . . . The difficulties of arrangement he had overcome skilfully and fairly. Into his company he had instilled some at least of the speed which the passionate, soaring, plunging poem demands. In the part of Agnes . . . Miss Phyllis Relph did well, especially in that wonderful scene where Agnes, having learned from Brand to make the last sacrifice by giving away all her dead baby's clothes to the gipsy woman, soars clean above Brand's head and points him the way to his own goal. Miss Mignon Clifford gave a very lively and understanding portrait of Gerd, the wild girl. . . . As to the Brand of Mr H. A. Saintsbury, we are in a difficulty. In appearance and bearing, he was so wholly unlike our idea of Brand that we have not yet found our way about his performance. It seemed, we must admit, very experienced, very clever, and nothing more. But we can quite believe that what we saw as a mincing, prelatical Brand, entirely lacking the burliness, the vitality, the passion of the man, had good qualities, which would emerge on further acquaintance.'

On 11 December 1936, Hilton Edwards produced *Brand* at the Gate Theatre, Dublin, with Michael Mac Liammoir as Brand and Meriel Moore as Agnes. The Cambridge A.D.C. presented it at Cambridge in December 1945, in a production by John Prudhoe, with Richard Bebb-Williams as Brand, Ann Mankowitz as Agnes, and Lyndon Brook as Ejnar. A version by James Forsyth was broadcast in the B.B.C. Third Programme on 11 December 1949, with Ralph Richardson as Brand, Sybil Thorndike as Brand's mother, Margaret Leighton as Agnes, and Louise Hutton as Gerd, and again on 30 December 1956, this time with Stephen Murray as Brand, Fay Compton as Brand's mother, Ursula Howells as Agnes and June Tobin as Gerd. Both productions were by Val Gielgud. Apart from the solitary performance in 1912, however, London had to wait until 8 April 1959 to see a full production of *Brand*. On that date it was presented at the Lyric Opera House, Hammersmith, by the 59 Theatre Company, in a production by Michael Elliott, with the cast named on page 20.

In 1906, when Ibsen was dying, Christopher Bruun, the man who had largely inspired the character of Brand nearly half a century before, came to visit him. The two had remained friends, and Bruun had baptized Ibsen's grandchild. They had always kept off the subject of religion, but now, in the presence of death, Bruun tentatively touched on the subject of Ibsen's relationship to God. Ibsen's answer was short and characteristic. 'You leave that to me!' he growled; and Bruun did.

MICHAEL MEYER

Note on the Translation

Ibsen composed *Brand* in rhymed octosyllabics, varying his rhyming scheme with extraordinary skill. If one listens to the play in Norwegian, one almost forgets that rhyme is being used, although it plays an important part in giving an epigrammatic point to key statements, and reinforcing the strength and dignity of the language.

The present translation avoids rhyme, but otherwise keeps closely to Ibsen's text, except where cuts have been made. Ibsen, writing in 1865, included long discussions on topical issues, such as the Schleswig-Holstein war, the need for land reform, and the danger of an industrial revolution. Although these sections still read vividly as satirical verse, they digress from the main thread of the play, and have been omitted. Other cuts have been made for the sake of dramatic concision, though these are fewer and shorter than might have been supposed necessary.

I gladly express my thanks to Michael Elliott for much patient advice; also to the 59 Theatre Company for commissioning this translation.

M.M.

This translation was commissioned by the 59 Theatre Company, and presented by them on 8 April 1959, at the Lyric Opera House, Hammersmith. The cast was:

BRAND	Patrick McGoohan
A GUIDE	Robert Bernal
GUIDE'S SON	William McLaughlin
AGNES	Dilys Hamlett
EJNAR	Harold Lang
GERD	Olive McFarland
MAYOR	Patrick Wymark
WOMAN FROM THE HEADLAND	June Bailey
A VILLAGER	Fulton MacKay
SECOND VILLAGER	Frank Windsor
BRAND'S MOTHER	Enid Lorimer
DOCTOR	Peter Sallis
GIPSY WOMAN	Anita Giorgi
SEXTON	Robert Bernal
SCHOOLMASTER	Frank Windsor
PROVOST	Peter Sallis

Produced by Michael Elliott. Designed by Richard Negri.

The action takes place in and around a village on the west coast of Norway, and in the mountains above it.

Time: the middle of the last century.

ACT   I   High in the mountains
ACT   II   Scene   I   A village by the fjord
            Scene   II   A farm above the fjord
ACT III   Outside Brand's house
ACT   IV   Inside Brand's house
ACT   V   Scene   I   The new church
            Scene   II   By the highest farm above the village
            Scene III   High in the mountains

Act One

In the snow, high up in the wilds of the mountains. Mist hangs densely. It is raining, and nearly dark. BRAND, *dressed in black, with pack and staff, is struggling towards the west. His companions, a* GUIDE *and the* GUIDE'S YOUNG SON, *follow a short distance behind.*

GUIDE (*shouts after* BRAND).
    Hi, there, stranger! Don't go so fast!
    Where are you?
BRAND. Here.
GUIDE. You'll lose your way. This mist's so thick
    I can hardly see the length of my staff.
SON. Father, there's a crack in the snow!
GUIDE. A crevasse!
BRAND. We have lost all trace of the path.
GUIDE (*shouts*). Stop, man, for God's sake. The glacier's
    As thin as a crust here. Tread lightly.
BRAND (*listening*). I can hear the roar of a waterfall.
GUIDE. A river has hollowed its way beneath us.
    There's an abyss here too deep to fathom.
    It will swallow us up.
BRAND. I must go on. I told you before.
GUIDE. It's beyond mortal power. Feel!
    The ground here is hollow and brittle.
    Stop! It's life or death.
BRAND. I must. I serve a great master.
GUIDE. What's his name?
BRAND. His name is God.
GUIDE. Who are you?
BRAND. A priest.

GUIDE (*goes cautiously closer*).
>Listen, priest. We've only one life.
>Once that's lost, we don't get another.
>There's a frozen mountain lake ahead,
>And mountain lakes are treacherous.

BRAND. We will walk across it.

GUIDE. Walk on water? (*Laughs.*)

BRAND. It has been done.

GUIDE. Ah, that was long ago. There are no miracles now.
>You sink without trace.

BRAND. Farewell. (*Begins to move on.*)

GUIDE. You'll die.

BRAND. If my master needs my death
>Then welcome flood and cataract and storm.

GUIDE (*quietly*). He's mad.

SON (*almost crying*).
>Father, let's turn back. There's a storm coming on.

BRAND (*stops, and goes back towards them*). Listen, guide.
>Didn't you say your daughter has sent you word
>That she is dying, and cannot go in peace
>Unless she sees you first?

GUIDE. It's true, God help me.

BRAND. And she cannot live beyond today?

GUIDE. Yes.

BRAND. Then, come!

GUIDE. It's impossible. Turn back.

BRAND (*gazes at him*).
>What would you give for your daughter to die in peace?

GUIDE. I'd give everything I have, my house and farm, gladly.

BRAND. But not your life?

GUIDE. My life?

BRAND. Well?

GUIDE. There's a limit. I've a wife and children at home.

BRAND. Go home. Your life is the way of death.
>You do not know God, and God does not know you.

GUIDE. You're hard.

SON (*tugging at his coat*). Come on, father.

GUIDE. All right. But he must come too.

BRAND. Must I? (*Turns. A hollow roar is heard in the distance.*)

SON (*screams*). An avalanche!

BRAND (*to the* GUIDE, *who has grabbed him by the collar*). Let go!

GUIDE. No.

BRAND. Let go at once!

GUIDE (*wrestling with* BRAND). No, the Devil take me – !

BRAND (*tears himself loose, and throws the* GUIDE *in the snow*).

>   He will, you can be sure. In the end.

GUIDE (*sits rubbing his arm*).

>   Ah! Stubborn fool! But he's strong.
>   So that's what he calls the Lord's work.
>   (*Shouts, as he gets up.*) Hi, priest!

SON. He's gone over the pass.

GUIDE. I can still see him. (*Shouts again.*) Hi, there!
>   Where did we leave the road?

BRAND (*from the mist*).

>   You need no signpost. Your road is broad enough.

GUIDE. I wish to God it was.
>   Then I'd be warm at home by nightfall.

He and his SON *exeunt towards the east.*

BRAND (*appears higher up, and looks in the direction in which
        they have gone*).

>   They grope their way home. You coward!
>   If you'd had the will and only lacked the strength,
>   I would have helped you. Footsore as I am,
>   I could have carried you on my tired back
>   Gladly and easily. (*Moves on again.*)
>   Ha; how men love life! They'll sacrifice
>   Anything else, but life – no, that must be saved.

He smiles, as though remembering something.

When I was a boy, I remember,

Two thoughts kept occurring to me, and made me laugh.
An owl frightened by darkness, and a fish
Afraid of water. Why did I think of them?
Because I felt, dimly, the difference
Between what is and what should be; between
Having to endure, and finding one's burden
Unendurable.
            Every man
Is such an owl and such a fish, created
To work in darkness, to live in the deep;
And yet he is afraid. He splashes
In anguish towards the shore, stares at the bright
Vault of heaven, and screams: 'Give me air
And the blaze of day.'
What was that? It sounded like singing.
Yes, there it is – laughter and song.
The sun shines. The mist is lifting.
Now I see the whole mountain plain.
A happy crowd of people stands
In the morning sunshine on the mountain top.
Now they are separating. The others
Turn to the east, but two go westwards.
They wave farewell.

The sun breaks more brightly through the mist. He stands looking down at the approaching figures.

                       Light shines about these two.
It is as though the mist fell back before them,
As though heather clothed every slope and ridge,
And the sky smiled on them. They must be
Brother and sister. Hand in hand they run
Over the carpet of heather.

EJNAR *and* AGNES, *warm and glowing, in light travelling clothes, come dancing along the edge of the crevasse. The mist has dispersed, and a clear summer morning lies over the mountain.*

EJNAR (*sings*). Agnes, my butterfly,
  You know I will capture you yet.
  Though you fly, it will not save you,
  For soon you'll be caught in my net.
AGNES (*sings, dancing backwards in front of him, evading him
      continuously*). If I am your butterfly,
  With joy and delight I shall play,
  But if you should catch me,
  Don't crush my wings, I pray.
EJNAR. On my hand I shall lift you,
  In my heart I shall lock you away,
  And for ever, my butterfly,
  Your joyful game you can play.

Without noticing it, EJNAR *and* AGNES *have come to the edge of
the crevasse, and now stand on the brink.*

BRAND (*calling down to them*).
  Stop! You're on the edge of a precipice!
EJNAR. Who's that shouting?
AGNES (*points upwards*). Look!
BRAND. That snowdrift's hollow.
  It's hanging over the edge of the precipice.
  Save yourselves before it's too late!
EJNAR (*throws his arms round her and laughs up at him*).
  We're not afraid.
AGNES.   We haven't finished
  Our game; we've a whole lifetime yet.
EJNAR. We've been given a hundred years
  Together in the sun.
BRAND.   And then?
EJNAR. Then? Home again. (*Points to the sky.*) To Heaven.
BRAND. Ah! That's where you've come from, is it?
EJNAR. Of course. Where else? Come down here,
  And I'll tell you how good God has been to us.
  Then you'll understand the power of joy.

Don't stand up there like an icicle. Come on down!
Good! First, I'm a painter,
And it's a wonderful thing to give my thoughts flight,
Charming dead colours into life
As God creates a butterfly out of a chrysalis.
But the most wonderful thing God ever did
Was to give me Agnes for my bride.
I was coming from the south, after a long
Journey, with my easel on my back –

AGNES (*eagerly*). As bold as a king, fresh and gay,
Knowing a thousand songs.

EJNAR. As I was coming through the pass, I saw her.
She had come to drink the mountain air,
The sunshine, the dew, and the scent of the pines.
Some force had driven me up to the mountains.
A voice inside me said:
'Seek beauty where the pine trees grow,
By the forest river, high among the clouds.'
There I painted my masterpiece,
A blush on her cheek, two eyes bright with happiness,
A smile that sang from her heart.
I asked her to marry me, and she said yes.
They gave a feast for us which lasted three days.
Everyone was there. We tried to slip away
Last night, but they followed us, waving flags,
Leaves in their hats, singing all the way.
The mist was heavy from the north,
But it fell back before us.

BRAND. Where are you going now?

EJNAR. Over that last mountain peak, westwards down
To the mouth of the fjord, and then home to the city
For our wedding feast as fast as ship can sail.
Then south together, like swans on their first flight –

BRAND. And there?

EJNAR.   A happy life

Together, like a dream, like a fairy tale.
For this Sunday morning, out there on the mountain,
Without a priest, our lives were declared free
Of sorrow, and consecrated to happiness.

BRAND. By whom?

EJNAR. By everyone.

BRAND. Farewell. (*Turns to go.*)

EJNAR (*suddenly looks closely at him in surprise*).
    No, wait. Don't I know your face?

BRAND (*coldly*). I am a stranger.

EJNAR. I'm sure I remember –
    Could we have known each other at school – or at
       home?

BRAND. Yes, we were friends at school. But then
    I was a boy. Now I am a man.

EJNAR. It can't be – (*Shouts suddenly.*) Brand! Yes, it's you!

BRAND. I knew you at once.

EJNAR.   How good to see you!
    Look at me! Yes, you're the same old Brand,
    Who always kept to yourself and never played
    With us.

BRAND.   No, I was not at home
    Among you southerners. I was
    Of another race, born by a cold fjord,
    In the shadow of a barren mountain.

EJNAR. Is your home in these parts?

BRAND. My road will take me through it.

EJNAR. Through it? You're going beyond, then?

BRAND. Yes, beyond; far beyond my home.

EJNAR. Are you a priest now?

BRAND. A mission preacher. I live
    One day in one place, the next in another.

EJNAR. Where are you bound?

BRAND (*sharply*). Don't ask that.

EJNAR. Why?

BRAND (*changes his tone*).

    Well, the ship which is waiting for you will take me too.

EJNAR. Agnes, he's coming the same way!

BRAND. Yes; but I am going to a burial feast.

AGNES. To a burial feast?

EJNAR. Who is to be buried?

BRAND. That God you have just called yours.

AGNES. Come, Ejnar.

EJNAR. Brand!

BRAND. The God of every dull and earthbound slave
    Shall be shrouded and coffined for all to see
    And lowered into his grave. It is time, you know.
    He has been ailing for a thousand years.

EJNAR. Brand, you're ill!

BRAND.   No, I am well and strong
    As mountain pine or juniper. It is
    Our time, our generation, that is sick
    And must be cured. All you want is to flirt,
    And play, and laugh; to do lip-service to your faith
    But not to know the truth; to leave your suffering
    To someone who they say died for your sake.
    He died for you, so you are free to dance.
    To dance, yes; but whither?
    Ah, that is another thing, my friend.

EJNAR. Oh, I see. This is the new teaching.
    You're one of those pulpit-thumpers who tell us
    That all joy is vanity, and hope
    The fear of hell will drive us into sackcloth.

BRAND. No. I do not speak for the Church. I hardly
    Know if I'm a Christian. But I know
    That I am a man. And I know what it is
    That has drained away our spirit.

EJNAR (*smiles*). We usually have the reputation of being
    Too full of spirit.

BRAND.   You don't understand me.

It isn't love of pleasure that is destroying us.
It would be better if it were.
Enjoy life if you will,
But be consistent, do it all the time,
Not one thing one day and another the next.
Be wholly what you are, not half and half.
Everyone now is a little of everything;
A little solemn on Sundays, a little respectful
Towards tradition; makes love to his wife after Saturday
Supper, because his father did the same.
A little gay at feasts, a little lavish
In giving promises, but niggardly
In fulfilling them; a little of everything;
A little sin, a little virtue;
A little good, a little evil; the one
Destroys the other, and every man is nothing.

EJNAR. All right. I agree that we are sinful.
But what has that to do with Him
You want to bury – the God I still call mine?

BRAND. My gay friend, show me this God of yours.
You're an artist. You've painted him, I hear.
He's old, isn't he?

EJNAR.   Well – yes.

BRAND.   Of course.
And grey, and thin on top, as old men are?
Kindly, but severe enough to frighten
Children into bed? Did you give him slippers?
I hope you allowed him spectacles and a skull-cap.

EJNAR (angrily). What do you mean?

BRAND.   That's just what he is,
The God of our country, the people's God.
A feeble dotard in his second childhood.
You would reduce God's kingdom,
A kingdom which should stretch from pole to pole.
To the confines of the Church. You separate

Life from faith and doctrine. You do not want
To live your faith. For that you need a God
Who'll keep one eye shut. That God is getting feeble
Like the generation that worships him.
Mine is a storm where yours is a gentle wind,
Inflexible where yours is deaf, all-loving,
Not all-doting. And He is young
And strong like Hercules. His is the voice
That spoke in thunder when He stood
Bright before Moses in the burning bush,
A giant before the dwarf of dwarfs. In the valley
Of Gideon He stayed the sun, and worked
Miracles without number – and would work
Them still, if people were not dead, like you.

EJNAR (*smiles uncertainly*). And now we are to be created anew?

BRAND. Yes. As surely as I know that I
Was born into this world to heal its sickness
And its weakness.

EJNAR. Do not blow out the match because it smokes
Before the lantern lights the road.
Do not destroy the old language
Until you have created the new.

BRAND. I do not seek
To create anything new. I uphold
What is eternal. I do not come
To bolster dogmas or the Church.
They were born and they will die.
But one thing cannot die; the Spirit, not created, but
        eternal,
Redeemed by Christ when it had been forfeited
In the first fresh spring of time. He threw a bridge
Of human faith from flesh back to the Spirit's source.
Now it is hawked round piecemeal, but from these
        stumps
Of soul, from these severed heads and hands,

A whole shall rise which God shall recognize,
Man, His greatest creation, His chosen heir,
Adam, young and strong.

EJNAR (*interrupts*). Goodbye. I think we had better part.

BRAND. Go westwards. I go to the north. There are two
Roads to the fjord. One is as short as the other.
Farewell.

EJNAR. Goodbye.

BRAND (*turns as he is about to descend*).
There is darkness and there is light. Remember,
Living is an art.

EJNAR (*waving him away*). Turn the world upside down.
I still have faith in my God.

BRAND.   Good; but paint him
With crutches. I go to lay him in his grave.

He goes down the path. EJNAR *goes silently and looks after him.*

AGNES (*stands for a moment as though abstracted; then starts and
looks round uneasily*). Has the sun gone down?

EJNAR. No, it was only
A cloud passing. Soon it will shine again.

AGNES. There's a cold wind.

EJNAR.   It was a gust
Blowing through the gap. Let's go down.

AGNES. How black the mountain has become, shutting
Our road to the south.

EJNAR.   You were so busy singing
And playing, you didn't notice it until
He frightened you with his shouting. Let him follow
His narrow path. We can go on with our game.

AGNES. No, not now. I am tired.

EJNAR.   Yes, so am I;
And the way down isn't as easy
As the way we've come. Look, Agnes! You see
That blue streak over there with the sun on it?

That is the sea. And the dark smoke drifting along
The fjord, and that black speck which has just appeared
Off the headland? That is the steamer; yours,
And mine. Now it is moving into the fjord.
Tonight it will steam out into the open sea,
With you and me on board. Now the mist veils it,
Heavy and grey. Look, Agnes! Did you see
How the sea and sky seemed to paint each other?

AGNES (*gazes abstractedly*). Yes. But – did you see – ?

EJNAR. What?

AGNES (*speaks softly, as though in church*).
      How, as he spoke, he grew?

She goes down the path. EJNAR *follows.*

The scene changes to a path along the mountain wall, with a wild abyss beyond, to the right. Higher up, behind the mountain, can be glimpsed higher peaks, covered with snow. BRAND *comes along the path, descends, stops half-way on a projecting rock, and looks down into the abyss.*

BRAND. Yes. Now I know where I am. Every boathouse,
      Every cottage; the landslide hill,
      The birchtrees on the fjord, the old brown church,
      The elder bushes along the river bank.
      I remember it all
      From childhood. But it looks greyer now,
      And smaller. The snowdrift on the mountain
      Hangs further out than it used to. It cuts
      Even more from the valley's meagre strip of sky;
      It lowers, threatens, shadows, steals more sun.

He sits down and gazes into the distance.

The fjord; was it as grim and narrow as this?
A storm is blowing up. There's a ship
Running for shelter. And there to the south

Under the shadow of a crag, I can see
A boat-house and a jetty, and behind them
A red cottage. The widow's cottage!
My childhood home!
                    Memories swarm upon me,
And memories of memories. There, among
The stones on the shore, I lived my childhood alone.

A heavy weight lies on me, the burden
Of being tied to another human being
Whose spirit pointed earthwards. Everything
That I desired so passionately before
Trembles and fades. My strength and courage fail me,
My mind and soul are numbed.
Now, as I approach my home, I find
Myself a stranger; I awake bound, shorn,
And tamed, like Samson in the harlot's lap.

He looks down again into the valley.

What is all that activity?
From every cottage pour men, women and children.
Long lines of people wind up the narrow streets,
Towards the old church. (*Stands up.*)
                    Oh, I know you through and through,
Dull souls and slovenly minds. Your prayers
Have not the strength nor the agony to reach
To Heaven – except to cry:
'Give us this day our daily bread!' That
Is now the watchword of this country, the remnant
Of its faith. Away from this stifling pit;
The air down here is poisoned, as in a mine.
Here no breeze can ever stir.

He is about to go when a stone thrown from above rolls down the path close to him.

BRAND (*shouts up*). Hallo, there! Who is throwing stones?

GERD, *a fifteen-year-old girl, runs along the mountain crest with stones in her apron.*

GERD. He screeched! I hit him!
 No, there he sits unhurt, rocking
 On that fallen branch.

She throws a stone again, and screams.

                    Here he comes again,
 As savage as before. Help! Ah!
 He's tearing me with his claws!
BRAND. In God's name – !
GERD. Ssh! Who are you? Stand still, stand still,
 He's flying away.
BRAND. Who is flying away?
GERD. Didn't you see the hawk?
BRAND. Here? No.
GERD. The big ugly bird with the red and gold
 Circled eye?
BRAND. Where are you going?
GERD. To church.
BRAND (*pointing downwards*). But there's the church.
GERD (*smiles scornfully at him, and points downwards*). That?
BRAND. Yes. Come with me.
GERD. No, that's ugly.
BRAND. Ugly? Why?
GERD. Because it's small.
BRAND. Do you know a bigger one?
GERD. A bigger one? Oh, yes. Goodbye. (*Begins to climb.*)
BRAND. Is your church up there? That leads into the moun-
 tains.
GERD. Come with me, and I'll show you a church
 Built of ice and snow.
BRAND.   Of ice and snow?

Now I understand. I remember,
When I was a boy, up among the peaks and summits,
At the head of a valley, there was a chasm.
People called it the Ice Church.
A frozen mountain lake was its floor.
And a great piled snowdrift stretched like a roof
Over the split in the mountain wall.

GERD. Yes, it looks like rocks and ice, but really
It's a church.

BRAND.   Never go there.
A gust of wind can bring the roof crashing down.
A scream, a rifle-shot, is enough.

GERD (*not listening*). Come with me, and I'll show you a herd
Of reindeer which was buried by an avalanche,
And wasn't seen again till the spring thaw.

BRAND. Don't go there. It's unsafe.

GERD (*pointing down into the valley*).
Don't go there. It's ugly!

BRAND. God's peace be with you.

GERD.   No, come with me!
Up there, cataract and avalanche sing Mass.
The wind preaches along the wall of the glacier,
And the hawk can't get in; he swoops down
On to the Black Peak and sits there
On my church steeple like an ugly weathercock.

BRAND. Wild is your way, and wild your soul,
Poor, broken instrument.

GERD.   Here he comes
With his clattering wings; I must get inside.
Goodbye! In the church, I'm safe.
Ah! How angry he is! (*Shrieks.*)
Don't come near me! I'll throw stones at you!
I'll hit you if you try to claw me.

She runs off up the mountain side.

BRAND (*after a pause*). Another churchgoer!
    On the mountain, or in the valley?
    Which is best? Who gropes most blindly?
    Who strays farthest from home? The light of heart
    Who plays along the edge of the crevasse?
    The dull of heart, plodding and slow because
    His neighbours are so? Or the wild of heart,
    In whose broken mind evil seems beautiful?
    This triple enemy must be fought.
    I see my calling. It shines forth like the sun.
    I know my mission. If these three can be slain,
    Man's sickness will be cured.
    Arm, arm, my soul. Unsheath your sword.
    To battle for the heirs of Heaven!

He descends into the valley.

Act Two

Down by the fjord. Steep mountains surround it, and the ruined church stands nearby on a small hill. A storm is building up. VILLAGERS (men, women and children) are gathered in groups on the shore and hillside. In the midst of them, the MAYOR is seated on a stone. The SEXTON is helping him to dole out corn and other food. Some way off, EJNAR and AGNES stand surrounded by a group of people. Boats lie on the shingle.

BRAND appears on the hill by the church, unnoticed by the crowd.

A MAN (*forcing his way through the crowd*).
    Get out of the way!

A WOMAN. I was first!

MAN (*pushing her aside*). Make way!
    (*Pushes his way to the* MAYOR.)
    Here, fill my sack!

MAYOR. Be patient.

MAN. I must go home. I've four children starving – five!

MAYOR (*sardonically*). Don't you know how many?

MAN. One was dying when I left.

MAYOR. Well, be patient. You're on the list, I take it?

He glances through his papers.

    No. Yes, here you are. Lucky for you. (*To* SEXTON.)
    Give number twenty-nine his. Now, now, good people,
    Be patient. Nils Snemyr?

SECOND MAN. Yes?

MAYOR. You must take a quarter less than you had last time.
    You've one less mouth to feed.

SECOND MAN. Yes, Ragnhild died yesterday.

MAYOR (*makes a note*). One less. Well, a saving's a saving.

EJNAR (*to* AGNES). I've given all I have – I've emptied
    My pockets and my purse.

MAYOR (*catches sight of* BRAND, *and points up at him*).
    Ha, a new arrival! Welcome!
    We've had drought and famine here, and now floods,
    So open your purse and give what you can.
    We've very little left; five small fishes
    Don't feed many hungry mouths nowadays.

BRAND. Better than ten thousand issued in the name of idolatry.

MAYOR. I didn't ask you for advice.
    Words are no good to hungry men.

EJNAR. Brand, you can't know how the people have suffered.
    The harvest's failed, there's been famine and sickness.
    People are dying –

BRAND. Yes, I can see that. These sunken eyes
    Tell me what judge holds court here.

MAYOR. And yet you stand there hard as stone?

BRAND (*comes down among the crowd, and speaks earnestly*).
    If your life here was languid and easy,
    I could pity your cries for bread. When day follows day
    Ploddingly, like mourners at a funeral,
    Then a man may well suppose that God has struck him
    From His book. But to you He has been merciful,
    He has made you afraid, He has scourged you
    With the whip of death. The precious gift He gave you,
    He has taken away –

SEVERAL VOICES (*threateningly*). He mocks us in our need!

MAYOR. He abuses us who give you bread!

BRAND (*shakes his head*).
    Oh, could my heart's blood heal and refresh you,
    I would pour it till my veins were dry.
    But to help you now would be sin. God
    Shall lift you out of your distress. A living people
    Sucks strength from sorrow. The weak brace their backs,
    Knowing that the strife will end in victory.

But where extremity breeds no courage, the flock
Is not worthy of salvation.

A WOMAN.   A storm is breaking
Over the fjord. His words awake the thunder!

ANOTHER WOMAN. He tempts God!

BRAND. *Your* God will perform no miracles for you!

WOMEN. Look at the sky! The storm is rising!

CROWD. Drive him out of the village! Drive him out!
Stone him! Kill him!

The VILLAGERS *gather threateningly round* BRAND. *The*
MAYOR *tries to intervene.* A WOMAN, *crazed and dishevelled,*
runs down the hillside.

WOMAN (*screams*).
Help me, in the name of Jesus Christ, help me!

MAYOR. What is the matter? What do you want?

WOMAN. A priest, a priest! Where can I find a priest?

MAYOR. We have no priest here.

WOMAN. Then all is lost, lost!

BRAND. Perhaps one could be found.

WOMAN (*clutches his arm*).
Where is he? Tell me! Where is he?

BRAND. Tell me why you need him, and he will come.

WOMAN. Over the fjord – my husband –
Three children, starving – we had no food.
No! Tell me he is not damned!

BRAND. Explain.

WOMAN. My breasts were dry – no one would help us –
God would not help us – my youngest child was dying.
It drove him mad. He killed the child.

CROWD (*fearfully*). Killed his own child!

WOMAN. At once, he realized what he had done.
His grief burst forth like a river, and he turned
His hand on himself. Cross the fjord and save
His soul! He cannot live, and dare not die.

He lies clasping the child's body, shrieking
The Devil's name.

BRAND (*quietly*). Your need is great.

EJNAR (*pale*). Can it be possible?

MAYOR. He doesn't belong to my district.

BRAND (*sharply, to the* VILLAGERS).

Unmoor a boat and row me over.

A MAN. In this storm? No one would dare.

BRAND. Unmoor a boat!

SECOND MAN. Impossible! Look!

The wind's blowing from the mountain! The fjord is
seething!

BRAND. The soul of a dying sinner does not wait
For wind and weather.

He goes to a boat, and unties the sail.

Will you risk your boat?

MAN. Yes, but wait –

BRAND. Good. Now, who will risk his life?

MAN. Not I.

ANOTHER MAN. Nor I.

OTHERS. It's certain death.

BRAND.   Your God will help
No one across. But mine will be on board!

WOMAN. He will die unshriven.

BRAND (*shouts from the boat*). I only need one man,
To bale and work the sail. Come, one of you!
You gave food just now! Won't anyone give his life?

CROWD (*retreating*). You can't ask that!

A MAN (*threateningly*).

Get out of the boat! Don't tempt the Lord!

CROWD. The storm's rising!

BRAND (*holding himself fast with the boathook, shouts to the*
WOMAN). All right, then, you come. But hurry!

WOMAN (*shrinks back*). I? When no one – !

BRAND. Let them stay.

WOMAN. No, I can't.

BRAND. Can't?

WOMAN. My children – !

BRAND (*laughs contemptuously*). You build on sand!

AGNES (*turns with flaming cheeks to* EJNAR, *and lays her hand on his arm*). Did you hear?

EJNAR. Yes. He is strong.

AGNES. God bless you! You know your duty. (*Cries to* BRAND) Here is one who is worthy to go with you.

BRAND. Come on, then.

EJNAR (*pales*). I?

AGNES. Go! I want you to. My eyes were blind; now they see.

EJNAR. A week ago, I would gladly have given my life
And gone with him –

AGNES (*trembling*). But now?

EJNAR. I am young, and life is dear. I cannot go.

AGNES (*draws away from him*). What?

EJNAR. I dare not.

AGNES. This storm has driven us apart.
All God's ocean lies between us now.
(*Cries to* BRAND.) I will come.

BRAND. Good! Come on, then.

WOMEN (*in terror, as she runs on board*).
Help! Jesus Christ have mercy!

EJNAR (*tries desperately to seize her*). Agnes!

CROWD (*rushing forward*). Come back!

BRAND. Where is the house?

WOMAN. Over there, on the headland.

The boat moves away from the shore.

EJNAR (*cries after them*).
Remember your family! Remember your mother!
Save your life!

AGNES. We are three on board!

The boat sails away. The VILLAGERS *gather on the hillside and gaze after them.*

MAN. The squall's caught them!

ANOTHER MAN. The water's boiling like pitch!

EJNAR. What was that cry above the storm?

WOMAN. It came from the mountain.

ANOTHER WOMAN. There! It's the witch, Gerd, laughing and shouting at him!

FIRST WOMAN. Blowing a buck's horn, and throwing stones!

SECOND WOMAN. Hooting!

FIRST MAN. Howl and trumpet, you ugly troll! He's well protected.

SECOND MAN. Next time he asks, I'll sail with him in a hurricane.

FIRST MAN (*to* EJNAR). What is he?

EJNAR. A priest.

SECOND MAN. Mm. Well, whatever he is, he's a man. Tough and strong. And brave.

FIRST MAN. That's the sort of priest we need.

VILLAGERS. Yes, that's the sort of priest we need.

They look out to sea.

On the headland, outside a hut. The day is far advanced. The fjord lies still and shining. AGNES *is seated down by the shore. After a moment,* BRAND *comes out of the door.*

BRAND. That was death. It has washed away the stains
Of fear. Now he lies, freed from his pain,
His face calm and peaceful. But those two children
Who sat huddled in the chimney corner
Staring with huge eyes,
Who only looked and looked, whose souls
Received a stain which all the toil of time

Will not wash out, even when they themselves
Are bent and grey,
Must grow up in the memory of this hour.
And what chain of sin and crime will not stretch on
From them, link upon link? Why?
The hollow answer echoes: 'They were their father's
Sons'. Silence cannot erase this,
Nor mercy. Where does responsibility
For man's inheritance from man begin?
What a hearing that will be when the great assizes sits!
Who shall bear witness where every man is guilty?
Shall the answer: 'I am my father's son'
Be admitted then?
Deep-dizzy riddle of darkness, which none can solve.
Men do not understand what a mountain of guilt
Rises from that small word: Life.

Some of the VILLAGERS *appear, and approach* BRAND.

FIRST MAN. We meet again.

BRAND. He no longer needs your help.

MAN. There are still three mouths to fill –

BRAND. Well?

MAN. We haven't much to offer, but we've brought a few
        things –

BRAND. If you give all you have, but not your life,
     You give nothing.

MAN. I would give it now, if it could save his life.

BRAND. But not to save his soul?

MAN. We are only working people.

BRAND. Then turn your eyes away from the light
     Beyond the mountains. Bend your backs to the yoke.

MAN. I thought you would tell us to throw it off.

BRAND. Yes, if you can.

MAN. You can give us the strength.

BRAND. Can I?

MAN. Many people have pointed the way, but you
Walked in it.

BRAND (*uneasily*). What do you want with me?

MAN. Be our priest.

BRAND. I?

MAN. You are the sort of priest we need.

BRAND. Ask anything of me, but not that.
I have a greater calling. I must speak to the world.
Where the mountains shut one in, a voice is powerless.
Who buries himself in a pit when the broad fields beckon?
Who ploughs the desert when fertile soil awaits him?

MAN (*shakes his head*):
I understood your deeds, but not your words.

BRAND. Ask no further; my time here is finished. (*Turns to go.*)

MAN. Is your calling dear to you?

BRAND. It is my life.

MAN. If you give all, but not your life,
You give nothing.

BRAND. One thing a man cannot give: his soul.
He cannot deny his calling.
He dare not block that river's course;
It forces its way towards the ocean.

MAN. Yet if it lost itself in marsh or lake,
It would reach the ocean in the end, as dew.

BRAND (*looks steadfastly at him*).
Who gave you power to speak like that?

MAN. You did. In the storm.
When you risked your life to save a sinner's soul,
Your deed rang in our ears like a bell. (*Lowers his voice.*)
Tomorrow, perhaps, we shall have forgotten it.

BRAND. Where there is no will, there is no calling. (*In a hard
voice.*)
If you cannot be what you would be,
Turn your face to the earth, and till it well.

MAN (*looks at him for a moment*).

    May you be cursed for quenching the flame you lit,
    As we are cursed, who, for a moment, saw.

He goes. The others follow him silently.

BRAND (*gazing after him*).

    Silently they go, their spirits bowed,
    As Adam walked from Paradise.
    No! I have dared to take upon myself
    The salvation of Man. That is my work.
    I must leave this narrow valley; I cannot fight
    My battle here.

He turns to go, but stops as he sees AGNES *sitting on the shore.*

    See how she sits and listens, as though the air
    Were full of song. So she sat in the storm. (*Goes towards her*)
    What are you looking at, girl? The fjord's crooked course?

AGNES (*without turning*).

    No. Not the fjord's course, nor the earth's.
    Both are hidden from me now.
    But I see a greater earth, its outline
    Sharp against the air.
    I see oceans and the mouths of rivers.
    A gleam of sunshine pierces through the mist.
    I see a fiery red light playing about the mountain peaks.
    I see a boundless waste of desert.
    Great palm trees stand, swaying in the sharp winds.
    There is no sign of life;
    It is like a new world at its birth.
    And I hear voices ring;
    'Now shalt thou be lost or saved.
    Thy task awaits thee; take up thy burden.
    Thou shalt people this new earth.'

BRAND. What else?

AGNES (*lays a hand on her breast*).
> I feel a force waking within me;
> And I sense Him who watches over us,
> Sense that He looks down
> Full of sadness and of love.
> A voice cries: 'Now shalt thou create and be created.
> Thy task awaits thee. Take up thy burden.'

BRAND. Yes. Within, within. There is the way,
> That is the path. In oneself is that earth,
> Newly created, ready to receive God.
> There shall the vulture that gnaws the will be slain;
> There shall the new Adam be born.
> A place on the earth where one can be wholly oneself;
> That is Man's right; and I ask no more. (*Reflects for a
>   moment.*)
> To be wholly oneself! But how,
> With the weight of one's inheritance of sin?
> Who is that climbing the hill? Who is she –
> Her body crooked and bent?
> What icy gust, what cold memory from childhood
> Numbs me? Merciful God!

BRAND'S MOTHER *climbs over the hilltop and stands there, half
visible, shading her eyes with her hand and peering about her.*

MOTHER. They said he was here. (*Approaches him.*)
> Curse the sun, it half blinds me.
> Is that you, my son?

BRAND. Yes, mother.

MOTHER (*rubs her eyes*).
> Ugh! It's enough to burn one's eyes out.

BRAND. At home I never saw the sun
> From the leaves' fall to the cuckoo's song.

MOTHER (*laughs quietly*). No, it's good there – dark and cold.
> It makes you strong, and afraid of nothing.

BRAND. Good day. My time is short.

MOTHER. Yes, you were always restless; ran away and left me —

BRAND. You wanted me to leave.

MOTHER. It was best. You had to be a priest. (*Looks at him
    more closely.*)

Hm! You've grown big and strong. But mark my words.
Take care of your life!

BRAND. Is that all?

MOTHER. All? What could be dearer than life?

Look after yours, for my sake — I gave it to you. (*Angrily.*)
I've heard about your crossing the fjord this morning.
In that storm! You are my only son,
The last of our family. You must live
To carry on my name, and all I've lived
And worked for. You'll be rich, you know, one day.

BRAND. I see. So that's why you came to look for me?

MOTHER. Keep away! (*Draws back.*) Don't come near me!

I'll hit you with my stick! (*More calmly.*) Listen to me.
I'm getting older every year. Sooner or later
I've got to die, and then you'll get all I have.
It's not much, but it's enough.
You shall have it all, my son. The whole inheritance.

BRAND. On what conditions?

MOTHER. Only one. That you don't throw your life away.

Pass on our name to sons and grandsons.
That's all I ask.

BRAND.   Let's be clear about one thing.

I have always defied you, even when I was a child.
I have been no son to you, and you have been
No mother to me.

MOTHER.   I don't ask for sentiment.

Be what you want — be hard, be stubborn, be cold —
I shan't weep. But guard your inheritance.
Never let it leave our family.

BRAND (*takes a step towards her*).

And if I should decide to scatter it to the winds?

MOTHER. Scatter it?

    The money I've drudged all my life to save?

BRAND (*nodding slowly*). Scatter it to the winds.

MOTHER. If you do, you scatter my soul with it.

BRAND. But if I should?

    If I should come to your bedside one evening,
    When a candle stands at the foot of your bed;
    When, clasping a psalmbook in your hands,
    You lie, sleeping your first night with death –

MOTHER (*goes towards him tensely*). Who gave you this idea?

BRAND. Shall I tell you?

MOTHER. Yes.

BRAND. A memory from childhood. Something
    I cannot forget. It was an autumn evening.
    Father was dead. I crept in to where he lay
    Pale in the candlelight. I stood
    And stared at him from a corner. He was holding
    A psalmbook. I wondered why he slept so deeply,
    And why his wrists were so thin; and I remember
    The smell of clammy linen. Then I heard
    A step on the stair. A woman came in.
    She didn't see me, but went straight to the bed,
    And began to grope and rummage. She moved the head,
    And pulled out a bundle; then another. She counted,
    And whispered: 'More, more!' Then she pulled out
    From the pillows a packet bound with cord,
    She tore, she fumbled at it with greedy fingers,
    She bit it open with her teeth, searched on,
    Found more, counted, and whispered: 'More, more!'
    She wept, she prayed, she wailed, she swore.
    At last she had emptied every hiding-place.
    She slunk out of the room like a damned soul,
    Groaning: 'So this was all!'

MOTHER. I needed the money; and God knows
    There was precious little. I paid dearly enough for it.

BRAND. Yes, dearly. It cost you your son.

MOTHER. Maybe. But I paid a bigger price than that.
I think I gave my life. I gave something
Which is dead now; something foolish and beautiful.
I gave – I hardly know what it was –
People called it love. I remember
What a hard struggle it was. I remember
My father's advice. 'Forget the village boy',
He said, 'Take the other. Never mind that he's old
And withered. He's clever. He'll double his money.'
I took him, and it only brought me shame.
He never doubled his money. But I've worked
And slaved since then, so that now I'm not so poor.

BRAND. And do you remember, now you are near your grave,
That you gave your soul, too?

MOTHER. I remember. But I made my son a priest.
When my time comes, you must look after my soul,
In return for your inheritance.

BRAND.   And the debt?

MOTHER. Debt? What debt? I won't leave any debts.

BRAND. But if you should? I must answer every claim.
That is a son's duty when his mother
Is laid in her grave.

MOTHER.   There's no such law.

BRAND. Not in the statutes; but it must be obeyed.
Blind woman, learn to see! You have debased
God's coinage, you have squandered the soul He lent you,
You were born in His image, and you
Have dragged it in the mire. That is your debt.
Where will you go when God demands His own?

MOTHER (timidly). Where shall I go? Where?

BRAND. Have no fear. Your son
Takes all your debt on him. God's corroded image
Shall be burnt clean in me. Go to your death
In comfort. My mother shall not sleep debt-bound.

MOTHER. And my sins?

BRAND. No; only your debt; you yourself must answer
   For your sins. You must repent or perish.

MOTHER (*uneasily*). I'd better go back home
   Under the shadow of the glacier.
   In this hot glare, rank thoughts sprout like weeds.
   The stench is enough to make you giddy.

BRAND. Go back to your shadows. I am near.
   If you feel drawn towards the light
   And wish to see me, send, and I will come.

MOTHER. Yes, to judge me.

BRAND.   No, as a son
   To love you, and as a priest to shrive you.
   I shall shield you against the chill wind
   Of fear. I shall sit at the foot of your bed
   And cool the burning in your blood with song.

MOTHER. Do you promise that?

BRAND. I shall come in the hour of your repentance. (*Goes
      closer to her.*)
   But I, too, make one condition.
   Everything that binds you to this world
   You must renounce; and go naked to your grave.

MOTHER. Ask anything else! Not what I love most!

BRAND. Nothing less can mitigate His judgment.

MOTHER. My life wasted, my soul lost,
   And soon my life's savings will be lost too.
   I'll go home then,
   And hug the little I can still call mine.
   My treasure, my child of pain,
   For you I tore my breast until it bled.
   I will go home and weep like a mother
   At the cradle of her sick child.
   Why was my soul made flesh
   If love of the flesh is death to the soul?
   Stay near me, priest. I don't know how I shall feel

When my time is near. If I must lose everything
At least let me keep it as long as I can.

Goes.

BRAND (*looking after her*).
　　Your son will stay near, to answer your call.
　　And if you stretch your withered, freezing hand,
　　He will warm it. (*Goes down to* AGNES.) This evening
　　Is not as the morning was. Then I was eager
　　For battle. I heard distant trumpets bray,
　　And longed to swing the sword of wrath
　　To kill the demon of untruth,
　　Filling the earth with the noise of war.
AGNES (*turns, and looks up at him with shining eyes*).
　　The morning was pale; but the evening glows.
　　This morning I laughed; my laughter was a lie.
　　I lived for that the loss whereof is gain.
BRAND. This morning visions flocked to me
　　Like wild swans, and lifted me on their broad wings.
　　I looked outwards, thinking my path lay there.
　　I saw myself as the chastiser of the age,
　　Striding in greatness above the tumult.
　　The pomp of processions, hymns
　　And incense, silken banners, golden cups,
　　Songs of victory, the acclaim
　　Of surging crowds, glorified my life's work.
　　But it was an empty dream, a mountain mirage
　　Made by the sun in the morning mist.
　　Now I stand in a deep valley, where darkness
　　Falls long before evening. I stand between
　　The mountain and the sea, far from the tumult
　　Of the world. But this is my home.
　　My Sunday song is over, my winged steed
　　Can be unsaddled. My duty lies here.

There is a higher purpose than the glory of battle.
To hallow daily toil to the praise of God.

AGNES. And that God who was to fall?

BRAND.   I shall bury him.
But secretly, in each man's soul, not openly
For all to see. I thought I knew the way
To cure man's sickness, but I was wrong.
I see it now.
It is not by spectacular achievements
That man can be transformed, but by will.
It is man's will that acquits or condemns him.

He turns towards the village, where the evening shadows are beginning to fall.

You men who wander dully in this damp
Hill-locked valley which is my home. Let us see
If we can become tablets on which God can write.

He is about to go, when EJNAR *appears, and stops him.*

EJNAR. Stop! Give me back what you took from me.

BRAND. Her? There she sits.

EJNAR (*to* AGNES). Choose between the sunny plains and this
dark corner of sorrow.

AGNES. I have no choice.

EJNAR. Agnes, Agnes, listen to me.
Out on the shining water, the white sails
Cut from the shore, the high prows pearled with spray.
They fly towards harbour in our promised land.

AGNES. Sail west or east, but think of me as one dead.
Go, and God be with you, fair tempter.

EJNAR. Agnes, come with me as a sister.

AGNES (*shakes her head*). All God's ocean lies between us.

EJNAR. Then come home with me to your mother.

AGNES (*calmly*). He is my teacher, my brother and my friend.
I shall not leave him.

BRAND (*takes a step towards them*).
    Young woman, think carefully before you decide.
    Locked between mountain and mountain, shadowed by
        crag
    And peak, shut in the twilight of this ravine,
    My life will flow like a sad October evening.
AGNES. The darkness no longer frightens me. A star
    Pierces through the night.
BRAND.   Remember, I am stern
    In my demands. I require All or Nothing.
    No half-measures. There is no forgiveness
    For failure. It may not be enough
    To offer your life. Your death may be required also.
EJNAR. Stop this mad game, leave this man of dark law.
    Live the life you know you can.
BRAND. Choose. You stand at the parting of the ways.
EJNAR. Choose between storm and calm,
    Choose between joy and sorrow, night and morning.
    Choose between death and life.
AGNES (*rises*). Into the night; through death.
    Beyond, the morning glows.

She goes after BRAND. EJNAR *stares after her for a moment as though lost, bows his head, and turns back towards the fjord.*

Act Three

Three years later. A small garden at the parsonage. High moun-
tains tower above it; a stone wall surrounds it. The fjord is visible
in the background, narrow and mountain-locked. The door of the
house leads into the garden. It is afternoon.

BRAND *is standing on the step outside the house.* AGNES *is seated*
on the step below him.

AGNES. My dearest husband, again your eye travels anxiously
    Along the fjord.
BRAND.   I am waiting for a message.
AGNES. You are uneasy.
BRAND. I am waiting for a message from my mother.
    For three years I have waited faithfully,
    But it has never come. This morning
    I heard for certain that her hour is near.
AGNES (*quiet and loving*).
    Brand, you ought to go to her without waiting
    For any message.
BRAND (*shakes his head*). If she does not repent,
    I have no words to say to her, no comfort
    To offer her.
AGNES.   She is your mother.
BRAND. I have no right to worship gods in my family.
AGNES. You are hard, Brand.
BRAND. Towards you?
AGNES. Oh, no!
BRAND. I told you it would be a hard life.
AGNES (*smiles*).
    It has not been so; you have not kept your word.
BRAND. Yes; this place is cold and bitter. The rose
    Has faded from your cheek; your gentle spirit freezes.

The sun never warms this house.

AGNES. It dances so warmly and mildly on the shoulder
　　Of the mountain opposite.

BRAND. For three weeks
　　In the summer. But it never reaches the valley.

AGNES (*looks steadily at him, and rises to her feet*).
　　Brand, there is something you are afraid of.

BRAND. I? No, you.

AGNES. No, Brand. You.

BRAND. You have a secret fear.

AGNES. So have you.

BRAND. You tremble, as though on the edge of a precipice.
　　What is it? Tell me.

AGNES. Sometimes I have trembled – (*Stops.*)

BRAND. For whom?

AGNES. For our son.

BRAND. For Ulf?

AGNES. You have, too?

BRAND. Yes, sometimes. No, no!
　　He cannot be taken from us. God is good.
　　My son will grow well and strong. Where is he now?

AGNES. Sleeping.

BRAND (*looks in through the door*).
　　Look at him; he does not dream of sickness
　　Or sorrow. His little hand is round and plump.

AGNES. But pale.

BRAND. Pale, yes. But that will pass.

AGNES. How peacefully he sleeps.

BRAND. God bless you, my son. Sleep soundly. (*Closes the door.*)
　　You and he have given me light and peace
　　In my work. You have made every moment of sorrow,
　　Every difficult task, easy to bear.
　　Your courage has never failed me; his childish play
　　Gives me strength.
　　I thought my calling would be a martyrdom,

But success has followed me on my journey.

AGNES. Yes, Brand, but you deserve success.
You have fought and suffered, have toiled and drudged.
I know you have wept blood silently.

BRAND. Yes, but it all seemed easy to me. With you
Love came like a sunny spring day to warm my heart.
I had never known it before. My father and mother
Never loved me. They quenched any little flame
That faltered from the ashes. It was as though
All the gentleness I carried suppressed within me
Had been saved so that I could give it all to you
And him.

AGNES.   Not only to us. To others too.

BRAND. Through you and him. You taught me
Gentleness of spirit. That was the bridge to their hearts.
No one can love all until he has first loved one.

AGNES. And yet your love is hard.
Where you would caress, you bruise.
Many have shrunk from us, at your demand
Of: All or Nothing.

BRAND. What the world calls love, I neither know nor want.
I know God's love, which is neither weak nor mild.
It is hard, even unto the terror of death;
Its caress is a scourge. What did God reply
In the olive grove when His Son lay in agony
And cried, and prayed: 'Take this cup from me'?
Did He take the cup of pain from his lips?
No child; he had to drink it to the dregs.

AGNES. Measured by that yardstick, we all stand condemned.

BRAND. No man knows whom the judgment shall touch.
But it stands written in eternal letters of fire:
'Be steadfast to the end!' It is not enough
To bathe in the sweat of anguish; you must pass
Through the fire of torture. That you *cannot*
Will be forgiven; that you *will* not, never.

AGNES. Yes, it must be so. Oh, lift me, lift me
    To where you climb. Lead me towards your high heaven.
    My longing is great, my courage weak.
    I grow dizzy, my feet are tired
    And clogged with earth.

BRAND. Listen, Agnes. There is but one law
    For all men: no cowardly compromise!
    If a man does his work by halves,
    He stands condemned.

AGNES (*throws her arms round his neck*).
    Lead, and I shall follow.

BRAND. No path is too steep for two to climb.

The DOCTOR *comes down the path and stops outside the garden wall.*

DOCTOR. Hullo, I never expected to see
    Lovebirds in this cold valley.

AGNES. Dear doctor, are you here? Come in!

She runs down and opens the garden gate.

DOCTOR. No, I won't! You know quite well
    I'm angry with you! Burying yourselves
    In this damp cellar, where the wind from the mountain
    Cuts through body and soul like a knife.

BRAND. Not through the soul?

DOCTOR. No? Well – no, it almost seems so. Well,
    I must be off – I've got to visit a patient.

BRAND. My mother?

DOCTOR. Yes. Care to come with me?

BRAND. Not now.

DOCTOR. You've been to see her already, perhaps?

BRAND. No.

DOCTOR. You're a hard man. I've struggled all the way
    Across the moor, through mist and sleet,
    Although I know she pays like a pauper.

BRAND. May God bless your energy and skill.

    Ease her suffering, if you can.

DOCTOR. I hope He may bless my sense of duty.

    I came as soon as I heard she needed me.

BRAND. She sends for you; I am forgotten.

    I wait, wait.

DOCTOR. Don't wait for her to send for you. Come now, with
      me.

BRAND. Until she sends for me, I know no duty there.

DOCTOR (*to* AGNES). Poor child, you have a hard master.

BRAND. I am not hard.

AGNES. He would give his blood if it could wash her soul.

BRAND. As her son, I shall pay her debts.

    They are my inheritance.

DOCTOR. Pay your own!

BRAND. One man may pay for the sins of many.

DOCTOR. Not when he himself is a beggar.

BRAND. Whether I am rich or a beggar, I have the will;

    That is enough.

DOCTOR (*looks sternly at him*).

    Yes, in your ledger your credit account

    For strength of will is full, but, priest,

    Your love account is a white virgin page.

He goes.

BRAND (*watching him go*).

    Love! Has any word been so abused

    And debased? It is used as a veil to cover weakness.

    When the path is narrow, steep and slippery,

    It can be cut short – by love.

    When a man walks on the broad road of sin,

    There is still hope – in love.

    When he sees his goal but will not fight towards it,

    He can conquer – through love.

    When he goes astray, knowing what is right,

He may yet find refuge in love!

AGNES. Yes, love is a snare. And yet –
  I sometimes wonder – is it?

BRAND. First there must be will.
  You must will your way through fear, resolutely,
  Joyfully. It is not
  Martyrdom to die in agony on a cross;
  But to *will* that you shall die upon a cross,
  To will it in the extremity of pain,
  To will it when the spirit cries in torment,
  That is to find salvation.

AGNES (*clings to him*).
  Oh, Brand. When the path becomes too steep for me,
  You must give me strength.

BRAND. When the will has triumphed, then comes the time for
    love.
  But here, faced by a generation
  Which is lax and slothful, the best love is hate. (*In terror.*)
  Hate! Hate! But to will that simple word
  Means universal war.

  He rushes into the house.

AGNES. He kneels by the child; he rocks his head
  As though he wept. He presses himself
  Against the cot like a man desperate for comfort.
  What a deep well of love exists in his soul!
  He can love his child; the snake of human weakness
  Has not yet bitten that small heart.

BRAND (*comes out on to the steps*). Has no message come?

AGNES. No, no message.

BRAND (*looks back into the house*).
  His skin is dry and hot, his temple throbs,
  His pulse beats fast. Don't be afraid, Agnes –

AGNES. Oh, God!

BRAND. No, don't be afraid. (*Shouts down the road.*) The
    message! At last!

A MAN (*through the garden gate*).
    Father, you must come now!

BRAND (*eagerly*). At once! What message does she send?

MAN. A strange message. She raised herself in bed,
    Leaned forward, and said: 'Bring the priest,
    I will give half my goods for the sacrament.'

BRAND. Half!

MAN. Half.

BRAND. Half? Half! She meant all!

MAN. Maybe; but I heard her clearly.

BRAND (*seizes him by the arm*).
    Dare you swear, on the day of judgment,
    That she used that word?

MAN. Yes.

BRAND (*sternly*). Go and say that this is my reply.
    No priest will come; no sacrament.

MAN. You can't have understood. Your mother sent me.

BRAND. I know but one law for all mankind.
    I cannot discriminate.

MAN. Those are hard words.

BRAND. She knows what she must offer: All or Nothing.

MAN. Priest!

BRAND. Say that the least fragment of the golden
    Calf is as much an idol as the whole.

MAN. I will give her your answer as gently as I can.
    She'll have one comfort: God is not as hard as you.

He goes.

BRAND. Yes; they always comfort themselves
    With that illusion. A psalm and a few tears
    Just before the end, and all will be forgiven.
    Of course! They know their old God; they know
    He is always ready to be bargained with.

The MAN *has met a* SECOND MAN *on the path. They return together.*

BRAND. Another message?

FIRST MAN. Yes.

BRAND. Tell me.

SECOND MAN. She says she will give nine-tenths of her wealth.

BRAND. Not all?

SECOND MAN. No.

BRAND. She knows my answer: no priest, no sacrament.

SECOND MAN. She begged – in pain!

FIRST MAN. Priest, remember – she gave you birth!

BRAND. Go and tell her:
'The table for the bread and wine must be clean.'

The MEN *go.*

AGNES (*clings tightly to him*).
Brand, sometimes you frighten me. You flame
Like the sword of God.

BRAND (*with tears in his voice*). Does not the world fight me
With its stubborn apathy?

AGNES.   Your terms are hard.

BRAND. What other terms would you dare offer?

AGNES. Could anyone meet them?

BRAND. No, you are right. So false,
So empty, so flat, so mean has man become.

AGNES. And yet, from this blind, stumbling generation,
You demand: All or Nothing?

BRAND. He who seeks victory must not weaken;
He who has sunk most low may rise most high.

He is silent for a moment; when he speaks again, it is with a changed voice.

And yet, when I stand before a simple man
And make that demand, I feel as though I were floating

In a storm-wracked sea on a shattered spar.
Go, Agnes, go in to the child.
Sing to him, and give him sweet dreams.

AGNES (*pale*).
What is it, Brand? Your thoughts always return to him.

BRAND. Oh, nothing. Take good care of him.

AGNES. Give me a text.

BRAND. Stern?

AGNES. No, gentle.

BRAND (*embracing her*). He who is without stain shall live.

AGNES (*looks up at him with shining eyes*). Yes!
There is one sacrifice which God dare not demand.

He goes into the house.

BRAND. But if He should dare? If He should test me
As He tested Abraham?

MAYOR (*over the garden gate*). Good afternoon.

BRAND. Ah, his worship the Mayor.

MAYOR. We don't see each other often.
So I thought – but perhaps this is a bad time?

BRAND (*indicates the house*). Come in.

MAYOR. Thank you.

BRAND. What do you want?

MAYOR. Your mother's sick, I hear; very sick.
I'm sorry to hear that.

BRAND. I don't doubt it.

MAYOR. *Very* sorry.

BRAND. What do you want?

MAYOR. Well, I – er – I've a little suggestion to make.
I hope you don't mind my broaching the subject
At this sad time?

BRAND. Now is as good as any other time.

MAYOR. Well, I'll come straight to the point. You're going
To be quite well off now – I may even say rich.
You won't want to bury yourself in this little

Backwater any longer, I presume,
Now that you have the means to live elsewhere?

BRAND. In other words: go?

MAYOR. If you like to put it that way.
I think it would be better for all concerned.
Don't misunderstand me! I admire your gifts
Greatly, but wouldn't they be better suited
To a more sophisticated community?

BRAND. A man's native soil is to him as the root
Is to the tree. If he is not wanted there,
His work is doomed, his song dies.

MAYOR. If you insist on staying, of course I can't force you
          to go.
But don't overstep the limits of your calling.

BRAND. A man must be himself.
Only thus can he carry his cause to victory.
And I shall carry mine to victory.
This people whom you and your like have lulled
To sleep shall be awakened. You have softened
And debased the good metal of their souls.
I declare war on you and everything
You stand for.

MAYOR.   War?

BRAND.   War.

MAYOR. If you sound the call to arms, you will be
The first to fall.

BRAND.   One day it will be clear
That the greatest victory lies in defeat.

MAYOR. Think, Brand. If you stay,
And lose this battle, your life will have been wasted.
You have all the good things of the world –
Money, a child, a wife who loves you. Why
Wage your crusade in this backwater?

BRAND. Because I must.

MAYOR. Go to rich cities where life is not so hard,

And order them to bleed. We do not want to bleed
But only to earn our bread in the sweat of our brows,
Prising a living out of these rocky hillsides.

BRAND. I shall stay here. This is my home, and here
I shall begin my war.

MAYOR. You're throwing away a great opportunity.
And remember what you stand to lose if you should fail.

BRAND. I lose myself if I weaken.

MAYOR. Brand, no man can fight a war alone.

BRAND. My flock is strong. I have the best men on my side.

MAYOR (*smiles*). Possibly. But I have the most.

He goes.

BRAND (*watching him go*).
There goes a typical man of the people;
Full-blooded, right-thinking, well-meaning, energetic,
Jovial and just. And yet, no landslide, flood
Or hurricane, no famine, frost or plague
Does half the damage in a year that that man does.
How much spiritual aspiration
Has he not stifled at birth? (*Suddenly anxious.*)
Why does no message come? Ah, doctor! (*Runs to meet
    him.*)
Tell me – my mother – ?

DOCTOR. She stands before her judge.

BRAND. Dead? But – penitent?

DOCTOR. I hardly think so. She clung fast
To her worldly goods until God took her from them.

BRAND. What did she say?

DOCTOR. She mumbled: God is not so cruel as my son.

BRAND (*sinks down on the bench*).
That lie that poisons every soul, even
At the threshold of death, even in the hour of judgment.

He buries his face in his hands.

DOCTOR (*goes close to him, looks at him and shakes his head*).
　　You want to resurrect an age that is dead.
　　You still preach the pact Jehovah
　　Made with man five thousand years ago.
　　Every generation must make its own pact with God.
　　Our generation is not to be scared by rods
　　Of fire, or by nurses' tales about damned souls.
　　Its first commandment, Brand, is: Be humane.
BRAND (*looks up at him*). Humane! That word excuses all our
　　　　weakness.
　　Was God humane towards Jesus Christ?

　　He hides his head and sits in silent grief.

DOCTOR (*quietly*). If only you could find tears!
AGNES (*comes out on to the step; pale and frightened she whispers
　　　　to the* DOCTOR).
　　Come inside. Please.
DOCTOR. What is it, child?
AGNES. I am afraid.
DOCTOR. What? Why?
AGNES (*takes him by the hand*). Come!

　　They go into the house, unnoticed by BRAND.

BRAND (*quietly to himself*).
　　She died unrepentant; unrepentant
　　As she had lived. Is not this God's finger pointing?
　　If I weaken now, I am damned tenfold. (*Gets up.*)
　　Henceforth I shall fight unflinchingly for the victory
　　Of the spirit over the weakness of the flesh.
　　The Lord has armed me with the blade of His word;
　　He has inflamed me with the fire of His wrath.
　　Now I stand strong in my will;
　　Now I dare, now I can, crush mountains.

The DOCTOR *comes hurriedly out on to the steps, followed by*
AGNES.

DOCTOR. Put your affairs in order and leave this place.

BRAND. If the earth trembled, I would still remain.

DOCTOR. Then your child will die.

BRAND (*uncomprehendingly*). My child! Ulf? My child?

He rushes towards the house.

DOCTOR (*restraining him*). No, wait!
Listen to me! There's no light or sunshine here.
The wind cuts like a polar blast;
The clammy mist never lifts. The child is weak;
Another winter here will kill him.
Go, Brand, and your son will live.
But do it quickly. Tomorrow, if you can.

BRAND. Tonight – today – now.
Come, Agnes, lift him gently in his sleep.
Let us fly south. Oh Agnes, Agnes,
Death is spinning its web about our child.
Wrap him warmly; it will soon be evening,
And the wind is cold.

AGNES *goes into the house.*

The DOCTOR *watches* BRAND *silently as he stands motionless,
staring in through the door. Then he goes up to him, and places a
hand on his shoulder.*

DOCTOR. So merciless towards your flock, so lenient towards
           yourself.

BRAND. What do you mean?

DOCTOR. You threatened your mother: 'Unless you renounce
           everything
And go naked to your grave, you are lost.'
Now you are the shipwrecked soul clinging
To your upturned boat, overboard now
Go all your threats of damnation. You fly south,
Away from your flock and your calling.
The priest will not preach here again.

BRAND (*clasps his head in his hands' distraught*).
  Am I blind now? Or was I blind before?
DOCTOR. You act as a father should. Don't think I blame you.
  I find you bigger now with your wings clipped
  Than when you were the Angel of God. Goodbye.
  I have given you a mirror; look at it, and ask yourself:
  'Is this a man who would storm the gates of Heaven?'

  He goes.

BRAND (*is silent for a moment, then cries suddenly*).
  Was I wrong then, or am I now?

AGNES *comes out of the door with her cloak over her shoulders
and the child in her arms.* BRAND *does not see her. She is about
to speak to him, but stands as though numbed by fear as she sees
the expression on his face.* A MAN *rushes in through the garden
gate. The sun is setting.*

MAN. Father, father, listen to me. You've an enemy.
BRAND (*puts his hand on his heart*). Yes, here.
MAN. Be on your guard against the mayor.
  He's spreading rumours. He's saying the parsonage
  Will soon be empty, that you will turn your back on us
  Now that your rich mother is dead.
BRAND. And if I did?
MAN. Then – you've been lying to us all!
BRAND. Have I?
MAN. How many times haven't you told us that God
  Sent you here to fight for us? That it's better
  For a man to die than to betray his calling?
  This is your calling, here, among us.
BRAND. Here the people are deaf. Their hearts are dead.
MAN. You know better. You've shown us the light.
BRAND. For every one who has found the light, ten remain in
      darkness.
MAN. I am that one; and I say to you:

'Go if you can!' I can't help myself
From the book; you have dragged me up from the abyss.
See if you dare let me fall! You can't!
If you let me go, my soul is lost. Goodbye.
I am not afraid. My priest and my God will not fail me.

He goes.

BRAND. Every word I say echoes back at me
    Like thunder from the mountain wall.
AGNES (*takes a step towards him*). I am ready.
BRAND. Ready? For what?
AGNES. To go.

GERD *runs down the path and stops outside the garden gate.*

GERD (*claps her hands and shouts gleefully*). Have you heard?
        The parson's flown away!
    The trolls and demons are swarming out of the hillsides,
    Black and ugly. Big ones, small ones – oh!
    How sharply they can strike! They nearly
    Tore my eye out. They've taken half my soul.
    But I can manage with what's left.
BRAND. Child, you talk crazily. Look at me; I am still here.
GERD. You? Yes, you, but not the priest.
    My hawk swept down the mountainside
    From Black Peak. Bridled, saddled, wild and angry,
    Hissing down the evening wind. And on his back
    A man rode. The priest, it was the priest!
    The village church stands empty, locked and barred.
    Its time is up; it's ugly.
    My church's time has come now. There stands my priest,
    Big and strong, in his white cloak woven of ice.
    Come along with me!
BRAND. Stricken soul, who sent you to bewilder me
    With talk of idols?

GERD (*comes in through the gate*).
> Idols? There's one, do you see him?
> See those hands and feet under the blanket.
> Man, there's an idol!

BRAND. Agnes, Agnes!
> I fear a Greater One has sent her to us.

GERD. Can you see the thousand trolls
> The village priest drowned in the sea?
> That grave can't hold them; they're groping their way
>   ashore,
> Cold and slimy. Look at the troll children!
> They're only skin-dead; see how they grin
> As they push up the rocks that pinned them down.

BRAND. Get out of my sight!

GERD. Listen! Can you hear that one laughing
> As he sits astride the crosspoint where the road
> Swings up to the moor, writing down in his book
> The name of every soul that passes? He has them all.
> The old church stands empty, locked and barred.
> The priest flew away on the hawk's back.

She leaps over the gate and disappears among the rocks. Silence.

AGNES (*goes across to* BRAND; *says quietly*). Let us go, Brand.
>   It is time.

BRAND (*stares at her*). Which way? (*Points towards the gate, then
>   towards the door of the house.*)
> That way – or that?

AGNES. Brand! Your child, your child!

BRAND. Answer me;
> Was I not a priest before I was a father?

AGNES. I cannot answer.

BRAND. You must. You are the mother.

AGNES. I am your wife. I shall do as you command me.

BRAND. I cannot choose! Take this cup from me!

AGNES. Ask yourself if you have a choice.

BRAND (*seizes her hand*). You must choose, Agnes.
AGNES. Do as your God bids you.

Silence.

BRAND. Let us go. It is late.
AGNES (*tonelessly*). Which way? (BRAND *is silent. She points
  towards the gate.*)
 That way?
BRAND (*points towards the door of the house*). No. That.
AGNES (*lifts the child high in her arms*).
 Oh, God! This sacrifice You dare demand
 I dare to raise towards Your heaven.
 Lead me through the fire of life.

She goes into the house.

BRAND (*stands staring silently for a moment, then bursts into tears
  and throws himself down on the step*).
 Jesus! Jesus! Give me light!

Act Four

In the parsonage. It is Christmas Eve. In the rear wall is the front door of the house; in one side wall is a window, in the other is another door.

AGNES, dressed in mourning, is standing at the window, staring out into the darkness.

AGNES. Still no sign of him. No sign.
    Oh, how hard it is to wait
    Listening to the silence. The snow falls soft and thick,
    Binding the church in a tight shroud. (*Listens.*)
    Ssh! I hear the gate creak.
    Footsteps. (*Runs to the door and opens it.*)
    Is it you? Come in, come in.

BRAND enters, covered in snow. He begins to take off his travelling clothes.

AGNES (*embraces him*). Oh, how long you've been away.
        Don't leave me,
    Don't leave me. I cannot shake off
    The black shadows of night alone.
BRAND. You have me back now, child.

He lights a single candle, which illumines the room feebly.

                                    You are pale.

AGNES. I am tired. I have watched and yearned.
    I've bound some branches together, just a few;
    It was all I had saved
    From the summer, to decorate the Christmas tree.
    His branches, I called them, because he liked
    Their leaves. He had some of them for his wreath.

She bursts into tears.

Look, it is half covered with snow,
In the –
BRAND. In the graveyard.
AGNES. That word!
BRAND. Dry your tears.
AGNES. Yes, I will. But be patient.
My soul still bleeds, the wound is fresh,
I have no strength. It will be better soon.
BRAND. Is this how you honour Our Lord's birthday?
AGNES. I know, Brand. But give me time, you must give me
time.
Think, last Christmas he was so well and strong,
And now he –
BRAND (*sharply*). Lies in the graveyard.
AGNES (*screams*). Don't say it!
BRAND. It must be said. Shouted – if you are afraid of it.
AGNES. It frightens you more than you will admit.
Your brow is wet. I know what it cost you to say it.
BRAND. It is only the spray from the fjord.
AGNES. And what is that in your eyes? Melted snow?
No, it is warm.
BRAND.   Agnes, we must both be strong.
We must strengthen each other, fight our way
Step by step together. Out on the fjord
An hour ago, I was a man. The water
Seethed around us, the mast shook,
Our sail was slit and blew far to leeward,
Every nail in the boat screeched,
Rocks were falling on either side from the slopes.
My eight men sat at their oars like corpses,
But I exulted in it. I grew stronger.
I took command. I knew
A Great One had baptized me to my calling.

AGNES. It is easy to be strong in the storm,
   Easy to live the warrior's life.
   But to sit alone in silence, nursing one's grief,
   Performing dull and humble tasks, is harder.
   I am afraid to remember, yet I cannot forget.
BRAND. Your task is not small or humble, Agnes.
   It was never as great as it is now.
   Listen. I want to tell you something
   That has come to me in our sorrow.
   It is as though there lay a kind of joy
   In being able to weep – to weep!
   Agnes, then I see God closer
   Than I ever saw Him before.
   O, so near that it seems as though I might touch Him,
   And I thirst to cast myself into His bosom,
   To be sheltered by His strong, loving, fatherly arms.
AGNES. O Brand, always see Him so,
   As a God you can approach,
   More like a father, less like a master.
BRAND. I must see Him great and strong,
   As great as Heaven. I must fight
   In the heat of the day, keep watch through the cold night.
   You must give me love. Your task is not small.
AGNES. Brand, last night, when you were away,
   He came into my room, rosy-cheeked,
   Dressed in his little shirt; tottered
   Towards my bed, and stretched out his arms,
   Smiled, and called: 'Mother', but as though he were asking
   To be warmed. I saw it – oh! I shivered –
BRAND. Agnes!
AGNES. Yes. The child was freezing.
   He must be cold out there, under the snow.
BRAND. His body is under the snow, but the child is in heaven.
AGNES. Why do you tear open the wound?
   What you call his body is still my child to me.

I cannot separate the two.

BRAND. Your wound must remain open and bleed,
Before it can be healed.

AGNES. Yes, but you must be patient. I can be led,
But not driven. Stay near me, Brand.
Give me strength. Speak to me gently.
The God you taught me to know is a warrior God.
How dare I go to Him with my small sorrow?

BRAND. Would you have found it easier to have turned
To the God you worshipped before?

AGNES. No. I shall never turn to that God again.
And yet sometimes
I long to be where light and sunshine are.
Your kingdom is too big for me. Everything here
Is too big for me; you, your calling,
This mountain that hangs over us, our grief,
Our memories. Only the church is too small.

BRAND. The church? Why is it too small?

AGNES. I can't explain it. I feel it. The church is too small.

BRAND. Many people have said the same to me.
Even the mad girl I met on the moor
Said it. 'The church is ugly
Because it is too small', she screamed.
She couldn't explain either. Many women
Have said it since. 'Our village church is too small.'
Agnes! You can find the right road blindfold
Where I pass by the turning.
Our Lord's church is small. Well, it must be rebuilt.
Again you guide me. You see how much I need you.
It is I who say to you. 'Do not leave me, Agnes.'

AGNES. I shall shake off my sorrow, I will dry my tears.
I will bury my memories. I will be wholly your wife.

She turns to go.

BRAND. Where are you going?

AGNES (*smiles*). I must not forget my household duties,
    Least of all tonight. Do you remember
    Last Christmas you said I was wasteful, because
    I had a candle burning in every window;
    Green branches and pretty things,
    Toys on the Christmas tree, singing and laughter?
    Brand, this year I shall put lights everywhere
    Again, to remind us that it is Christmas.
    I shall make the house as bright as I can
    For Christ's birthday. Now do you see any tears in my
        eyes?
BRAND (*embraces her*).
    Light the candles, child. That is your task.
AGNES (*smiles sadly*).
    Build your big church. But have it built by the spring.

She goes.

BRAND. O God, give her strength. Take from me the cup,
    The bitterest cup, of bending her to Thy law.
    I have strength. I have courage.
    Lay upon me a double portion of Thy load.
    Only be merciful unto her.

A knock upon the door. The MAYOR *enters.*

MAYOR. Well, you've beaten me.
BRAND. Beaten you?
MAYOR. Yes. I reckoned I'd beat you, father.
    Well, I proved a bad prophet.
BRAND. Well?
MAYOR. I'm in the right. But I shan't fight you any longer.
BRAND. Why?
MAYOR. Because you've got the people on your side.
BRAND. Have I?
MAYOR. You know that. And no man's fool enough
    To fight a war alone.

BRAND. Well, what do you intend to do?

MAYOR. I'm going to build.

BRAND. Build, did you say?

MAYOR. Yes. For my own sake.
As well as for the village. Election time
Will soon be here, and I must show the people
That I have their best interests at heart.
Otherwise they may elect some worthless fellow
In my place. So I thought I'd discuss with you
What would be the best measures to improve
The welfare of our poor parishioners.

BRAND. You want to abolish poverty?

MAYOR. Certainly not. Poverty's a necessity
In every society; we've got to accept that.
But with a little skill it can be kept
Within limits, and moulded into decent forms.
I thought, for example, we might build
A poorhouse. And while we're at it, we might combine it
With other amenities under the same roof;
A gaol, a hall for meetings and banquets,
With a platform for speeches, and guest rooms
For distinguished visitors –

BRAND. But the money – ?

MAYOR. Ah! That's the problem, as always, and that
Is what I wanted to talk to you about.
I need your help to raise it.

BRAND. I myself am going to build.

MAYOR. What? You? Steal my plan?

BRAND. Not exactly. (*Points out of the window.*) Look. Can
you see that?

MAYOR. What? That great ugly building?
That's your cowshed, isn't it?

BRAND. Not that. The little ugly one.

MAYOR. What? The church?

BRAND. I shall rebuild it.

MAYOR. Rebuild the church?

BRAND. Make it great.

MAYOR. The devil you don't! That'd ruin my plan.
We'd never get the people to subscribe to both.

BRAND. That church must come down.

MAYOR. It's always been acceptable to the people,
At least in the old days.

BRAND. Possibly, but now that time is past.
It is too small.

MAYOR. Too small? Well, I've never seen it full.

BRAND. That is because there is not space enough in it
For a single soul to rise.

MAYOR. Brand, take my advice. Leave the church alone.
It's an ancient monument! You can't
Just knock it down to satisfy a whim.
It'd be shameful, horrible, barbaric –
Besides, where will you get the money?

BRAND. I will build it with my own money.
My inheritance. All I have, to the last penny,
Shall be given to this work.

MAYOR. My dear Brand, I am dumbfounded. Such munificence
Is without precedent, even in the rich cities.
I am dumbfounded. Very well,
I withdraw my project. Make your plans.
I'll see what support I can work up for you.
We shall build the church together.

BRAND. Will you give up your plan?

MAYOR. Yes. I'd be a fool not to. If I went round
Asking for contributions for my plan,
While they knew that you were paying for yours
Out of your own pocket, whom do you think
They'd support? No, I'm with you,
I'm all for your plan. I'm very taken with it.
It's quite excited me. What a lucky chance
I happened to come and visit you this evening!

BRAND. But remember. The old church must come down.

MAYOR. You know, now that I see it in the moonlight,
　　　　With all this snow on it, it does look a bit
　　　　Tumbledown.

BRAND.　　　　　　What?

MAYOR.　　　　　　　　　Brand, it is too old.
　　　　I can't think why I didn't notice it before.
　　　　We mustn't let our reverence for the past,
　　　　Or our piety, warp our judgment.

BRAND.　　　　　　　　　　　　　But suppose
　　　　Our parishioners should refuse to pull it down?

MAYOR. You leave that to me.
　　　　If I don't succeed in persuading the fools to agree,
　　　　I'll pull it down with my own hands, beam by beam.
　　　　Well, I must be off. (*Takes his hat.*) I shall have to see about
　　　　Those ragamuffins I arrested this morning.

BRAND. Ragamuffins?

MAYOR. Gipsies. I discovered them just outside the village.
　　　　Dreadful people.
　　　　I tied them up and locked them in a stable.
　　　　Two or three gave me the slip, unfortunately.
　　　　The trouble is, they belong to the parish
　　　　In a kind of way. They're my responsibility. (*Laughs.*)
　　　　Yours, too. Did you ever hear folk talk
　　　　Of that penniless lad who wanted to marry your mother?
　　　　She sent him packing, of course. He went
　　　　Half out of his mind. In the end he married
　　　　A gipsy girl, and added another one
　　　　To their numbers before he died.

BRAND. A child?

MAYOR. Yes, the gipsy Gerd. So, in a sense,
　　　　The woman who brought you into the world
　　　　Brought her here too, for the girl was conceived
　　　　As a result of his love for your mother.
　　　　Well, I mustn't stay any longer. I'll be seeing you

Again soon. Goodbye, goodbye!
Remember me to your good wife! Happy Christmas!

He goes.

BRAND. Will atonement never cease?
How strangely, how wildly the threads of fate are woven!
My poor, innocent son, so you were killed
For my mother's greed. A mad, stricken girl
Born of my mother's sin, made me choose to stay.
And so you died.
For I the Lord thy God am a jealous God
And visit the sins of the fathers upon the children
Even unto the third and fourth generation. (*Turns from
    the window.*)
The God of Justice watches over us.
He demands retribution. (*Begins to pace up and down the
    room.*) Prayer! Prayer!
How easily that word slips through our lips!
Men pray to be allowed to add their weight
To Christ's burden, they stretch their hands towards
    heaven
While they stand knee-deep in the mire of doubt.

He stops, and reflects silently.

And yet – when I was afraid – when I saw my son
Fall into his last sleep, and his mother's kisses
Could not bring back the smile to his cheek,
Did I not pray then? Whence came that sweet delirium,
That stream of song, that melody
That sounded from afar, and floated by,
And bore me high and set me free? Did I pray?
Was I refreshed by prayer? Did I speak with God?
Did He hear me? Did He look down
On this house of grief where I wept? I do not know.
Now all is shut and barred. Darkness has fallen

On me again, and I can find no light,
No light. (*Cries.*) Light, Agnes! Bring me light!

AGNES *opens the door and enters with the Christmas candles. Their
bright light illumines the room.*

BRAND. Light!
AGNES. Look, Brand! The Christmas candles.
BRAND (*softly*). Ah, the Christmas candles.
AGNES (*putting them on the table*). Have I been long?
BRAND. No, no.
AGNES. How cold it is in here. You must be freezing.
BRAND. No.
AGNES (*smiles*). How proud you are.
    You will not admit that you need light and warmth.
BRAND. Hm! Will not!
AGNES (*speaks quietly as she decorates the room*).
    Last Christmas he groped
With his tiny fingers at their clear flames.
He stretched forward from his little chair and asked:
'Mother, is it the sun?' (*Moves the candles slightly.*)
They will stand here.
                    Now their light falls
On his – on the –! Now from where he sleeps,
He can see their warmth through the window pane.
Now he can peep quietly in, and see
The bright glow of our Christmas room.
But the window pane is misted. Wait a moment.
Wait a moment! It will soon be clear.

She wipes the window.

BRAND. What are you doing, Agnes?
AGNES. Ssh! Quiet!
BRAND. Close the shutters.
AGNES. Brand!
BRAND. Shut them! Shut them tightly!

AGNES. Why must you be so hard? It is not right.

BRAND. Close the shutters.

AGNES (*closes them and bursts into tears*).

 How much more will you demand of me?

BRAND. Unless you give all, you give nothing.

AGNES. I have given all.

BRAND (*shakes his head*). There is more.

AGNES (*smiles*). Ask. I have the courage of poverty.

BRAND. You have your grief, your memories,

 Your sinful longing for what is gone.

AGNES. Take them, take them!

BRAND. Your sacrifice is worthless, if you grieve.

AGNES (*shudders*). Your Lord's way is steep and narrow.

BRAND. It is the way of the will. There is no other.

AGNES. But the way of mercy?

BRAND. Is built of sacrificial stones.

AGNES (*trembling*).

 Now those words of the scripture open before me

 Like a great abyss.

BRAND. Which words?

AGNES. He dies who sees Jehovah face to face.

BRAND (*throws his arms round her and holds her tightly*).

 Oh, hide, hide. Do not look at Him. Close your eyes.

AGNES. Shall I?

BRAND (*releasing her*). No.

AGNES. Brand!

BRAND. I love you.

AGNES. Your love is hard.

BRAND. Too hard?

AGNES. Do not ask. I follow where you lead.

BRAND. You are my wife, and I have the right to demand

 That you shall devote yourself wholly to our calling.

 He turns to go.

AGNES. Yes. But don't leave me.

BRAND. I must. I need rest and quiet.
Soon I shall begin to build my church. (*Embraces her.*)
All peace be with you.

He goes towards the door.

AGNES. Brand, may I open the shutters just a little?
Only a little? Please, Brand.
BRAND (*in the doorway*). No.

He goes into his room.

AGNES. Shut. Everything is shut.
Even oblivion is shut to me.
I cannot forget, and I am forbidden to weep.
I must go out. I cannot breathe
In this shuttered room alone. Out? But where?
Will not those stern eyes in heaven follow me?
Can I fly from the empty silence of my fear?

She listens for a moment at BRAND'S *door.*

He is reading aloud. He cannot hear what I say.
No help, no advice, no comfort. (*Goes cautiously to the
    window.*)
Shall I open the shutters, so that the clear light
May hunt the horrors of night from his black bed-
    chamber?
No, he is not down there. Christmas
Is the children's time. He will be allowed to come here.
Perhaps he stands outside now, stretching up his hands
To tap at his mother's window, and finds it closed.
Ulf, the house is closed;
Your father closed it. I dare not open it now.
You and I have never disobeyed him.
Fly back to heaven. There is light
And happiness, there children play.
But do not let anyone see you cry. Do not say

Your father shut you out. A little child
Cannot understand what grown people must do.
Say he was grieved, say he sighed,
Tell them it was he who plucked the pretty leaves
To make your wreath. (*Listens and shakes her head.*)
        No, I am dreaming.
There is much to be done before we two
Can meet. I must work, work silently.
God's demand must be fulfilled. I must
Make myself hard. I must make my will strong.
But tonight is Christmas, a holy night.
I will bring out my relics of love
And happiness, whose worth only a mother can know.

She kneels by a chest of drawers, opens a drawer and takes out various objects. As she does this, BRAND *opens his door and is about to speak to her when he sees what she is doing and remains silent.* AGNES *does not see him.*

AGNES. Here is the veil. Here is the shawl
In which he was carried to his christening.
Here is the shirt. Dear God!

She holds it up, looks at it, and smiles.

How pretty it is. How smart he looked in it
When he sat in church. Here is his scarf,
And the coat he wore when he first went out of doors.
It was too long, but it soon became too small.
Ah, and here are the clothes I wrapped him in
To keep him warm on the long journey south.
When I put them away, I was tired to death.
BRAND. Spare me, God. I cannot destroy this last idol.
Send another, if it be Thy will.
AGNES. It is wet. Have I been crying?
How rich I am to have these treasures still!

There is a loud knock at the door. AGNES *turns with a cry, and sees* BRAND. *The door is flung open, and a* GIPSY WOMAN *in rags rushes in with a child in her arms.*

GIPSY (*sees the child's clothes on the floor, and shouts at* AGNES).
               Share with me, rich mother.

AGNES. You are far richer than I.

GIPSY. Oh, you're like the rest. Full of words.

BRAND (*goes towards her*). Tell me what you want.

GIPSY. Not you, you're the priest. I'd rather go back
    Into the storm than have you preach at me.
    Can I help being what I am?

AGNES. Rest, and warm yourself by the fire.
    If your child is hungry, it will be fed.

GIPSY. Gipsies mustn't stay where there's light and warmth.
    We must wander, we must be on the road.
    Houses and homes are for you others.
    Just give me a rag to wrap him in. Look at him,
    He's half naked and blue with cold.
    The wind's made his body raw.

BRAND. Agnes.

AGNES. Yes?

BRAND. You see your duty.

AGNES. Brand! To her? No!

GIPSY. Give them to me. Give them all to me.
    Rags or silks, nothing's too poor or too fine
    As long as it's something to wrap him in
    And keep him warm.

BRAND. Choose, Agnes.

GIPSY. Give them to me.

AGNES. It is sacrilege. A sin against the dead.

BRAND. If you fail now, he will have died for nothing.

AGNES. Come, woman, take them. I will share them with you.

BRAND. Share, Agnes? Share?

AGNES. Half is enough. She needs no more.

BRAND. Would half have been enough for your child?

AGNES. Come, woman. Take them. Take the dress
    He wore to his baptism. Here is his shirt, his scarf,
    His coat. It will keep the night air from your child.

GIPSY. Give them to me.

BRAND. Agnes, have you given her all?

AGNES. Here is his christening robe. Take that, too.

GIPSY. Good. That seems to be all. I'll go.
    I'll wrap him up outside. Then I'll be on my way. (*Goes.*)

AGNES. Tell me, Brand. Haven't I given enough now?

BRAND. Did you give them willingly?

AGNES. No.

BRAND. Then your gift is nothing. The demand remains.

He turns to go.

AGNES (*is silent until he is almost at the door, then cries*). Brand!

BRAND. What is it?

AGNES. I lied. (*Shows him a child's cap.*)
    Look. I kept one thing.

BRAND. The cap?

AGNES. Yes.

BRAND. Stay with your idols. (*Turns.*)

AGNES. Wait!

BRAND. What do you want?

AGNES (*holds out the cap to him*). Oh, you know.

BRAND (*turns*). Willingly?

AGNES. Willingly.

BRAND. Give it to me. The woman is still outside. (*Goes.*)

AGNES *stands motionless for a moment. Gradually the expression on her face changes to one of exultation.* BRAND *comes back. She runs joyfully towards him, and throws her arms round his neck.*

AGNES. I am free, Brand! I am free!

BRAND. Agnes!

AGNES. The darkness is past. The mist has stolen away.
   The clouds have gone. Through the night, beyond death,
   I see the morning.
BRAND. Agnes! Yes; you have conquered.
AGNES. Yes, I have conquered now. Conquered death
   And fear. He was born to die. Ulf is in heaven.
   If I dared, if I could, I would not beg for him back again.
   Giving my child has saved my soul from death.
   Thank you for guiding my hand. You have fought for me
   Unflinchingly. Now the weight has fallen on you –
   Of All or Nothing. Now you stand
   In the valley of choice.
BRAND. Agnes, you speak in riddles. Our struggle is over.
AGNES. Have you forgotten, Brand?
   He dies who sees Jehovah face to face.
BRAND. No! Agnes, no! You shall not leave me.
   Let me lose everything else, everything,
   But not you. Don't leave me, Agnes!
AGNES. Choose. You stand where the road divides.
   Quench the light that burns in me. Give me back
   My idols. The woman is still outside.
   Let me go back to my blindness. Push me back
   Into the mire where till now I have sinned.
   You can do anything. You are free to.
   I have no strength to oppose you. If you will,
   And dare do it, I am your wife as before.
   Choose.
BRAND. Agnes, you must not go back.
   Oh, far from this place, far from our memories of sorrow,
   You will find that life and light are one.
AGNES. Do you forget the thousand souls here
   Whom God has called you to save? Whom your God bade
        you lead
   Home to the fountain of redemption? Choose.
BRAND. I have no choice.

AGNES (*embraces him*).

> Thank you for this. Thank you for everything.
> I am tired now. I must sleep.

BRAND. Sleep, Agnes. Your day's work is ended.

AGNES. The day is ended, and the candle is lit for the night.

> The victory took all my strength.
> O, but God is easy to praise! Goodnight, Brand.

BRAND. Goodnight.

AGNES. Goodnight. Thank you for everything.

> Now I want to sleep. (*Goes.*)

BRAND. Soul, be steadfast to the end.

> The victory of victories is to lose everything.
> Only that which is lost remains eternal.

Act Five

Six months later. The new church is ready, and stands decorated for the ceremony of consecration. The river runs close by. It is early morning, and misty. The SEXTON *is hanging garlands outside the church. After a few moments, the* SCHOOLMASTER *enters.*

SCHOOLMASTER. Good morning! My word!
  The village has come to life today.
  People are pouring in from miles around.
  The whole fjord's white with sails.
SEXTON. Yes. The people have woken up.
  It's not like the old days. Then we slept.
  Life used to be peaceful. Now they have
  To change everything. Well, I don't know.
SCHOOLMASTER. Life, sexton, life.
SEXTON. What has life to do with us?
SCHOOLMASTER. Ah, we are not ordinary parishioners.
  We are public officials. Our task
  Is to keep church discipline and instruct the young,
  And stand aloof from all controversy.
SEXTON. The priest's the cause of it all.
SCHOOLMASTER. He's no right to be. But he's no fool. He knows
  What impresses people. So he builds his church.
  As soon as people see something being done,
  They go crazy. It doesn't matter what it is,
  As long as something's being done.
SEXTON. Ssh!
SCHOOLMASTER. What is it?
SEXTON. Quiet!
SCHOOLMASTER. Good gracious, someone's playing the organ.

SEXTON. It's him.

SCHOOLMASTER. Who? The priest?

SEXTON. Exactly.

SCHOOLMASTER. He's out early. He doesn't sleep well these
    days.

SEXTON. He's been gnawed by loneliness ever since he lost his
    wife.
    He tries to keep his sorrow to himself,
    But it breaks out now and then. Listen!
    Every note sounds as though he were weeping
    For his wife and child.

SCHOOLMASTER. It's as if they were talking.

SEXTON. As if one were weeping, the other consoling.
    The new church hasn't brought him much happiness.

SCHOOLMASTER. Or any of us. The day the old church fell
    It seemed to take with it everything
    In which our life had been rooted.

SEXTON. They shouted: 'Down with it, down with it!'
    But when the beams began to fall,
    They dropped their eyes guiltily, as though a sacrilege
    Had been committed against the old house of God.

SCHOOLMASTER. As long as the new church was unfinished
    They still felt they belonged to the old.
    But, as the spire climbed upwards, they grew uneasy.
    And now, yes, now the day has come.
    How quiet everything is. They are afraid,
    As though they had been summoned to elect
    A new God. Where is the priest?
    I feel frightened.

SEXTON. So do I, so do I!

SCHOOLMASTER. We must not forget ourselves. We are men,
    Not children. Good morning. My pupils are waiting.

He goes.

SEXTON. I must get to work. Idleness is the Devil's friend.

He goes.

The organ, which has been subdued during the preceding dialogue, peals once loudly, ending in a harsh discord. A few moments later, BRAND *comes out of the church.*

BRAND. No. I can find no harmony. Only discord.
 The walls and roof imprison the music,
 As a coffin imprisons a corpse.
 I have tried, I have tried; the organ has lost its tongue.
 I lifted its voice in prayer, but it was thrown back
 Broken, like the note of a cracked and rusted bell.
 It was as if the Lord God stood enthroned
 On high in the choir, and cast it down in His wrath,
 Refusing my petition.
 'I shall rebuild the Lord's house and make it greater' –
 That was my boast. Is this what I envisaged?
 Is this the vision I once had
 Of a vault spanning the world's pain?
 If Agnes had lived, it would have been different.
 She would have banished my doubts.
 She could see greatness where I saw only smallness.

He sees the decorations.

 Garlands. Flags. They have set up my name in gold.
 God, give me light, or else bury me
 A thousand fathoms in the earth.
 Everyone praises me, but their words burn me.
 If I could hide myself. If only I could hide.
MAYOR (*enters in full uniform, and hails* BRAND *triumphantly*).
 Well, the great day's arrived! Warmest congratulations,
 My noble friend! You are a mighty man.
 Your name will soon be famous throughout the land.
 Congratulations! I feel moved, deeply moved,
 But very happy. And you?
BRAND. As though a hand were pressed around my throat.

MAYOR. Well, we mustn't have that. You must preach your
    best
    This morning. The new church has marvellous acoustics.
    Everyone I've spoken to is full of admiration.

BRAND. Really?

MAYOR. Yes. The provost himself was quite amazed,
    And praised them highly. What a noble building
    It is! What style! What size!

BRAND. You think that?

MAYOR. Think what?

BRAND. That it seems big?

MAYOR. Seems? Why, it is big.

BRAND. Yes, so it is.
    We have only exchanged an old lie for a new.
    They used to say: 'How old our church is!' Now
    They squeal: 'How big! How wonderfully big!'
    They must be told the truth. The church, as it stands,
    Is small. To hide that would be to lie.

MAYOR. God bless my soul, what strange words! What do you
    mean?
    But I've news for you. That's why I came.
    Your fame has spread, and now you have attracted
    Favourable attention in the highest circles.
    Royalty! You're to receive a decoration!
    It will be presented to you this morning.
    The Grand Cross.

BRAND. I am already crushed beneath a heavier cross.
    Let who can take that from me.

MAYOR. What? You don't seem very excited by the news.

BRAND. Oh, it's useless.
    You don't understand a word I say.
    I'm tired. Go and chatter to someone else.

He turns and walks towards the church.

MAYOR. Well, really! He must have been drinking. (*Goes.*)

BRAND. Oh, Agnes, Agnes, why did you fail me?
    I am weary of this game which no one wins
    And no one loses. I am tired of fighting alone.

Enter PROVOST.

PROVOST. Dear children! Blessed lambs! I beg your pardon –
    My sermon! I've been practising it all morning.
    Thank you, dear brother, thank you.
    My heartfelt thanks. Others more eloquent
    And wittier than I will thank you at greater length
    After luncheon. There will be many speeches.
    But, my dear Brand, you look so pale.
BRAND. My strength and courage failed me long ago.
PROVOST. Quite understandable.
    So many things to worry about, and no one
    To help you. But now the worst is over.
    Your fellow-priests are deeply proud of you,
    And the humble people are full of gratitude.
    Heartfelt gratitude. Everyone says the same
    About the church. 'What style! What size!'
    And the luncheon! My goodness, what a banquet!
    I was there just now, and watched them roasting the ox.
    You never saw a finer animal.
    They must have gone to a lot of trouble
    With meat as expensive as it is these days.
    But we mustn't ask about that. There was something else
    I wanted to talk to you about.
BRAND. Speak.
PROVOST. Well, now, you mustn't think I'm angry with you.
    You're young, you're new. You're from the city,
    And don't know country people's ways.
    To speak plainly, my complaint is this.
    You treat each one of your parishioners
    As though he were a separate spiritual problem.
    Between ourselves, that's a mistake.

You must treat all alike. We can't afford to discriminate.

BRAND. Explain yourself more clearly.

PROVOST. What I mean is this.
    The state sees religion as the best means
    Of improving the country's moral tone.
    The best insurance against unrest.
    Good Christian means good citizen.
    Now the state can only achieve this
    Through its officials; in this case, the priests.

BRAND. Go on.

PROVOST. Your church is of benefit to the state, and therefore
    You have a responsibility to the state.
    With the gift goes an obligation.

BRAND. By God, I never meant that.

PROVOST. Well, now, my friend, it's too late.

BRAND. Too late? We shall see about that.

PROVOST. I don't want to argue. I'm not asking you to do
    Anything wicked. I really can't see what worries you.
    You can minister just as well to the souls in your care
    By serving the state at the same time.
    Your job isn't to save every Jack and Jill
    From damnation, but to see that the parish as a whole
    Finds grace. We want all men to be equal.
    But you are creating inequality
    Where it never existed before. Until now
    Each man was a member of the Church.
    You have taught him to look upon himself
    As an individual, requiring special treatment.
    This will result in the most frightful confusion.
    The surest way to destroy a man
    Is to turn him into an individual.
    Very few men can fight the world alone.

BRAND. Do you know what you are asking me to do?
    You are demanding that, at the cock-crow of the state,
    I shall betray the ideal for which I have lived.

PROVOST. Betray an ideal? My dear Brand, nobody
    Is asking you to do anything of the sort.
    I'm just showing you your duty.
    I only ask you to subdue those talents
    Which are not useful to our community.
    Aspire to be a saint, but be a good fellow
    And keep such aspirations to yourself.
    Don't encourage others to imitate you.
    Why be obstinate? You'll suffer for it in the end.
BRAND. I can see the mark of Cain upon your brow.
    Cowardice, greed and worldly wisdom
    Have slain the pure Abel that once dwelt in you.
PROVOST. There's no call to get personal. I don't intend
    To prolong this argument. I merely beg you
    To consider your position if you want to get on.
    Every man must curb his individuality,
    Humble himself, and not always be trying
    To rise above his fellows. The man who fights alone
    Will never achieve anything of lasting value.
    Well, goodbye. I am going to preach a sermon
    On the duality of human nature,
    And must take a little light refreshment first. (*Goes.*)
BRAND. No. Not yet. They have not got me yet.
    This churchyard has had blood to drink.
    My light, my life, lie buried here,
    But they will not get my soul.
    It is terrible to stand alone.
    Wherever I look, I see death.
    It is terrible to hunger for bread
    When every hand offers me a stone.
    If only one person would share my faith,
    And give me strength, give me peace.

EJNAR, *pale and emaciated and dressed in black, comes down the road. He stops on seeing* BRAND.

BRAND. Ejnar! You!

EJNAR. Yes, that is my name.

BRAND. I have been longing to meet someone whose heart
    Was not of wood or stone. Come and talk to me.

EJNAR. I need no priest. I have found peace.

BRAND. You are angry with me for what happened
    When we last met.

EJNAR.   No, I do not blame you.
    You are the blind guide Our Saviour sent me
    When I was playing the world's wild game,
    Wandering in the vacant paths of sin.

BRAND. What language is this?

EJNAR.   The language of peace.
    The language a man learns when he shakes off
    The sleep of sin and wakes regenerated.

BRAND. Strange. I had heard –

EJNAR. I was seduced by pride, and belief
    In my own strength. But, God be praised,
    He did not abandon his foolish sheep.
    When the moment was ripe, He opened my eyes.

BRAND. How?

EJNAR. I fell.

BRAND. Fell?

EJNAR. Yes, into drunkenness and gambling.
    He gave me a taste for cards and dice –

BRAND. And you call this the Lord's doing?

EJNAR. That was my first step towards salvation.
    Then He took my health from me, my talent
    For painting, and my love of merriment.
    I was taken to hospital, where I lay sick
    A long while, lay as though in flames.
    I thought I saw in all the rooms
    Thousands of huge flies. At last they let me go,
    And I became a child of the Lord.

BRAND. And then?

EJNAR. I became a preacher of total abstinence,
    And am now a missionary.

BRAND. A missionary? Where?

EJNAR. In Africa. I am on my way there now.
    I must go. My time is short.

BRAND. Won't you stay for a while? As you see,
    We have a feast-day here.

EJNAR.   Thank you, no.
    My place is with the black souls. Goodbye.

BRAND. Don't you want to ask what happened to – ?

EJNAR. To whom? Ah, that young woman
    Who held me struggling in her net of lust,
    Before I became cleansed by the True Faith.
    Yes, what's happened to her?

BRAND. The next year, she became my wife.

EJNAR. Such matters do not concern me.

BRAND. Our life together was richly blessed
    With joy, and sorrow. Our child died –

EJNAR. A triviality.

BRAND. Perhaps you are right. He was lent, not given.
    And we shall meet again. But then
    She left me, too. Their graves grow green
    Side by side.

EJNAR. Vanity, Brand, vanity.

BRAND. That too?

EJNAR. All that is important is how she died.

BRAND. In hope of the dawn, with the heart's wealth untouched,
    Her will steadfast even to her last night,
    Grateful for all that life had given her
    And had taken away, she went to her grave.

EJNAR. Vanity, vanity, man. How was her faith?

BRAND. Unshakable.

EJNAR. In whom?

BRAND. In her God.

EJNAR. Her God cannot save her. She is damned.

BRAND. What are you saying?

EJNAR. Damned, poor soul.

BRAND (*calmly*). Go your way, fool.

EJNAR. The prince of darkness will have you in his clutches.
    You will burn, like her, in everlasting fire.

BRAND. You dare to pronounce judgment on her and me,
    Poor, sinning fool?

EJNAR. My faith has washed me clean.

BRAND. Hold your tongue.

EJNAR. Hold yours. I smell sulphur here,
    And glimpse the Devil's horns upon your brow.
    I am a grain of God's immortal wheat,
    But you are chaff upon the wind of Judgment.

    He goes.

BRAND (*stares after him for a moment, then his eyes flame and he
    cries*).
    And that was the man who was to give me strength!
    Now all my bonds are broken. I shall march
    Under my own flag, even if none will follow.

MAYOR (*enters in haste*).
    Hurry, Brand! The procession is lined up
    Ready to move towards the church.

BRAND. Let them come.

MAYOR. Without you? Listen, the crowd is shouting for you.
    Go and calm them, or I fear they'll grow violent.

BRAND. I shall stay here.

MAYOR. Are you mad? Use your influence to control them.
    Ah, it's too late.

*The crowd streams in, forcing its way through the decorations
towards the church.*

CROWD. Father! Brand! Where is the priest?
    Look! There he is! Open the church, father! Open the
        church!

PROVOST (*to* MAYOR). Cannot you control them?

MAYOR. They won't pay any attention to me.

BRAND. At last a current has stirred this stagnant pool.
    Men, you stand at the crossroads! Will yourselves to be
      new!
    Destroy everything in you that is rotten!
    Only then can the great temple be built,
    As it must and shall.

PRIESTS AND OFFICIALS. The priest is mad. He is mad.

BRAND. Yes, I was. I was mad to think
    That to double the church's size would be enough.
    I did not see that it was All or Nothing.
    I lost myself in compromise. But today
    The Lord has spoken. The trump of doom
    Has sounded over this house. Now all doubt is past.
    People! Compromise is the way of Satan!

CROWD (*in fury*). Away with them, they have blinded us.
    Away with them, they have stolen our spirit.

BRAND. No. Your enemy lurks within you, binding you;
    A worm sapping your strength.
    Why have you come to the church? Only
    To gape at the show, to gape at its steeple,
    To listen to the organ and the bells,
    Enjoy the glow of high-sounding speeches.
    This was not what I dreamed.
    I dreamed that I might build a church so great
    That it would embrace, not just faith and doctrine,
    But everything in life
    Which God has given as a part of life.
    The day's toil, the evening's rest, the night's
    Sorrows, the fresh delights of burning youth,
    The river that flows below, the waterfall
    That roars between the rocks, the cry of the storm,
    And the soft voices that call from the sea.
    These should be one with the Word of God,
    With the organ music and the people's singing.

The thing that stands here is a lie, a monstrous lie!
Away with it!
CROWD. Lead us! Lead us! Lead us to victory!
PROVOST. Do not listen to him. He is not a true Christian.
BRAND. No, you are right. I am not a true Christian.
Neither are you, nor is anyone here.
A true Christian must have a soul,
And show me one who has kept his soul!
You grind away God's image, live like beasts,
Then join the grovelling queue to beg for grace.
Has He not said that only if ye are
As little children can ye enter the kingdom?
Come then, both men and women;
Show yourselves with fresh children's faces
In the great church of life!
MAYOR. Open the door!
CROWD (*cries as though in anguish*).
No, not this church! Not this church! The church of life!
BRAND. Our church is boundless. It has no walls.
Its floor is the green earth,
The moorland, the meadow, the sea, the fjord.
Only heaven can span its roof.
There, life and faith shall melt together.
The day's toil there is a flight among the stars,
Is one with children's play round the Christmas tree,
Is one with the dance of the king before the ark.

*A storm seems to shake the crowd. Some turn away, but most of
them press closer round* BRAND.

CROWD. You give us light! We have lived in darkness!
Show us the Church of Life! Life and faith must be one!
PROVOST. Stop him, stop him! He will take our flock from us.
MAYOR (*quietly*). Keep calm, man. Let him rave.
BRAND (*to* CROWD). Away from this place! God is not here.
His kingdom is perfect freedom.

He locks the church door, and stands with the keys in his hand.

I am priest here no longer. I withdraw my gift.

He throws the keys into the river.

If you want to enter, creep in through the cellars.
Your backs are supple.

MAYOR (*quietly, relieved*).
Well, that's the end of his decoration.

PROVOST. He'll never be a bishop now.

BRAND. Come, all you who are young and strong!
Leave this dead valley! Follow me to victory!
One day you must awaken! Arise
From your misery! Arise from your half-life!
Slay the enemy within you!

MAYOR. Stop! Stop!

CROWD. Show us the way! We will follow!

BRAND. Over the frozen ocean of the moor!
We shall wander through the land, freeing
Our souls, purifying, crushing our weakness.
Be men, be priests, renew God's faded image.
Make the earth your temple.

The CROWD, *including the* SCHOOLMASTER *and the* SEXTON,
swarm around him. They raise BRAND *high on their shoulders.*

CROWD. A vision! Follow him! Arise!
Leave the valley! Up to the moor!

They stream up through the valley. A few remain behind.

PROVOST. Are you blind? Can't you see that the devil is in his
words?

MAYOR. Turn back, turn back!
You belong to the calm waters of this village.
Good people, stop! He will lead you to destruction.
Listen! They will not answer, the swine!

PROVOST. Think of your homes and houses.

CROWD. A greater house shall be built.

MAYOR. How will you live?

CROWD. The chosen people found manna in the wilderness.

PROVOST (*gazes after them with folded hands, and says quietly*).

They have left me. My flock has abandoned me.

MAYOR. Do not fear, my lord. Victory will soon be ours.

PROVOST (*almost in tears*).

Victory? But our flock has left us.

MAYOR. We are not beaten. Not if I know my sheep.

He goes after them. The PROVOST *follows.*

By the highest farm above the village. A bleak mountain landscape towers behind. It is raining. BRAND *appears over the hillside, followed by the crowd of men, women and children.*

BRAND. Forward! Forward! Victory lies ahead.

Forget your village. Leave it in its hollow.

The mist has buried it. Forget that you were beasts.

Now you are men of the Lord. Climb onward, climb!

A MAN. Wait, wait. My old father is tired.

ANOTHER. I have eaten nothing since yesterday.

SEVERAL. Yes, give us food. Quench our thirst.

BRAND. We must cross the mountain first. Follow me.

MAN. The path's too steep. We'll never get there by nightfall.

SEXTON. The Ice Church lies that way.

BRAND. The steep path is the shortest.

A WOMAN. My child is sick.

ANOTHER WOMAN. My feet are sore.

A THIRD. Water, water, we are thirsty.

SCHOOLMASTER. Give them strength, priest. Their courage
is failing.

CROWD. Perform a miracle, father. A miracle.

BRAND. Your slavery has branded you vilely.

You demand your wage before your work is done.

Rise up, shake off your sloth.

If you cannot, go back to your graves.

SCHOOLMASTER. He is right, victory must be won first.

The reward will follow.

BRAND. You will be rewarded, my people,

As surely as a God watches keen-eyed over this world.

CROWD. He prophesies! He prophesies!

OTHERS IN THE CROWD. Tell us, priest, will the battle be hard?

Will it be long? Will it be bloody?

A MAN. Will we have to be brave?

SCHOOLMASTER. There's no question of our lives being endangered?

A MAN. What will be my share of the reward?

A WOMAN. My son will not die, will he, father?

SEXTON. Will victory be ours by Tuesday?

BRAND (*stares at them bewildered*).

What are you asking? What do you want to know?

SEXTON. First, how long shall we have to fight?

Secondly, how much will it cost us?

Thirdly, what will be our reward?

BRAND. That is what you want to know?

SCHOOLMASTER. Yes; you didn't tell us.

BRAND (*angrily*). Then I shall tell you now.

CROWD. Speak! Speak!

BRAND. How long will you have to fight? Until you die!

What will it cost? Everything you hold dear.

Your reward? A new will, cleansed and strong,

A new faith, integrity of spirit;

A crown of thorns. That will be your reward.

CROWD (*screams in fury*). Betrayed! You have betrayed us!

You have tricked us!

BRAND. I have not betrayed or tricked you.

CROWD. You promised us victory. Now you ask for sacrifice.

BRAND. I have promised you victory,

And I swear it shall be won through you.

But we who march in the first rank must fall.

CROWD. He wants us to die! To save people who haven't been
    born!

BRAND. The only road to Canaan lies through a desert.

That desert is self-sacrifice. Death is the only victory.

I consecrate you soldiers of the Lord.

SCHOOLMASTER. We can't go back.

SEXTON. And we daren't go on.

WOMEN (*pointing in terror down the road*).

Look! The provost!

SCHOOLMASTER. Now don't be frightened.

Enter PROVOST.

PROVOST. My children! My sheep! Listen to the voice

Of your old shepherd. Do not listen

To this man. He would trick you with false promises.

CROWD. That's true.

PROVOST. We understand weakness. We forgive those

Who truly repent. Look into your hearts

Before it is too late.

Can you not see the black art he has used

To get you into his power?

CROWD. Yes. He has bewitched us.

PROVOST. Think, my children. What can you achieve,

Humble people born in a humble village?

Were you created to shake the world,

To right wrongs, liberate the oppressed?

You have your humble tasks allotted you;

To attempt more is presumptuous and wrong.

Would you intervene between the hawk and the eagle?

Would you challenge the wolf and the bear?

You will only be preyed on by the ruthless and the mighty,

My sheep, my children.

CROWD. Yes. It's true. He's right.

BRAND. Choose, men and women. Choose.

SOME OF THE CROWD. We want to go home.

OTHERS. Too late, too late. Let us go on.

MAYOR (*hurries in*). What luck that I managed to find you!

WOMEN. Oh, sir, please don't be angry with us.

MAYOR. No time for that. Just you come with me.
    A marvellous thing has happened for the village.
    If you behave sensibly, you will all be rich by nightfall.

CROWD. What? How?

MAYOR. A shoal of fishes has entered the fjord –
    Millions of them!

CROWD. What?

MAYOR. Do you want to spend the night on this mountain?
    Such a shoal has never entered our fjord before.
    A better time is dawning for us, my friends.

BRAND. Choose between him and God.

PROVOST. A miracle! A miracle! A sign from Heaven!
    I have often dreamed that this might happen.
    Now it has. We have been given a sign.

BRAND. If you turn back now, you are lost.

CROWD. A shoal of fishes!

MAYOR. Millions of them!

PROVOST. Food for your children! Gold for your wives!

SEXTON. Will I be allowed to keep my job?

SCHOOLMASTER. Will my school be taken from me?

PROVOST. Use your good influence with the people, and you
    will find us lenient.

MAYOR. Away, away! Don't waste time!

SEXTON. To the boats, to the boats!

SOME OF THE CROWD. What about the priest?

SCHOOLMASTER. The priest? Leave the lunatic.

CROWD. Yes – he lied to us!

PROVOST. He refused his old mother the sacrament.

MAYOR. He killed his child.

SEXTON. And his wife too.

WOMEN. Shame on him! The scoundrel!

PROVOST. A bad son, a bad father, a bad husband.
Where could you find a worse Christian?

CROWD. He pulled our church down. He locked us out of the
new one.

BRAND. I see the mark of Cain on every brow.
I see where you will all end.

CROWD (*roars*). Don't listen to him!
Drive the hell-brand away from the village!
Stone him! Kill him!

They stone BRAND *and drive him up the mountain. Gradually
his pursuers return.*

PROVOST. Oh, my children! Oh, my sheep!
Return to your firesides. Repent of your rash folly,
And you will find that the simple life is good.
Farewell – and good luck to your fishing!

SEXTON. They are true Christians. They are gentle and
merciful.

SCHOOLMASTER. They go their way and let us go ours.

SEXTON. They don't ask us to sacrifice our lives.

SCHOOLMASTER. They are wise.

The CROWD *goes down towards the village.*

PROVOST. God's miracle has saved us.

MAYOR. What miracle?

PROVOST. The shoal of fishes.

MAYOR. Oh, that. A lie, of course.

PROVOST. A lie? Really? Well, I –

MAYOR. I hope your reverence will think it excusable,
In view of the importance of the issue.

PROVOST. Of course, of course. Quite excusable.

MAYOR (*scratches his nose*).
I wonder, though, whether their treatment of him
Wasn't a little inhumane?

PROVOST. The voice of the people is the voice of God.
　　Come!
　　They go.

*Among the peaks. A storm is gathering, hunting the clouds slowly
across the snowfields. Black peaks are visible here and there; then
they are veiled again in mist.* BRAND *appears, blood-stained and
beaten.*

BRAND (*stops and looks back*). A thousand started with me
　　　　　from the valley;
　　Not one has followed me to the mountain top.
　　All of them have the craving in their hearts,
　　But the sacrifice frightens them.
　　Their will is weak; their fear is strong.
　　Someone once died to save their souls,
　　So nothing more is required of them.

　　He sinks down on a stone.

　　It was not for us that He drained the cup of agony,
　　Not for us that the thorn-crown scarred His brow.
　　It was not for us that the lance pierced His side,
　　Not for us that the nails burned
　　Through His hands and feet. We are small and mean.
　　We are not worthy. We defy the call to arms.
　　It was not for us that He carried His cross.

*He throws himself down into the snow and covers his face. After
a while he looks up.*

　　Have I been dreaming? Am I awake?
　　Everything is hidden in mist. Was it all
　　Only a sick man's vision? Have we forgotten
　　The image in whose likeness we were made?
　　Is Man defeated after all? (*Listens.*)
　　Ah! There is a sound in the air like singing.

VOICES (*murmur in the storm*).
　　You can never be like Him, for you are flesh.
　　Do His will, or forsake Him, you are lost, lost.
BRAND. Lost. Lost? I can almost believe it.
　　Did He not reject my prayer in the church?
　　Did He not take from me all I had,
　　Closed every path that might have led me to light?
　　Made me fight until my strength was finished,
　　And then let me be defeated?
VOICES (*louder*). Worm, you will never be like Him.
　　You have drained the cup of death.
　　Follow or forsake Him, your work is doomed.
BRAND (*weeps quietly*). Ulf and Agnes, come back to me.
　　I sit alone on the mountain top.
　　The north wind blows through me, spectres haunt me.

He looks up. A gap opens in the mist, revealing the FIGURE OF A
WOMAN, *wrapped in a light cloak. It is* AGNES.

FIGURE (*smiles, and opens her arms towards him*).
　　Brand, I have come back to you.
BRAND. Agnes? Agnes! (*Moves towards her.*)
FIGURE (*screams*). Stop! A gulf lies between us.
　　　　(*Gently.*) You are not dreaming. You are not asleep.
　　You have been sick, my dear. You have been mad.
　　You dreamed your wife was dead.
BRAND. You are alive? Praise be to – !
FIGURE (*quickly*). Ssh! We have not much time.
　　Come with me, come with me.
BRAND. But – Ulf?
FIGURE. He is alive, too.
BRAND. Alive?
FIGURE. It was all a dream. Your sorrows were a dream.
　　You fought no battle. Ulf is with your mother.
　　She is well, and he grows tall.
　　The old church still stands; you can pull it down, if you wish.

The villagers toil below, as they did before you came,
In the good old days.

BRAND. Good?

FIGURE. Yes. Then there was peace.

BRAND. Peace?

FIGURE. Quickly, Brand. Come with me.

BRAND. Ah, I am dreaming.

FIGURE. No longer. But you need tenderness and care.

BRAND. I am strong.

FIGURE. Not yet. Your dreams will lure you back again.
The mist will swallow you, and take you from me.
Your mind will grow confused again unless
You try the remedy.

BRAND. Oh, give it to me!

FIGURE. You have it.

BRAND. What is it?

FIGURE. Three words.
You must blot them out, wipe them from your memory.
Forget them.

BRAND. Say them!

FIGURE. All or Nothing.

BRAND (*shrinks*). Ah! That?

FIGURE. As surely as I live, and as surely as you shall sometime
die.

BRAND. Alas for us both; the drawn sword
Hangs over us as it hung before.

FIGURE. Be gentle, Brand. My breasts are warm.
Hold me in your strong arms.
Let us go and find the sun and the summer.

BRAND. The sickness will not come again.

FIGURE. It will come, Brand. Be sure.

BRAND (*shakes his head*).
No, I have put it behind me. The horror of dreams
Is past. Now comes the horror of life.

FIGURE. Of life?

BRAND. Come with me, Agnes.

FIGURE. Stop! Brand, what will you do?

BRAND. What I must. Live what till now I dreamed;
Make the illusion real.

FIGURE. Impossible! Remember where that road led you.

BRAND. I will tread it again.

FIGURE. That road of fear in the mist of dreams?
Will you ride it freely and awake?

BRAND. Freely and awake.

FIGURE. And let your child die?

BRAND. And let my child die.

FIGURE. Brand!

BRAND. I must.

FIGURE. And kill me?

BRAND. I must.

FIGURE. Quench the candles in the night,
And shut out the sun in the day?
Never pluck life's fruit, never be soothed
By song? I remember so many songs.

BRAND. I must. Do not waste your prayer.

FIGURE. Do you forget what reward your sacrifices brought
you?
Your hopes betrayed you, everyone forsook you.
Everyone stoned you.

BRAND. I do not suffer for my own reward.
I do not strive for my own victory.

FIGURE. Remember, an Angel with a flaming rod
Drove Man from Paradise.
He set a gulf before the gate.
Over that gulf you cannot leap.

BRAND. The way of longing remains.

FIGURE (*disappears; there is a clap of thunder, the mist gathers
where it stood, and a sharp and piercing scream is heard
as though from one in flight*).
Die! The world has no use for you!

BRAND (*stands for a moment as though dazed*).
　　It disappeared in the mist,
　　Flying on great rough wings across the moor
　　Like a hawk. It was a deceitful spirit;
　　The spirit of compromise.

GERD (*appears with a rifle*).
　　Did you see him? Did you see the hawk?

BRAND. Yes, child. This time I saw him.

GERD. Quick, tell me – which way did he fly?
　　We'll go after him. This time we'll get him.

BRAND. No weapon can harm him. You think you've killed him,
　　But the next moment he's after you,
　　As fierce as ever.

GERD. I stole the reindeer-hunter's rifle, and loaded it
　　With silver. I'm not as mad as they say.

BRAND. I hope you hit him. (*Turns to go.*)

GERD. Priest, you're limping. Your foot's hurt.
　　How did that happen?

BRAND. The people hunted me.

GERD (*goes closer*). Your forehead is red.

BRAND. The people stoned me.

GERD. Your voice used to be clear as song.
　　Now it creaks like leaves in autumn.

BRAND. Everything – everyone –

GERD. What?

BRAND. Betrayed me.

GERD (*stares at him*). Ah! Now I know who you are!
　　I thought you were the priest. Fie upon him and all the
　　　　others!
　　You're the Big Man. The Biggest of all.

BRAND. I used to think I was.

GERD. Let me see your hands.

BRAND. My hands?

GERD. They're scarred with nails. There's blood in your hair.
　　The thorn's teeth have cut your forehead.

You've been on the cross. My father told me
It happened long ago and far away.
But now I see he was deceiving me.
I know you. You're the Saviour Man!

BRAND. Get away from me!

GERD. Shall I fall down at your feet and pray?

BRAND. Go!

GERD. You gave the blood that will save us all.
　　　There are nail holes in your hands. You are the Chosen
　　　　　One.
　　　You are the Greatest of all.

BRAND. I am the meanest thing that crawls on earth.

GERD (*looks up; the clouds are lifting*).
　　　Do you know where you are standing?

BRAND (*stares unseeingly*). I stand upon the lowest stair.
　　　There is far to climb and my feet are sore.

GERD (*savagely*).
　　　Answer me! Do you know where you are standing?

BRAND. Yes, now the mist is lifting.

GERD. Yes, it is lifting. Black Peak points its finger towards
　　　　　heaven.

BRAND (*looks up*). Black Peak? The Ice Church?

GERD. Yes. You came to my church after all.

BRAND. I wish I were far away. Oh, how I long for light
　　　And sun, and the still tenderness of peace.
　　　I long to be where life's summer kingdoms are.
　　　　　(*Weeps.*)
　　　O Jesus, I have called upon Your name.
　　　Why did You never receive me into Your bosom?
　　　You passed close by me, but You never touched me.
　　　Let me hold one poor corner of Your garment
　　　And wet it with my tears of true repentance.

GERD (*pale*).
　　　What's the matter? You're crying! Hot tears.
　　　The ice in my memory is thawing into tears.

You're melting the snow on my church roof.
The ice-priest's cloak is sliding from his shoulders.
(*Trembles.*) Man, why did you never weep before?

BRAND (*serene and shining, as though young again*).
My life was a long darkness.
Now the sun is shining. It is day.
Until today I sought to be a tablet
On which God could write. Now my life
Shall flow rich and warm. The crust is breaking.
I can weep! I can kneel! I can pray! (*Sinks to his knees.*)

GERD (*looks up towards the sky and says timidly and quietly*).
Look, there he sits, the ugly brute. That's him
Casting the shadow. Can't you hear him beating
The sides of the peak with his great wings?
Now is the moment, now! If only the silver will bite!

*She throws the rifle to her cheek and fires. A hollow boom, like
thunder, sounds from high up on the mountain.*

BRAND (*starts up*). What are you doing?

GERD. I hit him! Look, he's falling! Hear how he groans!
Look at his white feathers floating
Down the mountain side! Ah!
He's rolling down on top of us!

BRAND (*sinks exhausted*).
Must each man die to atone for human sin?

GERD. Look how he tumbles and rolls!
Oh, I shan't be afraid any more.
Why, he's as white as a dove! (*Shrieks in fear.*)
Oh, the horrid, horrid roar!
Throws herself down in the snow.

BRAND (*shrinks before the onrushing avalanche*).
Answer me, God, in the moment of death!
If not by Will, how can Man be redeemed?
The avalanche buries him, filling the whole valley.

A VOICE (*cries through the thunder*). He is the God of Love.

Emperor and Galilean

Introduction

In the summer of 1864, soon after his arrival in Italy, Ibsen was staying with his friend Lorentz Dietrichson, a Norwegian art historian, in the village of Genzano outside Rome. Dietrichson tells how they spent the afternoons reading and chatting under the trees on the hills overlooking Lake Nemi, and how 'one day I was lying there reading Ammianus Marcellinus's account of Julian the Apostate's campaigns, and Ibsen became much interested in this. We began to talk of Julian, and I know that the idea of writing about this subject took root in his mind that day. At any rate, when I had finished reading, he said he hoped no one would write about it before he did.' That September, Ibsen wrote to Bjoernson: 'I . . . am planning a tragedy, *Julian the Apostate*, a task which I embrace with inordinate enthusiasm and which I think will bring me joy.'

He was also at this time engaged on a long epic poem about a priest, which in due course he abandoned and rewrote as a poetic drama, *Brand*. On finishing this in the autumn of 1865 he returned to Julian, but found his story too big a theme to fit into the span of a normal play. 'Why can't one write a drama in ten acts?' he asked Dietrichson. 'I can't find room in five.' *Emperor and Galilean* was in fact to fill ten acts, and was to take him nearly eight more years to complete; the malaise of contemporary Europe, and of Norway in particular, obsessed him too much for him to concentrate on the problems of a Roman apostate. He put it aside to write *Peer Gynt*, took it up again in 1868, but now found himself wanting to compose for the theatre again (he had written both *Brand* and *Peer Gynt* only to be read, not acted), and early in 1869, soon after moving from Rome to Dresden, wrote *The League of Youth*, a prose satire about politicians and the forerunner of his great plays on contemporary problems such as *A Doll's House* and *Ghosts*.

He seems not to have got down to the actual writing of *Emperor and Galilean* until late 1870 or early 1871. On 27 June of that year he informed his brother-in-law, Johan Thoresen, that he had now begun it, 'and hope to have it ready by Christmas ... I work blazingly fast, but only for a few hours each day.' On 12 July, he told his publisher, Fredrik Hegel: 'This book will be my masterpiece, and occupies all my thoughts and all my time. The positive view of things which the critics have so long demanded of me they will find here.' On 27 December, he was able to inform Hegel: 'Part One, 'Julian and the Philosophers', comprising three acts, is already finished and *fair-copied* ... I am now busily engaged on Part Two, and this will go more quickly and be much shorter. Part Three will, however, be somewhat longer; the whole thing will probably run to between 280 and 300 pages, all in prose, in a style mainly approximating to that of *The Pretenders*.'

Three weeks later, he told Hegel that he hoped to have the whole play finished by June, and although this proved over-optimistic, on 24 April 1872 he was still sanguine enough to write: 'I shall soon be ready with Part Two of Julian. The third and final section will go easily. The spring has now arrived, and I always work best in warm weather.' He worked hard on it on holiday in Berchtesgaden that July, and on 8 August wrote joyfully to Hegel that he had completed Part Two and that the third and final part 'is so clear in my mind that it will go very much quicker than the others'. On his return to Dresden in August, he was joined by his Danish admirer, the critic Georg Brandes, who asked Ibsen to read some at least of the play to him. 'At first', Brandes recalled in his autobiography, 'he could not be persuaded to read a line of it to me ... He said: "I never write a line without asking myself: 'What will G.B. think of this?' So how could I let you see it in the rough?" However, he shortly afterwards read me long extracts, including the scene between Julian and the mystic Maximus. His quiet voice lent itself well to the expression of what was powerful and disturbing.' Soon after this, he read the whole of Part One to Lorentz Dietrichson, who walked home 'quite shaken, and convinced that I had heard one of the most remarkable tragedies written since the time of Shakespeare. Its mighty figures haunted me even in my dreams.'

By the end of 1872, Ibsen had combined his original Parts One and Two into a single play of five acts, and had begun the draft of his final section, the ultimate Part Two. On 6 February 1873 he was able to tell Hegel: 'I have the great joy to be able to inform you that my great work is finished, and more happily so than anything I have previously written. The book is entitled *Emperor and Galilean: a World Drama in Two Parts*. It contains: Part One: *Caesar's Apostasy*, a play in five acts (170 pages). Part Two: *Emperor Julian*, a play in five acts (252 pages). Do not let the description "World Drama" alarm you: I shall begin fair-copying the play in a week and shall send you a weekly batch of 48 pages . . . This has been a Herculean labour for me: not the work itself, that has gone easily, but the pain it has cost me to live myself freshly and vividly into so distant and alien an age.'

Emperor and Galilean was published on 16 October 1873. 'The booksellers were so interested in this work', Hegel informed his other star author, Bjoernson, who may not have been overjoyed at the news, 'that the large edition . . . was almost entirely subscribed, and the rest were taken by the Copenhagen booksellers on the day of publication.' Critical reaction was generally favourable, though somewhat bewildered. Arne Garborg published a long pamphlet voicing the objections which were to be raised against Ibsen's plays in general as they gradually came to be translated and staged in other countries. 'It is', he wrote, 'with *Emperor and Galilean* as with all of Ibsen's works. One lays them down with a disagreeable feeling of dissatisfaction ... With each book Ibsen merely throws a new *problem* at the world ... from the standpoint he occupies he will never find the whole answer.' (Ibsen countered this objection, on another occasion, by declaring: 'I only ask. My task is not to answer.') Erik Boegh, a perceptive admirer of Ibsen, summed up many people's reaction when he stated in the Danish newspaper *Folkets Avis* that, while *Emperor and Galilean* was 'an interesting work' with 'certain scenes of great power', it was so unlike what one had expected that 'many of his friends and the friends of his muse will surely lay it down sighing: "Thank God Henrik Ibsen has finished *that*"': Ibsen's fellow-authors were less respectful than the critics. J.P. Jacobsen, the Danish novelist whom Rilke so revered, disliked it: 'There's no pace in the play, it's cold, the characters are without character.' So did Bjoernson, who found it 'a great disappointment', though he added a perceptive prophecy: 'I think he's finished with *Brand*-style writing [i.e., epic dramas not intended for the stage] ... and that we shall henceforth have what he will be a master of – plays of plot. We need them!'

Georg Brandes did not at first like it. 'I am sitting in agony over Ibsen's Julian', he wrote to his mother soon after the book's publication. 'I can't really bear the play, though of course there's a good deal in it.' He did not review it until the following year, and although his maturer verdict was kinder he still, as usual where Ibsen's work was concerned, found himself divided. He found the dialogue 'full of dramatic strength and fire' and felt that in the best scenes Ibsen had 'never written with greater effect, perhaps never as greatly'. But, like Garborg, he questioned Ibsen's metaphysics: 'His strength and originality lie in psychological insight, and not in the solution of metaphysical problems.' But he granted that 'it is full of splendid things, in the highest sense profound and poetic', and ended by declaring that the work confirmed one's hopes for Ibsen's future, and that 'never previously has he understood and portrayed history as he has here'. With few of these judgements would one disagree.

Ibsen was delighted with the book's reception. 'Who would have supposed that the whole large first edition would so soon disappear?', he wrote to Hegel on 13 November. 'From many letters from Norway I gather that none of my previous books has created such a stir up there. It has established itself in circles not normally concerned with literature.'

Of all Ibsen's plays, including even *When We Dead Awaken*, *Emperor and Galilean* is the one most under rated by posterity; indeed, it is unique among his major works in having been admired less by posterity than by his contemporaries. Ibsen himself several times referred to it as his masterpiece[1]; most subsequent commentators have rejected it as a failure. But few Ibsen commentators can have seen it, and fewer still seem able to read a play as a play, mentally excising (as a director of Shakespeare must) what on the stage would be tedious and superfluous. *Brand* was regarded as unactable in Britain until 1959, *When We Dead Awaken* until 1968; in some countries they are still so regarded, awaiting the director who can reveal their profound and exciting theatricality. The same is true of *Emperor and Galilean*. It has longueurs, especially in the first half of Part Two, but so have *Brand* and *Peer Gynt*; once one has stripped away the superfluous detail, a play is revealed which is a worthy successor to those two great dramas.

Emperor and Galilean is full of extraordinary scenes: the opening in Constantinople, with Julian and his brother waiting for the mad Emperor's hand to fall on them as on their eleven murdered kinsmen; Julian's confrontation with the philosopher Libanius who tempts him to forsake the

---

[1] See for example William Archer's introduction to the English translation of the play (London, 1907), p. xvi, and the report by Arnt Dehli printed in *Aftenposten*, 14 March 1928.

church for the debating-halls; Maximus' evocation of the ghosts of the 'corner-stones' of history, and Julian's sudden realisation that he himself is to be the third of these; Helena's revelation that she is pregnant by another man, and Julian's order to the doctor not to save her; and the great climax to Part One, when Helena's body lies in the church and the army outside grows mutinous while Julian hesitates to lead them against Rome until he has taken the final step of renouncing Christianity; he learns that Helena's body is working miracles because she was 'the pure woman' and, maddened by the falsity of this, he makes the sacrifice and appears with the blood of the beast on his forehead. The first three acts of Part Two mark a certain slackening of tension, and are over-weighted with grubbed-up knowledge which Ibsen does not carry very lightly; in any production, they would profit most by cutting. But the last two acts are of the quality of the whole of Part One; Julian's gradual submission to the force on which he has turned his back, but which he cannot evade, is as powerful and moving in its inevitability as the final acts of *Brand*, *Peer Gynt* or any of the great prose plays.

Emperor and Galilean marks a vital turning-point in Ibsen's development as a dramatist. Although it is on an epic scale like *Brand* and *Peer Gynt*, he wrote it in prose; it is both the last play of one period and the first of another. The conviction which had been growing in him for several years that he must abandon the poetic medium in which he had gained his greatest triumphs found expression in a letter he wrote on 15 January 1874 to Edmund Gosse. Gosse, in a review of the play published in the *Spectator* on 27 December 1873, had regretted Ibsen's abandonment of verse; and we must be grateful to Gosse that he wrote as he did, for his remarks stimulated Ibsen to a clear statement of his new policy.

'The illusion I wanted to produce', he informed Gosse, 'is

that of reality. I wished to produce the impression on the reader that what he was reading was something that had really happened. If I had employed verse, I should have counteracted my own intention, and prevented the accomplishment of the task I had set myself. The many ordinary and insignificant characters whom I have introduced into the play would have become indistinct, and indistinguishable from one another, if I had allowed all of them to speak in one and the same rhythmical measure. We are no longer living in the age of Shakespeare. Among sculptors, there is already talk of painting statues in the natural colours. Much can be said both for and against this. I have no desire to see the Venus de Milo painted, but I would rather see the head of a negro executed in black rather than white marble. Speaking generally, the style must conform to the degree of ideality which pervades the representation. My new drama is no tragedy in the ancient acceptation; what I desired to depict were human beings, and therefore I would not let them talk in "the language of the gods".[1]

In other words, *Emperor and Galilean* is at the same time Ibsen's farewell to the epic drama (at any rate until the final act of *John Gabriel Borkman* and *When We Dead Awaken*), and the forerunner of those naturalistic prose plays which were shortly to explode upon the nineteenth century like a series of bombs.

Despite the seeming remoteness of its theme, *Emperor and Galilean* is one of Ibsen's most personal statements, as self-analytical as *The Pretenders*, *Brand*, *The Master Builder* or *When We Dead Awaken*. Somewhat unexpectedly, he took pains to establish this fact. 'I have put a good deal of my own inner life into the play', he had written to Gosse on 14 October 1872, and again to Gosse on 20 February 1873: 'There is much self-anatomy in this book.' Three days later

---

[1] Edmund Gosse's translation.

he told Ludvig Daae that it contained 'more of my own personal experience than I would publicly admit'. The problem that baffled and finally destroyed Julian was one that was always at the back of Ibsen's mind, though he seldom if ever mentioned it: where to find a faith to replace the Christianity of his upbringing. The third quarter of the nineteenth century was, more than preceding ages, a time of revolt against conventional religious thinking, with Bible criticism and natural science marching hand in hand, and *Emperor and Galilean*, in its search for a 'third kingdom' (a phrase which had not yet acquired a sinister significance) was as much a book of its period as *The Origin of Species*, Renan's *Life of Jesus*, and *Das Kapital*. 'He who has once been under Him [Christ] can never be free', says Julian, and they are words that Ibsen himself, and many of his contemporaries, might have spoken.

It is a cliché that man is attracted by the qualities he lacks, and Ibsen's plays are permeated by a longing for what, in *Ghosts*, he was to term *livsglæde*, the joy of life. He deplored its absence in contemporary Christian teaching, which he probably (and with reason) blamed for his own inability to experience that joy; Brand and Pastor Manders, and those daunting lay preachers Roerlund, Gregers Werle and Kroll, denounce it as a sin; Bishop Nicholas and John Rosmer would like to enjoy it but cannot, as though castrated by their own church upbringing. To find a religion which would combine Christian ethics with the joy of life is a problem that has troubled many a piously educated man and woman; it was a problem which Ibsen personally was never to solve, and it is the central theme of *Emperor and Galilean* as it was to be the theme (or part-theme) of so many of his plays, whether explicitly as in *Ghosts* or *Rosmersholm*, or implicitly, as in *The Master Builder*, *John Gabriel Borkman* and *When We Dead Awaken*.

When Ibsen said that *Emperor and Galilean* contained

'more of my own personal experience than I would care to admit', I do not think there is much doubt that he was referring to the emotional strait-jacket in which he found himself confined, and from which, like his childhood Christianity, he could never escape. It is relevant to add here a remark that Professor Francis Bull once made to me: that his father, Edvard Bull, who was Ibsen's doctor during the latter's last years, once told his son that Ibsen was preternaturally shy about exposing his sexual organs even during medical examination. There was, indeed, much of Hedda Gabler in her creator.

Emperor and Galilean was, curiously, the first of Ibsen's plays to be published in Britain, in 1876 in a version by Catherine Ray. Ludvig Josephson, who had staged the first production of *Peer Gynt* at the Christiania Theatre in 1876, planned to present Part One in 1878, but was sacked before he could do so, and it was not until 1896 that an adaptation of it was performed at the Leipzig Stadttheater. It was first seen in Norway in 1903, when Part One was produced at the National Theatre in Christiania. To date, it has not been staged, even in part, in either Britain or the United States, though it has twice been heard on British radio, most recently in 1990. The late Michael Elliott, the greatest of Ibsen directors, admired it immensely and in 1962, when he was head of the Old Vic Theatre in London, commissioned Casper Wrede and Amund Hoenningstad to adapt it for the stage and myself to translate it, planning to present it during his next season. Unfortunately for us and for Ibsen, the National Theatre was created that year and took over the Old Vic as its headquarters. Elliott begged me not to publish our version until he had a chance to do it elsewhere, but the right circumstances for so huge an enterprise never arose (he suggested the idea to the Edinburgh Festival in the early eighties, but they turned it down). When Elliott died in 1984, and the Washington Square Press offered to publish my complete Ibsen translations in America, it seemed appropriate to include this, after it had languished in typescript for nearly a quarter of a century. I have, however, revised it considerably.

I make no apology for presenting this play, like *Brand*, in a cut version. Other translations of the complete texts are available for comparison, and judicious cutting reveals more clearly than the full texts the dramatic shape of the plays. About one fifth of Part One and almost half of Part Two have been deleted. Part One contains all its original scenes, but in Part Two, Act One has been completely cut apart from two long speeches, and Acts Two and Three, also heavily cut, have been combined with those speeches into a single act. The deleted passages deal in unnecessary detail with the squabbles between pagans and Christians following Julian's accession to the throne. Acts Four and Five, only slightly cut, are presented in this edition as Acts Two and Three. A section on pages 248–50 has been transposed from its original position ten pages further on, and on pages 242–3 the seven speeches beginning 'It was He Who laid the temple of Jerusalem in ruins' have been brought forward from the end of the scene.

Finally, one may note that *Emperor and Galilean* is much truer to the facts than most historical plays. In his 1907 introduction, William Archer states that Ibsen reproduced the main lines of Julian's career with 'extraordinary fidelity', much of the dialogue being borrowed almost word for word either from Julian's own writings or from other contemporary documents. Naturally, Ibsen took some liberties. The important character of Agathon is fictitious; there is no historical evidence of any intrigue between Gallus and Helena, nor for the symposium at Ephesus, though Maximus was rumoured to have caused Julian to undergo certain supernatural experiences. The great scene in the catacombs which concludes Part One is based on fact, for Julian is reported to have brought the high priest of the pagan mysteries (not Maximus) from Greece to Gaul and to have undergone the prescribed rites of pagan conversion before rebelling against Constantius. In Part Two, Julian, a very humane man by the standards of his age, is made far more ruthless a persecutor than even his enemies claimed; as Archer observed, 'a considerable part of his alleged oppression [of the Christians] lay in the withdrawal of extravagant privileges conferred on them by his predecessors.' Otherwise, *Emperor and Galilean* is good history in addition to being great drama.

Two translation problems may be noted. The Norwegian word *rige*, like the German *Reich*, means both 'empire' and 'kingdom'. In English one cannot use the word 'empire' in the last sentence of the Lord's Prayer, or write of 'the Roman Kingdom', so that one has to alternate between the two words. Secondly, the word 'Caesar' had, by the fourth century A.D., come to mean, not Emperor, but Crown Prince; thus, one cannot write: 'Render unto Caesar the things that are Caesar's.' The Norwegian for 'emperor' is *kejser*, which makes the transition easier in that language than it can be in English.

MICHAEL MEYER

Part One
Caesar's Apostasy

Characters

This translation of Part 1 was first broadcast on BBC Radio 3 on 30 March 1990, and repeated on 19 May 1991. The cast was:

THE EMPEROR CONSTANTIUS	Keith Drinkel
THE EMPRESS EUSEBIA	Sue Broomfield
THE PRINCESS HELENA, *sister to the* EMPEROR	Kathryn Hurlbutt
PRINCE GALLUS, *cousin to the* EMPEROR	Peter Gunn
PRINCE JULIAN, *younger half-brother to* GALLUS	Robert Glenister
MEMNON, *an Ethiopian, the* EMPEROR'S *personal slave*	Ben Onwukwe
POTAMON, *a goldsmith*	Norman Bird
FOKION, *a dyer*	Stephen Garlick
EUNAPIUS, *a barber*	David King
A FRUITSELLER	Dale Rapley
(AN OFFICER OF THE GUARD)	
(A SOLDIER)	
(A PAINTED WOMAN)	
(A MAN WITH TWISTED LIMBS)	
A BLIND BEGGAR	Garard Green
AGATHON, *son of a Cappadocian vine-grower*	Charles Simpson
LIBANIUS, *a philosopher*	Hugh Dickson
GREGOR OF NAZIANZ	David Timson
BASIL OF CAESAREA	Paul Downing
SALLUST OF PERUSIA	Stephen Tomkinson
HEKEBOLIUS, *a theologian*	Brett Usher
MAXIMUS, *a mystic*	Timothy West
EUTHERIUS, *a chamberlain*	Norman Bird
LEONTES, *a quaestor*	Peter Gunn
MYRRHA, *a slave-girl*	Marcia King

DECENTIUS, *a tribune*   Hugh Dickson
SINTULA, *master of the horse*   Dale Rapley
FLORENTIUS, *a general*   Brett Usher
SEVERUS, *a general*   David King
ORIBASES, *a doctor*   Garard Green
LAIPSO, *a centurion*   Stephen Garlick
VARRO, *a centurion*   Ben Onwukwe
MAUROS, *a standard-bearer*   Charles Simpson

SOLDIERS, CHURCHGOERS, PAGAN ONLOOKERS, COURTIERS, PRIESTS, STUDENTS, DANCING-GIRLS, SERVANTS, THE QUAESTOR'S ATTENDANTS, GALLIC WARRIORS, VISIONS *and* VOICES

Music by Christos Pittas
Directed by Martin Jenkins

ACT 1. Constantinople
ACT 2. Athens
ACT 3. Ephesus
ACT 4. Lutetia, in Gaul
ACT 5. Vienne, in Gaul

The action covers the period 351 to 361 A.D.

Act One

Easter night in Constantinople. An open place with trees, bushes and overturned statues, near the Imperial Palace. In the background, brilliantly illuminated, stands the Imperial Chapel. On the right, a marble balustrade, from which a flight of steps leads down to the water. Between pines and cypresses there is a view across the Bosphorus towards the coast of Asia. A service is in progress. MEMBERS OF THE IMPERIAL GUARD *stand on the steps of the Chapel. Great crowds of* WORSHIPPERS *are streaming in.* BEGGARS, CRIPPLES *and* BLIND PEOPLE *stand around the door.* PAGAN ONLOOKERS, FRUITSELLERS *and* WATERSELLERS *throng the scene. From the Chapel, the words of an anthem can be heard.*

EUNAPIUS (*a barber, hurries in and shoulders a*
    FRUITSELLER *aside*).Out of my way, pagan!
FRUITSELLER. Softly, master.
FOKION (*a dyer*). How dare you answer back a well-
    dressed Christian? A man of the Emperor's own faith!
EUNAPIUS (*pushes the* FRUITSELLER *over*). Into the gutter
    where you belong!
POTAMON (*a goldsmith*). That's right! Roll in the mud, like
    your gods!
FOKION (*hits him with his stick*). Take that – and that –
    and that!
EUNAPIUS (*kicks him*). And that, and that! I'll soften your
    godforsworn skin for you!

    The FRUITSELLER *runs out.*

FOKION (*ostentatiously, so as to be heard by the* OFFICER
    OF THE GUARD). It would be a good thing if someone

could report this incident to the blessed ears of our
Emperor. The Emperor has lately expressed his
displeasure at us Christian citizens associating
with pagans as though there were no distinction
between us.

POTAMON. You mean that order that has been posted in
the market-places? I've read that too. And I think
that, just as there is both pure gold and counterfeit –

EUNAPIUS. We should not all be rebuked; that's my
opinion. God be praised, there are still some zealous
spirits among us.

FOKION. We are far from zealous enough, my dear
brothers. Look how arrogantly these blasphemers
conduct themselves. How many of these riff-raff do
you suppose carry the sign of the cross and the fish
on their arm?

POTAMON. Yes – look at them milling and swarming on
the very steps of the Imperial Chapel.

FOKION. On this, the most sacred of nights –

EUNAPIUS. Obstructing pure members of the Church –

A PAINTED WOMAN (*in the crowd*). Is a Donatist pure?

FOKION. What? A Donatist! Are you a Donatist?

EUNAPIUS. Why – aren't you one?

FOKION. I? I! May lightning strike your tongue!

POTAMON (*makes the sign of the cross*). May boils and
pestilences – !

FOKION. A Donatist! You carrion! You rotten tree!

POTAMON. Well said, well said.

FOKION. Tinder for Satan's furnace!

POTAMON. Well said! Give it to him, dear brother, give it
to him!

FOKION (*pushes the* GOLDSMITH *away*). Hold your tongue!
Get away from me! I know you. You're Potamon the
Manichean!

EUNAPIUS. A Manichean! A stinking heretic! Fie, fie!

POTAMON (*holds up his paper lantern*). Aah! It's Fokion, the dyer from Antioch! The Cainite!

EUNAPIUS. Woe is me! I am fallen among liars and idolaters!

FOKION. Woe is me! I have helped the Devil's offspring!

EUNAPIUS (*hits him on the ear*). There's payment for your help!

FOKION (*hits him back*). You spineless dog!

POTAMON. May you both roast in Hell for ever!

> *They fight. The* CROWD *laugh and shout derisively at them.*

OFFICER OF THE GUARD (*shouts to the* SOLDIERS). The Emperor!

The FIGHTERS *are separated and hurry into the Chapel with the other* WORSHIPPERS. *The words of the anthem are heard from the high altar. The* COURT *enters from the left in stately procession.* PRIESTS *carrying censers walk first; then follow* SOLDIERS *and* TORCHBEARERS, COURTIERS *and the* IMPERIAL BODYGUARD. *In the middle of the procession is the* EMPEROR CONSTANTIUS. *He is 34, of aristocratic appearance, beardless and with brown, waved hair. His eyes are dark and distrustful; his walk and demeanour betray unease and debility. On his left walks the* EMPRESS EUSEBIA, *a pale and delicately built woman of the same age as the* EMPEROR. *Behind them walks* PRINCE JULIAN, *a youth of 19 who has not yet developed into full manhood. He has black hair, an incipient beard, and sparkling brown eyes which glance suddenly. His court dress sits ill on him; his manner is awkward, but intense and striking. The* EMPEROR's *sister, the* PRINCESS HELENA, *a voluptuous beauty of 25, walks behind him, attended by* MAIDENS *and* OLDER WOMEN. COURTIERS *and* SOLDIERS *bring up the rear. The* EMPEROR's *personal slave,* MEMNON, *a huge and magnificently dressed Ethiopian, is with the procession.*

CONSTANTIUS (*stops suddenly, turns to* JULIAN *and asks sharply*). Where is Gallus?

JULIAN (*turns pale*). Gallus? Why do you want Gallus?

CONSTANTIUS. Ah, I caught you there!

JULIAN. My lord – !

EUSEBIA (*takes the* EMPEROR's *hand*). Come, Constantius; come.

CONSTANTIUS. Your conscience cried out. What are you two plotting?

JULIAN. We?

CONSTANTIUS. You and Gallus.

EUSEBIA. Oh, come, come, Constantius.

CONSTANTIUS. What did the oracle answer?

JULIAN. The oracle? By our blessed Saviour –

CONSTANTIUS. If anyone lies about you, he shall burn at the stake. (*Pulls* JULIAN *aside*). Oh, let us remain friends, Julian. My dear kinsman, let us stay friends.

JULIAN. My dearest lord, all rests in your hands.

CONSTANTIUS. My hands – ?

JULIAN. Oh, hold them over us in benediction!

CONSTANTIUS. My hands? What were you thinking about my hands?

JULIAN (*seizes his hands and kisses them*). The Emperor's hands are white and cool.

CONSTANTIUS. What else should they be? What were you thinking? There – I caught you again!

JULIAN (*kisses them again*). They are like rose petals here in the moonlight.

CONSTANTIUS. Yes, Julian. Yes, yes.

EUSEBIA. Let us go. It is time.

CONSTANTIUS. To enter into the presence of God! I, I! Oh, pray for me, Julian! They will offer me the holy wine. I can see it! It dances in the golden chalice like the eyes of a serpent. (*Screams.*) Eyes of blood! Oh, Jesus Christ, pray for me!

EUSEBIA. The Emperor is sick –

HELENA. Where is Caesarius? The doctor, the doctor –
fetch him.

EUSEBIA (*beckons*). Memnon, good Memnon. (*Whispers to
the* SLAVE.)

JULIAN (*softly*). My lord, be merciful, and send me far
away from here.

CONSTANTIUS. Where would you like to go?

JULIAN. To Egypt. If you will agree. Many go to the desert
– into the great solitude.

CONSTANTIUS. Solitude? Oh? Solitude makes men brood. I
forbid you to brood.

JULIAN. I shan't brood, if only you will let me go. Here
my soul grows more troubled every day. Evil thoughts
crowd on me. For nine days I have worn a hair shirt,
but it has not protected me. For nine nights I have
scourged myself, but it has not driven them away.

CONSTANTIUS. We must be resolute, Julian. The Devil is
active in us all. Speak to Hekebolius –

MEMNON (*to* CONSTANTIUS). Time to go now.

CONSTANTIUS. No, no, I don't want to –

MEMNON (*takes him by the wrist*). Come, most gracious
lord. Come, I say.

CONSTANTIUS (*straightens himself and says with dignity*).
Into the house of God.

MEMNON (*quietly*). And afterwards – this other matter –

CONSTANTIUS (*to* JULIAN). Gallus shall attend on me.

JULIAN, *behind the* EMPEROR'*s back, clasps his hands
imploringly towards the* EMPRESS.

EUSEBIA (*quickly, whispers*). Don't be afraid!

CONSTANTIUS. Stay outside. Do not enter God's house in
your present state of mind. If you kneel before the
altar, it will be to call down evil on my head. Oh, my
dear kinsman, do not burden yourself with such a sin!

The PROCESSION *goes towards the Chapel. On the steps,* BEGGARS, CRIPPLES *and* BLIND PEOPLE *throng around the* EMPEROR.

A MAN WITH TWISTED LIMBS. Most mighty ruler of the world, let me touch the hem of your garment, that I may be made whole.

BLIND MAN. Pray for me, O thou the Lord's anointed, that I may regain my sight.

CONSTANTIUS. Have faith, my son. Give them silver, Memnon. Come, let us go in.

The PROCESSION *enters the Chapel; the door is closed. Gradually the* CROWD *disperses.* JULIAN *is left alone in one of the streets.*

JULIAN (*looks towards the Chapel*). What does he want with Gallus? Surely on this holy night he can't mean to – ? If one only knew! (*Turns and bumps against the* BLIND MAN, *who is walking away.*) Look where you're going, friend.

BLIND MAN. I am blind, my lord.

JULIAN. Still? Can you really not see even that shining star? O ye of little faith. Did not God's anointed promise to pray for your sight?

BLIND MAN. Who are you, that mock a blind brother?

JULIAN. A brother who shares your blindness and lack of faith. (*Turns to go out left.*)

A VOICE (*quietly, behind him, from among the bushes*). Julian, Julian.

JULIAN (*cries*). Ah!

VOICE (*closer*). Julian!

JULIAN. Don't move. I'm armed. Take care.

A YOUNG MAN (*humbly dressed, with a staff, appears among the trees*). Don't you remember Agathon?

JULIAN. Agathon! What are you saying? Agathon was a boy –

AGATHON. Six years ago. I knew you at once. (*Comes closer.*)

JULIAN. Agathon! Yes, by the Holy Cross, I really believe it is you.

AGATHON. Look at me. Have a good look –

JULIAN (*embraces and kisses him*). My old friend. My dearest friend! You here? But that's a miracle. You've come all the way from Cappadocia –

AGATHON. I arrived two days ago by ship from Ephesus. I've been trying to find you ever since. The palace guard wouldn't let me through the gates, and –

JULIAN. Did you mention my name to anyone? Or that you were looking for me?

AGATHON. No, I didn't dare. I –

JULIAN. Quite right. One should never let anyone know more than they need to. Come here, Agathon, into the moonlight, so that I can see you. Agathon, Agathon! How you've grown! How strong you look!

AGATHON. And you're paler.

JULIAN. I can't stand the air in the palace. I think it's unhealthy here. (*Sits down with him on a bench by the balustrade.*) 'Can any good come out of Cappadocia?', they say. Yes – friends can come. (*Gives him a long look.*) Incredible that I didn't recognize you at once. Of all my friends, you were the dearest. Things haven't changed between us, have they – ?

AGATHON (*kneels before him*). I kneel at your feet, now as then.

JULIAN. No, no, no!

AGATHON. Please let me.

JULIAN. Oh, Agathon, it's a blasphemy and a sin for you to kneel before me. If you knew how weighed down I am by guilt. I am a great source of grief to my dear teacher, Hekebolius. He could tell you! How rich and wavy your hair's grown! How are things with

Mardonius? His hair must be almost white by now.

AGATHON. It is completely white.

JULIAN. Mardonius! How magnificently he used to read
   Homer. I don't think anyone could equal him. Hero
   striving with hero; and the gods inspiring them from
   above. Yes, I saw it all.

AGATHON. In those days you wanted to become a great
   soldier.

JULIAN. Yes, those were happy days. We at our books and
   Gallus on his Persian horse. He used to gallop across
   the plain like the shadow of a cloud. Oh, but one
   thing you must tell me. The church –

AGATHON. Church?

JULIAN (*smiles faintly*). The one Gallus and I built, over
   the grave of the blessed martyr Mamas. Gallus
   finished his wing, but mine never quite came right.
   Why should Gallus succeed but not I? Oh, Agathon,
   when I see that church, I see the altar of Cain –

AGATHON. Julian!

JULIAN. God has washed his hands of me, Agathon.

AGATHON. You mustn't talk like that. Was not God strong
   in you when you led me out of darkness and gave me
   light for ever? And you were only a child at the time.

JULIAN. Yes. All that seems like a dream now.

AGATHON. It is as real as the promise of a new life.

JULIAN (*dully*). I wish I had that strength now. Where did
   I find those words of fire? The air was full of song; a
   ladder rose from earth to heaven. (*Stares.*) Did you
   see that?

AGATHON. What?

JULIAN. That falling star, there, behind those two
   cypresses. (*Is silent for a moment, then says suddenly.*)
   Did I tell you what my mother dreamed the night
   before I was born?

AGATHON. I don't remember –

JULIAN. No, no, of course. I didn't hear about it until
  later.

AGATHON. What did she dream?

JULIAN. My mother dreamed that she was giving birth
  to Achilles.

AGATHON (*eagerly*). Do you still believe in dreams?

JULIAN. Why do you ask?

AGATHON. It has to do with my reason for coming here.

JULIAN. You had some special reason – ? It didn't occur
  to me –

AGATHON. A strange reason. That's what makes me
  hesitant. And uneasy. There's so much I need to
  know first. About how things are here – about you –
  and the Emperor –

JULIAN (*looks him in the eyes*). Tell me the truth, Agathon.
  Whom have you spoken to here?

AGATHON. No one.

JULIAN. When did you get here?

AGATHON. I told you. Two days ago.

JULIAN. And at once you ask me – ! What do you want to
  know about the Emperor? Has someone asked you
  to – ? (*Clasps him.*) Oh, Agathon, my friend, forgive
  me.

AGATHON. What do you mean?

JULIAN (*stands up and listens*). Hush. No, it was nothing.
  Only a bird in the bushes. I'm very happy here. Why
  should you think otherwise? Why shouldn't I be
  happy? Haven't I all my family here? That is – all
  whom our gracious Saviour has protected beneath
  his wing.

AGATHON. And the Emperor treats you like a son?

JULIAN. The Emperor is beyond measure wise and good.

AGATHON (*has also risen*). Julian, is the rumour true that
  when the time comes you will be the Emperor's
  successor?

JULIAN (*quickly*). Don't say such dangerous things. Why
    are you asking me all these questions? I won't tell you
    anything till you tell me what you're doing in
    Constantinople.

AGATHON. I come in the service of the Lord our God.

JULIAN. If you love your Saviour and your own salvation,
    go back home. (*Leans out over the balustrade.*) Speak
    quietly, there's a boat down there. (*Pulls him across to
    the other side.*) Go back home, I tell you. Do you
    know what Constantinople has become during these
    past fifteen months? A blasphemous Babylon! Haven't
    you heard – don't you know that Libanius is here?

AGATHON. Who is Libanius? One of those false pagan
    teachers – ?

JULIAN. The most dangerous of them all.

AGATHON. More dangerous than that riddler Maximus?

JULIAN. Maximus? Don't talk about that impostor. Who
    knows anything for certain about Maximus? No, no,
    Agathon, Libanius is the most dangerous. His arrival
    here was presaged by signs. I myself saw the stars
    break from their orbits, plunge earthwards, and die as
    they fell. Everyone calls him a king among teachers of
    eloquence. Old men and youths flock to hear him. He
    binds their souls so that they have to follow him.
    Blasphemy flows like witchcraft from his lips – as
    bewitching as those tales of Greeks and Trojans –

AGATHON (*cries*). Oh, Julian! You have sought him too!

JULIAN (*recoils*). I? God protect me against such men! The
    rumour that I have sought Libanius by night or in
    disguise is false. I should be afraid even to come near
    him. All true believers who enter the presence of this
    man become apostates and blasphemers. And not only
    they. His words are borne from mouth to mouth,
    even into the Imperial Palace. His mocking wit, his
    impregnable logic, his foul lampoons, disturb my

prayers. Sometimes to my horror I feel my gorge
rising at the sight of the body and blood – ! (*In an
uncontrollable outburst.*) Were I the Emperor, I would
send you the head of Libanius on a charger!

AGATHON. But why does the Emperor allow this? How
can our pious and God-fearing Emperor – ?

JULIAN. The Emperor? Praised be the Emperor's faith and
piety! But the Emperor has no thought for anything
but this unfortunate Persian war. No one can think of
anything else. No one cares about the war which is
being waged here against the Prince of Golgotha. I
have begged Hekebolius and the Empress to get the
Emperor to banish him. But no, no. This man poisons
the air for us all. O blessed Jesus, if only I could flee
from all this heathen vileness! Living here is living in
the lions' den.

AGATHON (*appalled*). Julian, what are you saying?

JULIAN. Yes, it is true. Only a miracle can save us.

AGATHON. Then listen. That miracle has happened.

JULIAN. What do you mean?

AGATHON. I'll tell you, Julian; for I can no longer doubt
that you are the one who – ! What brought me to
Constantinople was a vision –

JULIAN. A vision!

AGATHON. A revelation from God –

JULIAN. Then in God's name, speak! Hush; someone's
coming. Stay here – try to look unconcerned –

*They remain standing by the balustrade. A tall, handsome,
middle-aged* MAN *dressed in a teacher's short cloak enters
along the avenue on the left. A group of* YOUNG MEN
*accompanies him; they all wear kilted cloaks, with ivy
garlands in their hair, and carry books, papers and
parchment. They are talking loudly and laughing.*

TEACHER. Don't drop anything in the water, my dear

Gregor. Remember that what you carry there is more precious than gold.

JULIAN (*close to him*). Excuse me, sir, but is any man-made thing more precious than gold?

TEACHER. Can gold buy wisdom?

JULIAN. True, true. But then you should not trust the treacherous waters.

TEACHER. The favour of man is more treacherous.

JULIAN. Wisely spoken. And where are you sailing to with your treasures?

TEACHER. To Athens. (*Begins to walk on.*)

JULIAN (*suppresses a laugh*). To Athens?

TEACHER (*stops*). Why do you laugh?

JULIAN. Would a wise man take owls to Athens?

TEACHER. In the monastic light of this Imperial city, my owls cannot fly. (*To one of the* YOUNG MEN) Your arm, Sallust. (*Makes to descend the steps.*)

SALLUST (*halfway down the steps, whispers*). By the gods, it is he!

TEACHER. He?

SALLUST. As truly as I live. I know him. I've seen him with Hekebolius.

TEACHER. Ah! (*Scrutinizes* JULIAN *unobtrusively.*) You smiled just now. What were you smiling at?

JULIAN. When you complained about monastic light, I wondered if it wasn't the princely light of the academy of logic that was shining too brightly in your eyes.

TEACHER. There is no room for envy under the short cloak.

JULIAN. What there is no room for cannot be hidden.

TEACHER. You have a sharp tongue, proud Galilean.

JULIAN. Why do you call me Galilean? What marks me out as a Christian?

TEACHER. Your courtier's cloak.

JULIAN. Beneath my cloak hides a philosopher: for I wear
an exceedingly coarse shirt. But, tell me, what do you
seek in Athens?

TEACHER. What did Pontius Pilate seek?

JULIAN. Cannot truth be found here, where Libanius lives?

TEACHER (*looks at him coldly*). Hm. Libanius, yes.
Libanius will soon be silent. Libanius, my lord, is
weary of the struggle.

JULIAN. Weary? He, the invulnerable, the all-conquering – ?

TEACHER. He is weary of waiting for his peer.

JULIAN. Now you jest, stranger. Where can Libanius hope
to find his peer?

TEACHER. He has been found.

JULIAN. Who? Where? Name him.

TEACHER. That might be dangerous.

JULIAN. Why?

TEACHER. Are you not a courtier?

JULIAN. And if I am?

TEACHER (*lowers his voice*). Would *you* dare to praise the
Emperor's heir-designate?

JULIAN (*shaken*). Ah!

TEACHER (*quickly*). If you betray me, I shall deny
everything.

JULIAN. I shall betray no one. Have no fear. The
Emperor's heir-designate, you say? I don't know
whom you mean. The Emperor has not named
anyone. But why did you jest just now? Why did you
speak of Libanius's peer?

TEACHER. Answer me truthfully. Is there at the Imperial
Court a youth who, by stern words and force, prayer
and persuasion, is barred from the light of the
academy?

JULIAN (*quickly*). That is to keep his faith pure.

TEACHER (*smiles*). Has this young man so little faith in his
faith? What does he know of his faith? What does a

soldier know of his shield before it has protected him
in battle?

JULIAN. True, true. But he has loving kinsmen and
teachers, who –

TEACHER. Words, words, my lord. Let me speak plainly. It
is for the Emperor's sake that his young kinsman is
kept from those who study wisdom. The Emperor is
not blessed with the gift of eloquence. The Emperor is
of course great; but he cannot endure that his
successor should dazzle the Empire –

JULIAN (confused). You dare to –?

TEACHER. Yes, yes. You are angry on your master's
behalf, but –

JULIAN. Far from it. On the contrary – that is – ! Listen, I
stand quite close to this young prince. I should dearly
like to know – (Turns.) Stand further off, Agathon. I
must speak privately with this man. (Walks a few
paces away with the TEACHER.) Dazzle, you said.
Dazzle the Empire? What do you know, what does
any of you know, about Prince Julian?

PHILOSOPHER. Can Sirius be hidden by a cloud? Will not
the driving wind open a rift here and there, so that – ?

JULIAN. No more of this, I pray you.

TEACHER. The palace and the church are like a double
cage in which the prince is held prisoner. But the
cage is not secure. Now and then he lets fall a cryptic
word. The court vermin – forgive me, my lord, I
mean the courtiers – repeat it to pour scorn on it.
Its inner meaning is not for those gentlemen –
forgive me, my lord, I mean, for most of them it
does not exist.

JULIAN. For no one. I promise you, for no one.

TEACHER. But it seems to exist for you. And it certainly
does for us. Yes, he could dazzle the Empire. Is it not
said that when he was a child in Cappadocia and was

debating with his brother Gallus he sided with the
gods and defended them against the Galilean?

JULIAN. That was only in jest – debating practice –

TEACHER. But what verbal skill the boy already had!
What beauty and grace of intellect –

JULIAN. You think so?

TEACHER. Yes. He could become an adversary whom we
could both fear and long for. Hekebolius fears for his
pupil's faith. Oh, I know it well – he has said as
much. But does he forget, that most conscientious
man, that in his youth he himself drank from those
springs which he would now forbid his pupil to
approach? Was it not from us that he learned that
verbal skill which he now wields with such praised
aptitude against us?

JULIAN. True, true.

TEACHER. Oh, Hekebolius is like the rest of you; his envy
is greater than his zeal. That is why Libanius has
waited in vain.

JULIAN (seizes his arm). What has Libanius said? For
God's – I beseech you, tell me.

TEACHER. He said: 'Watch that Galilean prince. He is a
spiritual Achilles.'

JULIAN. Achilles! (Whispers.) My mother's dream!

TEACHER. Yonder, in the open halls of the academy, lies
the battlefield. There the adversaries meet openly and
joyfully. Arrows of eloquence cut the air; the sharp
swords of knowledge sparkle; the blessed gods smile
down from the clouds –

JULIAN. Away from me with your pagan fancies –

TEACHER. And the heroes return to their tents, their arms
entwined, without rancour, their cheeks aglow, their
blood pulsing through every vein, crowned with
recognition, and with laurel. Ah, where is Achilles? I
do not see him. Achilles is wrathful –

JULIAN. Achilles is unhappy. But can I believe this? Oh, tell me – my brain grows dizzy – did Libanius say all this?

TEACHER. Why did Libanius come to Constantinople? For what reason but to seek the honoured friendship of a certain youth – ?

JULIAN (*excitedly*). Then why did he abuse and mock him? One does not scorn a man whose friendship one seeks.

TEACHER. Galilean lies, to sow hatred between the two champions.

JULIAN. Surely you won't deny that it was Libanius – ?

TEACHER. I deny it utterly.

JULIAN. You mean those lampoons weren't written by him?

TEACHER. Not one of them. They were all penned in the Imperial Palace and disseminated under his name –

JULIAN. Is it possible? Libanius didn't write them? None of them?

TEACHER. No.

JULIAN. Not even that vile piece about an Atlas with sloping shoulders – ?

TEACHER (*laughs*). That was conceived in the church, not in the halls of learning. You don't believe it? I tell you, it was Hekebolius –

JULIAN. Hekebolius?

TEACHER. Yes, Hekebolius, Hekebolius himself, to set his enemy against his pupil –

JULIAN (*clenches his fists*). Is it possible?

TEACHER. If this blinded and betrayed young man had known what kind of people we lovers of wisdom are, he would not have acted so harshly against us.

JULIAN. What do you mean?

TEACHER. Now it is too late. Good night, my lord. (*Turns to go.*)

JULIAN (*seizes his hand*). My friend and brother – who are you?

TEACHER. A man who is sad because he sees the chosen one of the gods destroyed.

JULIAN. What do you mean, the chosen one of the gods?

TEACHER. The uncreated in a changing world.

JULIAN. Your meaning is still dark to me.

TEACHER. There is a whole glorious world to which you Galileans are blind. In that world life is a festival at which every cup is full and foaming and every brow garlanded with roses. Dizzy bridges stretch from soul to soul, even to the most distant stars in the great room of the universe. I know the man who could be master of this mighty empire.

JULIAN (*fearfully*). At the cost of his salvation.

TEACHER. What is salvation? To return to one's beginning.

JULIAN. Oh, if I had the learning! If I had the weapons with which to challenge you –

TEACHER. Find those weapons, young man. The debating hall is a fencing-school where intellects and spirits are sharpened –

JULIAN (*shrinks*). Ah!

TEACHER. Farewell. You Galileans have driven truth into exile. See how we bear the blows of fate, our heads raised high and crowned with laurel. Thus *we* depart, shortening the night with song, awaiting the coming of Apollo.

He descends the steps, where his PUPILS *have been awaiting him. They are heard rowing away in the boat.*

JULIAN (*stares a long while over the water*). Who was that riddler?

AGATHON (*comes closer*). Listen to me, Julian –

JULIAN (*excited and disturbed*). *He* understood me! And Libanius himself – the great, incomparable Libanius – !

Oh, how sharp and bright the pagan eye must be!

AGATHON. He was sent to tempt you.

JULIAN (*ignores him*). I can't live any longer among these
people here. They mock me, they laugh behind my
back; nobody believes in what I carry within me.
Even Hekebolius – ! Oh, yes, I feel it. Christ is
abandoning me. I shall become evil here.

AGATHON. Oh, you don't understand. You are the one
whom God has chosen.

JULIAN (*walks up and down beside the balustrade*). I am
the one with whom Libanius wishes to measure his
strength! What a strange wish. Libanius regards *me* as
his peer. He is waiting for *me* –

AGATHON. Listen and obey. Christ is waiting for you.

JULIAN. My friend, what do you mean?

AGATHON. The vision that drove me to Constantinople –

JULIAN. Yes, yes – the vision. I'd almost forgotten about
that. A revelation, you said? Oh, tell me, tell me.

AGATHON. I was lying on my bed. I could neither wake
nor sleep. I felt hollow inside, as though my soul had
left me. Then, of a sudden, I saw before me on the
wall a white shining light, and in the radiance of the
light stood a man in a long cloak. Light shone from
his head. He gazed gently at me. Then he spoke, and
said: 'Rise, Agathon. Seek him who shall inherit
my kingdom. Bid him enter the den and wrestle with
the lions.'

JULIAN. Wrestle with the lions? Strange, strange. Oh, if it
were – ! The meeting with that philosopher – A
revelation; a message to me – ! Could I be the chosen
one?

AGATHON. It is most certain that you are.

JULIAN. To wrestle with the lions! Yes, I see. So be it,
Agathon. It is God's will that I shall seek out
Libanius –

AGATHON. No, no, hear me out!

JULIAN. Can you doubt it? Libanius – is he not strong like the mountain lion, and is not the debating hall – ?

AGATHON. I tell you, no. For the figure continued: 'Tell the chosen one that he shall shake the dust of the imperial city from his feet and never more enter its gates.'

JULIAN. You are sure of this, Agathon?

AGATHON. Yes, quite sure.

JULIAN. Not here, then. To wrestle with the lions? Where, where? Oh, where shall I find light?

> PRINCE GALLUS, *a handsome, powerfully built man of 25, with fair, waved hair, fully armed, enters along the avenue on the left.*

JULIAN (*goes towards him*). Gallus!

GALLUS. What is it? (*Points at* AGATHON.) Who is this person?

JULIAN. Agathon.

GALLUS. Which Agathon? You go around with so many kinds of – good God, it's the Cappadocian! Why, you've become a grown man –

JULIAN. Have you heard, Gallus? The Emperor has been asking for you.

GALLUS (*tensely*). Now? Tonight?

JULIAN. Yes, yes. He wants to speak with you. He seems extremely angry.

GALLUS. How do you know? What did he say?

JULIAN. He wanted to know what answer some oracle had given.

GALLUS. Ah!

JULIAN. Don't hide anything from me. What does it mean?

GALLUS. It means death or banishment.

AGATHON. Merciful Saviour!

JULIAN. I guessed as much. Oh, speak, speak.

GALLUS. What can I say? Do I know more than you? If
the Emperor has spoken of an oracle, then a certain
messenger must have been captured, or someone has
betrayed me –

JULIAN. Messenger? Gallus, what have you done?

GALLUS. Oh, I couldn't bear this fear and uncertainty any
longer. Let him do what he wants with me. Anything
is better than this –

JULIAN (*quietly, takes him aside*). Careful, Gallus. What is
this about the messenger?

GALLUS. I asked a question of the priests of Osiris
in Abydos –

JULIAN. Ah, the oracle. But that's a pagan –

GALLUS. I know one shouldn't have anything to do with
paganism, but – well, you may as well know. I asked
about the outcome of the Persian war –

JULIAN. What madness! Oh, Gallus – I see it in your eyes
– you asked something else too –

GALLUS. Wait! I didn't ask –

JULIAN. Yes, yes. You asked whether a great man would
live or die.

GALLUS. And if I did? What concerns us more closely
than that?

JULIAN (*clasps him*). Be quiet, you're mad!

GALLUS. Get away from me. Crawl before him if you
must – I can't stand it any longer. I want to cry it out
in every market-place – ! (*Shouts to* AGATHON.) Have
you seen him, Agathon? Have you seen the murderer?

JULIAN. Gallus! Brother!

AGATHON. Murderer!

GALLUS. The murderer in the red cloak – my father's
murderer, my stepmother's, my eldest brother's –

JULIAN. Hush, you will have us all killed.

GALLUS. Eleven heads in a single night – eleven corpses –
all our family. Oh, but never fear, his conscience

torments him – it trembles through his veins like a
nest of serpents –

JULIAN. Don't listen to him! Go, go!

GALLUS (*grasps* JULIAN *by the shoulder*). Wait. You look
pale and uneasy. Was it you who betrayed me?

JULIAN. I? Your brother?

GALLUS. Oh, brother, brother. Kinship protects no one in
our family. If you've been secretly spying on me, say
so. Who else could it be? Do you think I don't know
what people are whispering? The Emperor intends to
name you as his successor.

JULIAN. I swear to you, my beloved Gallus, that will never
happen. I don't want it. One mightier than the
Emperor has called me. Oh, believe me, Gallus, my
path has been marked out for me. I won't do it, I tell
you. O Lord of Hosts – I on the imperial throne? No,
no, no!

GALLUS (*laughs*). Well acted, mountebank.

JULIAN. Yes, you can laugh – you don't know what has
happened. I scarcely know myself. Oh, Agathon! If
this head should be anointed, would it not be an
apostasy – a mortal sin? Would not God's sacred oil
scald me like molten lead?

GALLUS. Then our noble kinsman would be balder than
Julius Caesar –

JULIAN. Don't talk like that. Render unto the Emperor
that which is the Emperor's –

GALLUS (*laughs*). The heir-designate rehearses his lines.

JULIAN (*weeps*). Oh, Gallus, if I could die, or be banished
in your place! My soul is wasting here. I ought to
forgive – but I can't. Evil grows in me – hatred and
revenge whisper in my ear –

GALLUS (*quickly, glancing towards the chapel*). Here
he comes.

JULIAN. Be careful, my dear brother. Ah, Hekebolius!

The door of the chapel has been thrown open. The
CONGREGATION *streams out. Some go away, others*
remain outside to watch the COURT PROCESSION *pass.*
Among them is the theologian HEKEBOLIUS *in priest's robes.*

HEKEBOLIUS (*as he is about to pass him, left*). Is that you,
    my Julian? Alas, you have been causing me much
    grief again lately. Christ is angry with you, my son.
    Your stubbornness offends him. There is no love in
    your heart, only worldly vanity –

JULIAN. Hekebolius, how could you write those vile
    slanders about me?

HEKEBOLIUS. I? I swear to you by all that is high
    and holy –

JULIAN. I can tell from your eyes you're lying. How could
    you write these things, I ask you – and pretend they
    are by Libanius?

HEKEBOLIUS. Very well, my beloved son. Since you know –

JULIAN. Oh, Hekebolius! You have lied to me. You have
    deceived and betrayed me –

HEKEBOLIUS. To prove, my son, how deeply I love you.
    What would I not do for the soul of one who shall
    some day be the Lord's anointed?

JULIAN. Oh, how blind I have been!

HEKEBOLIUS. The Emperor!

The EMPEROR CONSTANTIUS *enters from the chapel with all*
his TRAIN. *During the preceding dialogue,* AGATHON *has*
withdrawn among the bushes on the right.

CONSTANTIUS. Ah, this blessed sense of peace!

EUSEBIA. You feel strengthened, Constantius?

CONSTANTIUS. Yes, yes. I saw the dove hover above me. It
    took away that dreadful burden of guilt from my soul.
    Now, Memnon, I am no longer afraid to do what
    must be done.

MEMNON (*quietly*). Do it quickly, my lord.

CONSTANTIUS. There they both are. (*Goes towards them.*)

GALLUS (*gropes instinctively for his sword and cries*). Don't touch me!

CONSTANTIUS (*stretches out his arms*). Gallus! My kinsman! (*Embraces and kisses him.*) See, by the light of these Easter stars, I choose him who lies closest to my heart. Kneel, all of you. Acclaim Gallus Caesar!

General amazement among his RETINUE. *Involuntary exclamations are heard.*

EUSEBIA (*cries*). Constantius!

GALLUS (*astonished*). Caesar!

JULIAN. Ah! (*Seizes the* EMPEROR'*s hands, as though in joy.*)

CONSTANTIUS (*pushes him away*). Don't come near me! What do you want? Is not Gallus the elder? What hopes have you been building for yourself? Away, away with you!

GALLUS. I – Caesar?

CONSTANTIUS. My heir and my successor. Within three days you shall join the army in Persia. I know this Persian war is close to your heart –

GALLUS. Oh, most gracious lord – !

CONSTANTIUS. Thank me with deeds, beloved Gallus. King Sapores' army stands west of the Euphrates. I know how concerned you are for my life. So let it be your task to destroy him. (*Turns, seizes* JULIAN'*s hand in both of his and kisses him.*) Julian, my pious friend and brother – it must be so.

JULIAN. Blessed be the Emperor's will.

CONSTANTIUS. No petitions! But, yes – I've thought of you too. Know, Julian, that now you can breathe freely in Constantinople –

JULIAN. Yes, praised be Christ and the Emperor!

CONSTANTIUS. You know already? Who told you?

JULIAN. Know what, my lord?

CONSTANTIUS. That Libanius is banished.

JULIAN. Libanius – banished?

CONSTANTIUS. I have banished him to Athens.

JULIAN. Ah!

CONSTANTIUS. Yonder lies his ship. He sails tonight. I
    know you have long wanted this. I couldn't do it for
    you before, but now – ! Let this be some small
    compensation to you, my Julian –

JULIAN (*seizes his hand quickly*). My lord, grant me one
    favour more.

CONSTANTIUS. Ask what you will.

JULIAN. Let me go to Pergamon. You know that old
    Aedesius is teaching there –

CONSTANTIUS. A strange request. You wish to live among
    the pagans – ?

JULIAN. Aedesius is not dangerous. He is a noble old man,
    and very feeble –

CONSTANTIUS. And what do you want with him, brother?

JULIAN. I want to learn to wrestle with lions.

CONSTANTIUS. I understand your pious wish. And you are
    not afraid? You think you are strong enough – ?

JULIAN. The Lord our God has called me with a loud
    voice. Like Daniel, I go calm and joyful into the
    lions' den.

CONSTANTIUS. Julian!

JULIAN. Oh, let me go forth and cleanse the world.

GALLUS (*whispers to the* EMPEROR). Let him have his
    way, my lord. It will keep him from brooding on
    larger matters.

EUSEBIA. I beg you, Constantius, let him have his wish.

HEKEBOLIUS (*whispers*). Most mighty Emperor, let him go
    to Pergamon. I doubt the wisdom of caging him here.
    And now it doesn't matter so much if –

CONSTANTIUS. How could I refuse you anything at such a moment as this? Go, Julian, and God be with you.

JULIAN (*kisses his hands*). Oh, thank you, thank you!

CONSTANTIUS. And now to our feast of celebration. My Capuan cook has discovered some new Lenten dishes – carp-necks in Chian wine, and – Come. You shall walk behind me, Caesar Gallus.

The PROCESSION *begins to move.*

GALLUS (*quietly*). Helena, what a miraculous change of fortune!

HELENA. Oh, Gallus, now we can hope again.

GALLUS. I can scarcely believe it. Who can be responsible?

HELENA. Hush!

GALLUS. You, my love? Or who – who?

HELENA. Memnon's Spartan dog.

GALLUS. What do you mean?

HELENA. Memnon's dog. Julian kicked it. This is the slave's revenge.

CONSTANTIUS. Why so silent, Eusebia?

EUSEBIA (*quietly, weeping*). Oh, Constantius. Why this choice – why?

CONSTANTIUS. Eleven ghosts demanded it.

EUSEBIA. Alas for us. This will not appease the ghosts.

CONSTANTIUS (*shouts*). Flute-players! Why are the dogs silent? Play, play!

All go out left, except PRINCE JULIAN. AGATHON *comes out from among the trees.*

JULIAN. Gallus his successor! And I am free, free, free!

Act Two

In Athens. An open place surrounded by colonnades. Statues and a fountain. In a corner on the left the square is joined by a narrow street. Sunset.

BASIL OF CAESAREA, a slender young man, sits reading by a pillar. GREGOR OF NAZIANZ and other STUDENTS of the Academy walk up and down the colonnades in scattered groups. A larger GROUP runs noisily across the square and out to the right. Shouting is heard in the distance. BASIL goes out in the direction of the noise. As he does so, PRINCE JULIAN enters with a crowd of YOUNG MEN along the narrow street. His hair is uncombed and he wears a short cloak like the others. Among the STUDENTS is SALLUST OF PERUSIA.

CROWD. Long live the light of Athens! Long live the prince of wisdom and eloquence!

JULIAN. You waste your flattery. No more verses today.

SALLUST. When our leader is silent, our souls are empty, as on the morning after a night of feasting.

JULIAN. Then let it be something new. Let's hold a mock trial.

CROWD. Yes, yes, yes! Prince Julian in the seat of judgement!

JULIAN. I? No, there stands the man. Who is as learned in the law as Gregor of Nazianz?

SALLUST. That's true.

JULIAN. Up on the bench, my wise Gregor. I stand here accused.

GREGOR I beg you, my friend, let me stay out of this.

JULIAN. Up on the bench, I say. On the bench! Now. (*To the* OTHERS): What crime have I committed?

CROWD. Yes, what's it to be? You choose.

SALLUST. Let it be some Christian offence. Something
Galilean, as we pagans call it.

JULIAN. Right, something Galilean. I know! I've refused to
pay tax to the Emperor, so here I am, dragged by the
scruff of the neck, with my hands tied –

SALLUST (*to* GREGOR). Blind judge – since justice is blind
– behold this presumptuous man. He has refused to
pay the Emperor his lawful tax.

JULIAN. Your honour, I am a citizen of Greece. What does
a Greek citizen owe the Emperor?

GREGOR. Whatever the Emperor demands.

JULIAN. Right. But how much – now answer me as though
the Emperor himself were present – how much dare
the Emperor demand?

GREGOR. Everything.

JULIAN. That was indeed answered as though the Emperor
himself were present. But now comes the problem; for
it is written 'Render unto the Emperor that which is
the Emperor's, and unto God that which is God's.'

GREGOR. Well?

JULIAN. Then tell me, O wise judge, how much of what I
have belongs to God?

GREGOR. Everything.

JULIAN. And how much of what belongs to God may I
give to the Emperor?

GREGOR. My dear friends, let us have no more of
this game.

CROWD (*amid noise and laughter*). Yes, yes!
Answer him!

JULIAN. How much of what belongs to God dare the
Emperor demand?

GREGOR. I shall not answer. This is offensive to both God
and the Emperor. Let me go, please.

MANY VOICES. Form a ring around him!

JULIAN. Hold him! Stand here before me. Answer me now, all you who would serve both the Emperor and the muse of wisdom, has he not tried to shirk his duty as a servant of the Emperor?

CROWD. Yes, yes!

JULIAN. And what do you regard as fit punishment for such a crime?

VOICES. Death! Death in a wine-cask!

JULIAN. Let us consider. Let us answer as though the Emperor himself were present. What is the limit of the Emperor's power?

SOME OF THE CROWD. The Emperor's power is without limit.

JULIAN. I agree. But to try to evade what has no limits, my friends, is that not madness?

CROWD. Yes, yes! The Cappadocian is mad!

JULIAN. But what is madness? What did the Egyptian priests teach? They say that the divine riddle reveals itself in madmen. Our Gregor, in setting himself up against the Emperor, stands therefore in a special relationship to Heaven. Pour out libations to the Cappadocian! Let hymns be sung in praise of our brother Gregor! Let a statue be raised in honour of Gregor of Nazianz!

STUDENTS (*laughing and shouting*). Honour to the Cappadocian! Honour to the Judge of Cappadocia!

LIBANIUS *enters across the square, surrounded by* DISCIPLES.

LIBANIUS. Well, well! Do I see my brother Julian dispensing wisdom in the open forum?

JULIAN. Say rather madness, my friend. Wisdom has abandoned our city.

LIBANIUS. Has wisdom abandoned us?

JULIAN. It is about to. Are you not going down to the

Piraeus like all the rest?

LIBANIUS. I, brother? What should I do in the Piraeus?

JULIAN. Then you must be the only teacher in Athens who
does not know that a ship has just docked, filled to
the bulwarks with young men in search of learning –

LIBANIUS (*scornfully*). That ship is from Ephesus.

JULIAN. Doesn't gold weigh the same wherever it
comes from?

LIBANIUS. Gold? (*Laughs.*) Maximus keeps the true gold
for himself. He doesn't let them go. What kind of
students do we get from Ephesus? The sons of
shopkeepers and artisans.

JULIAN. Tonight at least one of your colleagues will have
no cause for disappointment.

LIBANIUS. My friend is jesting.

JULIAN. Your friend assures you that the two sons of the
Governor Milon are on board.

LIBANIUS (*seizes his arm*). What! Governor Milon's two
sons? The noble Milon who sent the Emperor seven
Persian horses and seven saddles embroidered
with pearls? Milon is a wealthy man. All his family
are wealthy.

JULIAN. Especially his two sons.

LIBANIUS. Then you were right, Julian. This ship has
brought gold from Ephesus. For are not the gifts of
the mind pure gold? Your news makes me restless.
These young men must be taken care of. My friends,
let us offer a welcoming hand to these two strangers,
help them to find teachers and accommodation, and –

SALLUST. Yes, yes.

STUDENTS. To the Piraeus! To the Piraeus!

SALLUST. We'll fight like wild boars for Milon's sons!

They all go out right with LIBANIUS. *Only* JULIAN *and*
GREGOR OF NAZIANZ *are left in the colonnade.*

JULIAN (*watches them go*). Look at them, skipping along
  like a pack of fauns. How they lick their lips at the
  thought of the feasting there'll be tonight!

GREGOR. Julian —

JULIAN. Look at me; I'm sober.

GREGOR. I know that. You're temperate in all things. And
  yet you live this life of theirs.

JULIAN. Why not? Which of us knows when the lightning
  will strike? So why not enjoy the noonday sun? Do
  you forget that I wasted my childhood and youth in a
  gilded prison? It became a habit for me, I might
  almost say a necessity, to live in fear. And now? This
  silence from the Emperor, as of the grave; this
  cunning silence. I left Pergamon without the
  Emperor's permission. The Emperor remained silent.
  I went without leave to Nicomedia; I sat there at the
  feet of Nikokles and his fellows; the Emperor let it
  happen. I came to Athens, sought out Libanius, whom
  the Emperor had forbidden me to see; the Emperor
  still says nothing. How am I to interpret this?

GREGOR. Perhaps he loves you, Julian.

JULIAN. Oh, you don't understand. I hate this power that
  dominates my life, terrible when it strikes, and still
  more terrible when it seems to sleep.

GREGOR. Be honest, my friend. Is it only this that has led
  you on such strange paths?

JULIAN. How do you mean, strange paths?

GREGOR. Is it true, as is rumoured, that you spend your
  nights studying the pagan mysteries at Eleusis?

JULIAN. Oh, rubbish. I promise you there's little to
  be gained from those riddling dreamers. Let's not talk
  of them.

GREGOR. Then it is true. Oh, Julian, how could you seek
  such shameful company?

JULIAN. I must live, Gregor! And this academic existence

isn't life. Libanius! I shall never forgive him for the fact that I once loved and admired him. When I first came here, how humbly, with what tremulous joy, I went to greet him, bowed down before him, kissed him and called him brother.

GREGOR. Yes, all we Christians thought you were going too far.

JULIAN. I envisaged a mighty duel between the two of us – the truth of the world against the truth of God. What became of it? I tell you, Gregor, Libanius is not a great man.

GREGOR. Yet all enlightened Greece declares he is.

JULIAN. Libanius has great learning, but he is not a great man. Only once have I seen Libanius great; that night in Constantinople. Then he was great because he had suffered a great injustice, and because a noble anger filled him. But here! Oh, what have I not witnessed here! And now he is writing letters to Gallus, to Caesar Gallus, the Emperor's heir, wishing him luck in his campaign against the Persians!

BASIL (*enters right*). Letters! Letters from Cappadocia!

GREGOR. Is there one for me?

BASIL. Here, from your mother.

GREGOR. My mother! (*Opens the letter and reads.*)

JULIAN (*to* BASIL). Is that from your sister?

BASIL (*who has come with an open letter in his hand*). Yes, Makrina. She has sad and strange news.

JULIAN. What? Tell me.

BASIL. First she writes of your noble brother, Gallus. He rules Antioch with a stern hand.

JULIAN. Yes, Gallus is hard. Did Makrina write: 'With a stern hand'?

BASIL (*looks at him*). Makrina writes: 'With a bloody hand.'

JULIAN. I feared as much.

GREGOR (*to* BASIL). Does Makrina say what is happening in Antioch?

BASIL. Not in detail. What's the matter? You look pale –

GREGOR. You knew the noble Alexandrian, Clematius?

BASIL. Yes, yes. What's happened to him?

GREGOR. He has been murdered, Basil.

BASIL. What?

GREGOR. They executed him without trial or sentence.

JULIAN. Who? Who has executed him?

GREGOR. Yes, who?

JULIAN (*quiet and pale*). Burn these dangerous letters. They could bring bad luck to us all.

BASIL. Such open violence – in the heart of a great city! Where are we, where are we?

JULIAN. Yes, you may well ask that. Where are we? A Christian murderer, a Christian – !

GREGOR. Curses will achieve nothing. What do you intend to do?

JULIAN. I?

GREGOR. You don't suppose it will end with the murder of Clematius. My mother writes that it is as though a stinking abyss had opened its jaws. Wives inform against their husbands, sons against their fathers, priests against their own congregations –

JULIAN. Oh, Gregor, if I could flee to the ends of the earth – !

GREGOR. Your place is at the earth's centre, Prince Julian.

JULIAN. What would you have me do?

GREGOR. You are the brother of this bloody Caesar. Go to him. Throw this deed in his face. Strike him to the ground in fear and guilt –

JULIAN (*recoils*). You must be mad!

GREGOR. Do you love your brother? Do you want to save him?

JULIAN. I loved Gallus as I loved no one.

GREGOR. Loved?

JULIAN. While he was my brother. But now – is he not Caesar? Gregor, Basil – oh, my dear friends, I tremble for my life, I breathe in fear of Caesar Gallus. Would you have me accuse him to his face when my very existence is a danger to him?

GREGOR. Why did you come to Athens? To fight for the truth of Christ against the lies of heathenism. What have you achieved?

JULIAN. Oh, the battle was never intended to be fought here.

GREGOR. No, not here. Not with debating points, or book against book. No, Julian, you must do battle on the field of life. You must risk your life.

JULIAN. Yes. I see.

GREGOR. How much of *you* belongs to God? How much dare the Emperor demand?

JULIAN (*quickly*). Well. Shall we go together?

GREGOR (*evasively*). I have my little circle; I have my family to take care of. My strength and talents extend no further.

JULIAN (*is about to reply; suddenly he listens towards the right, and cries*). To the Bacchanal!

BASIL. Julian!

JULIAN. To the Bacchanal, my friends!

> GREGOR *looks at him for a moment, then goes away left down the colonnade. A large crowd of* STUDENTS, *with the* NEWCOMERS *among them, rushes shouting and screaming into the square.*

BASIL (*comes closer*). Julian, will you listen to me?

JULIAN. Look, look! They have bathed their new friends, and anointed their hair. See how they swing their rods; how they howl and beat their breasts. What say'st thou, Pericles? I seem to see thy angry ghost –

BASIL. Come. Come.

JULIAN. Ah – look at that man they're driving naked
before them. Here come the dancing-girls. Ah! Do
you see what they're – !

BASIL. For shame, for shame. Turn your eyes away.

Evening has fallen. The whole CROWD *sits or lies down
in the square around the fountain. Wine and fruit are
brought.* PAINTED GIRLS *dance by torchlight.*

JULIAN (*after a short silence*). Tell me, Basil, why was the
pagan sin so beautiful?

BASIL. You are wrong, my friend. Beautiful poems and
stories have been written about the pagan sin. But it
was never beautiful.

JULIAN. How can you say that? Was not Alcibiades
beautiful when, hot with wine, he stormed by night
through the streets of Athens like a young god,
hammering on the citizens' doors while the women
trembled inside, sighing in breathless silence and
longing for nothing more than – ?

BASIL. Oh, Julian, I beg you, listen to me!

JULIAN. Was not Socrates beautiful in the symposium?
And Plato and all those other happy banqueters? And
yet they did things which would make those Christian
animals over there deny it on the Bible if anyone
accused them of it. Was the sin beautiful in Sodom
and Gomorrah? Did not Jehovah's fire avenge what
Socrates did not shrink from? Oh, as I live this life of
freedom and exultation, I sometimes wonder whether
truth is not the enemy of beauty.

BASIL. Can you pine for beauty at a moment like this?
Have you forgotten what Makrina wrote?

JULIAN (*turns away and puts his hands over his ears*). I
don't want to hear another word about those
hideous – ! Let's forget everything about Antioch.

What else does Makrina write?

BASIL. She writes of Maximus –

JULIAN (*alert*). The mystic?

BASIL. Yes, that strange man. He has turned up again, this
time in Ephesus. The whole countryside is in a
ferment. His name is on all lips. Either he is a
mountebank or he has made an unholy pact with
certain spirits. Even Christians are strangely attracted
by his blasphemous deeds and mysteries.

JULIAN. More, more; I pray you.

BASIL (*looks at the letter*). There's nothing more about
him. She only writes that in the reappearance of
Maximus she sees a sign that God is angry with us.
She believes that grievous retribution awaits us for
our sins.

JULIAN. Yes. Tell me, Basil, this sister of yours must be
a rare woman.

BASIL. She is indeed.

JULIAN. When you tell me of her letters, it is as though I
had at last found something I had long been seeking,
something perfect and complete. Tell me, does she
still intend to renounce the world and live in some
desert place?

BASIL. She is so determined.

JULIAN. Extraordinary. She, who seems to have been
blessed with everything. She is young and beautiful,
has great wealth awaiting her, and has, for a woman,
most uncommon wisdom. Do you know, Basil, I long
to see her. Why does she yearn for solitude?

BASIL. I told you, the man she was betrothed to died. She
still thinks of him as a husband who awaits her, and
to whom her purity is pledged.

JULIAN. It is strange how many are drawn to solitude in
these times. When you write to Makrina, tell her that
I too –

BASIL. She knows that, Julian. But she doesn't believe it.

JULIAN. Why not? What does she write?

BASIL (*hands him the letter*). Read there.

JULIAN (*reads*). 'Every time you write about the Emperor's young kinsman who is your friend, my heart is filled with a great joy.' Oh, Basil, read the rest of it to me.

BASIL (*reads*). 'Your account of the confidence and certainty with which he came to Athens seemed like a passage from the Ancient Scriptures. I believe he is the reincarnation of David, born to smite the heathen Goliath. May God's spirit be upon him in the battle and for all his days.'

JULIAN (*grasps his arm*). She too? What is it you all expect of me?

BASIL. Why do all believers pin their hopes on you?

JULIAN (*walks once or twice up and down the colonnade, stops, and puts out his hand for the letter*). Here, let me read it. (*Reads.*) 'May God's spirit be upon him in the battle and for all his days.' Oh, Basil, if only I could – ! But what sense is there in all these voices calling to me from east and west to save Christendom? Where is this Christendom that must be saved? In the Emperor, or in Caesar? Their deeds cry out: 'No, no!' In the great high-born families – those effeminate libertines who fold their hands over their full bellies and pipe: 'Was the Son of God created out of nothing?' Or is it to be found among the enlightened, men who like you and me have drunk beauty and wisdom from the pagan springs? Do not most of our brethren here incline towards the Aryan heresy which the Emperor himself so strongly favours? Or the ragged mob of the Empire that sacks temples and murders pagans and the children of pagans? Do they do that for Christ? (*Laughs.*) And then they fight among themselves for the goods of

those they have murdered. You might ask Makrina if
Christendom is to be found in solitude, on the pillar
where the saint awaits eternity on one leg. Or in the
cities? Whom of all these would Christ acknowledge
as His own if He returned again to earth?

BASIL. Seek the answer where it is always to be found in
times of trouble. In the Holy Scriptures.

JULIAN. The same counsel of despair. Books, always books.
When I asked Libanius, he said books, books. When I
come to you, it's books, books, books! I ask for bread
and you offer me a stone. I can't use books. It's life I
hunger for, communion with the spirit face to face.
Was it a book that opened Saul's eyes? Was it not a
torrent of light that smote him, a vision, a voice – ?
Oh, I stumble like Saul in the darkness. If Christ
wants anything of me, he must speak clearly. I want
to place my finger in his wounds –

BASIL. And yet it is written that –

JULIAN. Oh, I know everything that's written there. This
written word isn't the living truth. There must be a
new revelation. Or a revelation of something new.
There must, I tell you. The time is ripe. Yes, a
revelation. Oh, Basil, can't you pray for *that* to be
vouchsafed me? A martyrdom, if need be. Martyrdom
– the sweetness of the thought makes me dizzy – a
crown of thorns about my temples – ! (*Clasps his head
with both hands, seizes the garland of roses and tears it
off. Reflects a while, then says slowly.*) This. I'd
forgotten this. (*Throws the garland away.*) I've only
learned one thing in Athens.

BASIL. What, Julian?

JULIAN. The old beauty is no longer beautiful, and the
new truth is no longer new.

LIBANIUS *runs in along the colonnade from the right.*

LIBANIUS (*as he comes*). Now we have him, now we
    have him!

JULIAN. Him? I thought you had them both.

LIBANIUS. Both?

JULIAN. The sons of Milon.

LIBANIUS. Oh, yes, I have them too. But we have *him*, my
    dear Julian!

JULIAN. Whom, dear brother?

LIBANIUS. He has caught himself in his own net.

JULIAN. Ah, a philosopher?

LIBANIUS. The enemy of all philosophy.

JULIAN. Who, who?

LIBANIUS. Haven't you heard the news about Maximus?

JULIAN. Maximus? Oh, tell me.

LIBANIUS. He was bound to come to this in the end. The
    restless fool. Step by step towards madness –

JULIAN. Or the highest wisdom.

LIBANIUS. As you choose. But we must act now, we must
    not let this opportunity slip. You, most noble Julian,
    are the man. You are a close kinsman of the Emperor.

JULIAN. O excellent Libanius, since I am not omniscient,
    please explain –

LIBANIUS. Maximus has claimed that he can conjure up
    the spirits of the departed.

JULIAN (*grasps his cloak*). Libanius!

LIBANIUS (*shows him a letter*). My colleague Eusebius has
    written telling me details –

JULIAN. Spirits of the departed!

LIBANIUS. In Ephesus recently Maximus practised
    forbidden arts on the statue of Hecate. Eusebius
    writes that he himself was present. All around was as
    black as night. Maximus uttered strange incantations.
    Then he sang a hymn, which no one understood.
    Then the marble torch in the statue's hand began
    to flame –

JULIAN (*breathlessly*). Yes?

LIBANIUS. Then, in a clear bluish light, they all saw the
statue's face come alive and smile at them.

JULIAN. What else happened?

LIBANIUS. Many fell sick or went mad. But he – would
you believe it, Julian? – he continues on his dangerous
and sinful path.

JULIAN. Sinful? Does not all wisdom aim towards this end
– communion between spirit and spirit?

BASIL. My dear friend –

LIBANIUS. Fortunately we are no longer living in the age
of the blind bard. Maximus should know better than
that. Has not Plato – and we after him – satisfactorily
explained all that business? Is it not sinful in this
modern age to seek to obscure with riddles and misty
dreams this marvellous, tangible and, dare I say it,
painfully created structure of intelligence and
speculation which, after centuries of intellectual toil,
we scholars have –

JULIAN (*angrily*). Goodbye, Basil. I see a light on my path.

BASIL (*throws his arms around him*). I won't let you go! I'll
stop you –

JULIAN (*frees himself*). No one will stop me. Do not try to
prevent what must be.

LIBANIUS. My friend, my brother, where are you going?

JULIAN. To where torches light themselves and statues
smile! (*Runs out left down the colonnade.*)

LIBANIUS (*stares after him*). That princely youth is a
danger to scholarship.

BASIL (*half to himself*). Prince Julian is a danger to more
than that.

Act Three

Ephesus. A brightly lit room in PRINCE JULIAN'*s house. On the right is the entrance from the main hall; upstage, a smaller door concealed by a curtain. On the left, a door leads to the inner rooms of the house. The rear of the stage is bounded by a wall with a gap in it through which can be seen a small enclosed courtyard, furnished with small statues.* SERVANTS *are preparing an elaborate supper and setting cushions around the table.* JULIAN'*s chamberlain,* EUTHERIUS, *at the entrance of the room, is ceremoniously entreating* GREGOR OF NAZIANZ *and* BASIL OF CAESAREA *to enter.*

EUTHERIUS. Yes, yes, I assure you there is no mistake.

GREGOR. Impossible.

EUTHERIUS. He sent for me early this morning. 'Prepare a rich supper', he said, 'for this evening I shall be visited by two friends from Athens.' (*Glances towards the open door on the left, falls silent and takes a respectful step backwards.*)

BASIL. Is he there?

> EUTHERIUS *nods in reply; then he gestures to the* SERVANTS *to withdraw. They go out through the main door, right; he follows them. A few moments later,* PRINCE JULIAN *enters left. He is clad in a long, eastern robe; his demeanour is animated and betrays a state of strong inward excitement.*

JULIAN (*comes towards them and greets them warmly*).
You've come!

GREGOR. Julian!

BASIL. My friend and brother.

GREGOR. But explain to us how – ! Your servants greet us
  at the gate with music, seek to bathe us and anoint
  our hair, and garland us with roses –

JULIAN. I saw you last night. It was full moon, you know –
  and then my soul is always strangely alert. I was at
  my desk in the library and had fallen asleep, tired, oh,
  my friends, so tired, with reading and writing. Then
  the house was filled as though with a mighty wind.
  The curtain fluttered up, and I looked out into the
  night, far across the sea. I heard a sweet song; it came
  from two great birds with the faces of women. They
  flew towards the shore. There they alighted gently;
  the birds vanished like a white mist, and in a soft,
  trembling light, I saw you both.

GREGOR. Are you sure of all this?

JULIAN. Were you thinking about me? Did you talk about
  me last night?

BASIL. Why, yes – on the ship –

JULIAN. What time of night was that?

GREGOR. What time of night did you see this vision?

JULIAN. An hour after midnight.

GREGOR (*glances at* BASIL). Extraordinary!

JULIAN (*walks up and down, rubbing his hands*). You see?
  (*Laughs.*) You see?

BASIL (*watches him as he walks*). Then it's true – ?

JULIAN. What? What is true?

BASIL. The rumour that you practise clandestine arts here.

JULIAN. Oh, rumour always exaggerates.

BASIL (*seizes his hand*). Julian, in the name of our
  friendship, tell us the truth.

JULIAN. My dear friends, I am the happiest man on earth.
  And Maximus – yes, he deserves that name –
  Maximus is the greatest man who has ever lived.

GREGOR (*prepares to go*). We wanted only to see you,
  my lord.

JULIAN. I shrank too, before my eyes were opened and I
divined the true meaning of life.

BASIL. And what is the true meaning of life?

JULIAN. Maximus knows. In him is the new revelation.

BASIL. And you have seen it too?

JULIAN. Almost. It is about to be imparted to me. Tonight,
the last veil will be drawn aside. In this room, the
answer to the great enigma will be revealed. Oh, stay
with me, my brothers! Stay with me during this night
of agony and expectation! When Maximus comes, you
shall witness –

BASIL. Never!

GREGOR. We cannot!

JULIAN. At least stay until tomorrow –

GREGOR. Impossible. Our caravan leaves at dawn.

JULIAN. At dawn? Before midnight the day could dawn for
you. Oh, why so hesitant, my brothers? Why do you
stand there as though face to face with something
insuperable? I know what I know. In every generation
there has been one soul in whom the pure Adam has
been reborn. He was strong in Moses the lawgiver; he
had the power to conquer the world in Alexander the
Macedonian; he was all but fulfilled in Jesus of
Nazareth. But, you see, Basil – (*grasps his arm*) – all
of them lacked what I am promised – the pure woman!

BASIL (*tears himself free*). Julian, Julian! Are you that
same Julian who three years ago turned your back
on Constantinople?

JULIAN. I was blind then, as you are now. I knew only the
path that ends in dogma.

GREGOR. Do you know where your present path ends?

JULIAN. Where the path and the goal are one. For the last
time, Gregor, Basil, I beg you, stay with me. That
vision I had last night, that and much besides, proves
that a mysterious bond exists between us. Oh, Basil,

I had so much to say to you. You are the head of
your family, and who knows whether all that is
promised to me – whether it may not be through your
house that – ?

BASIL. Never! No one shall be drawn into your madness
and wild dreams with my consent.

JULIAN. Oh, how can you talk of consent? I see a hand
writing on the wall. Soon I shall decipher the writing.

GREGOR. Come, Basil.

JULIAN (*stretches out his arms*). Oh, my friends. My friends!

GREGOR. From this day a gulf is fixed between us. (*He
drags* BASIL *away. They both go out right.*)

JULIAN (*looks after them for a moment*). Yes, go. Go, go!
What is all your wisdom worth? You know only two
roads in Athens, the road to the school and the road
to the church. The third road, that leads to Eleusis
and beyond, you do not know; still less – ! Ah!

The curtain on the right is drawn aside. Two
SERVANTS *in eastern dress bring in a tall, veiled object,
which they place in the corner behind the table. A few
moments later,* MAXIMUS THE MYSTIC *enters through
the same door. He is a lean man of middle height with
a brown, hawk-like face. His hair and beard are
heavily flecked with grey, except for his thick eyebrows
and moustache, which have remained jet black. He
wears a pointed cap and a long black robe, and carries
a white staff in his hand. Without looking at* JULIAN,
*he goes over to the veiled object, stops, and gestures to
the* SERVANTS, *who silently leave.*

JULIAN (*softly*). At last!

MAXIMUS *removes the veil, revealing a bronze lamp
on a high tripod. Then he takes out a small silver pot
and pours oil into the bowl of the lamp. The lamp*

*catches fire of its own accord and burns with a strong
reddish fire.*

JULIAN (*tense and expectant*). Is it time?

MAXIMUS (*without looking at him*). Is your soul and your
body pure?

JULIAN. I have fasted and anointed myself,

MAXIMUS. Then let the night's high festival begin.

He makes a sign. DANCING GIRLS *and* FLUTE PLAYERS
*appear in the courtyard. They dance and play during
the ensuing dialogue.*

JULIAN. Maximus, what is this?

MAXIMUS. Roses in the hair! Sparkling wine! See, see the
beautiful limbs at play!

JULIAN. You mean this sensual turmoil is to accompany – ?

MAXIMUS. Sin exists only in the eye of the sinful.

JULIAN. Roses in the hair! Sparkling wine! (*Throws himself
down on one of the cushions by the table, empties a cup
of wine, puts it quickly down*). Ah! What was in
that wine?

MAXIMUS. A spark of the fire Prometheus stole. (*Lies
down on the other side of the table.*)

JULIAN. My senses are transposed. I hear brightness and
see music.

MAXIMUS. The wine is the soul of the grape. The freed yet
willing prisoner. Logos in Pan!

DANCING GIRLS (*sing in the courtyard*).
   Drink the blood of Bacchus and free thyself.
   Rock thyself on the river of our song.

JULIAN (*drinks*). Yes, yes, there is freedom in intoxication.
Can you explain this sense of blessedness?

MAXIMUS. To be intoxicated is to be wedded with the
spirit of Nature.

JULIAN. A sweet riddle. It tempts and seduces me – what

was that? Why did you laugh?

MAXIMUS. I?

JULIAN. I hear whispering on my left. The silk cushion
is rustling – (*leaps half up, pale.*) Maximus, we are
not alone.

MAXIMUS (*cries*). We are five at table!

JULIAN. A symposium with the spirits!

MAXIMUS. With the shades.

JULIAN. Name my guests.

MAXIMUS. Not now. Listen, listen.

JULIAN. What is that? A great wind blowing through
the house –

MAXIMUS (*cries*). Julian! Julian! Julian!

JULIAN. Speak, speak! What is happening to us?

MAXIMUS. The hour of annunciation is upon thee!

JULIAN (*leaps up and shrinks far back from the table*). Ah!

*The lamps on the table are all but extinguished. Over
the great bronze lamp a circle of bluish light rises.*

MAXIMUS (*throws himself full length on the floor*). Look at
the light!

JULIAN. There?

MAXIMUS. Yes, yes.

DANCING GIRLS (*sing softly in the courtyard*).
      Night, the all-seeing, stretches her web.
      Lust with her laughter tempts you in.

JULIAN (*stares at the light*). Maximus! Maximus!

MAXIMUS (*quietly*). Do you see anything?

JULIAN. Yes.

MAXIMUS. What do you see?

JULIAN. I see a shining face in the light.

MAXIMUS. Man or woman?

JULIAN. I don't know.

MAXIMUS. Speak to it.

JULIAN. Dare I?

MAXIMUS. Speak, speak!

JULIAN (*goes closer to it*). Why was I born?

A VOICE IN THE LIGHT. To serve the spirit.

MAXIMUS. Does it answer?

JULIAN. Yes, yes.

MAXIMUS. Ask more.

JULIAN. What is my task?

VOICE. Thou shalt establish the kingdom.

JULIAN. Which kingdom?

VOICE. The kingdom.

JULIAN. And by which path?

VOICE. The path of freedom.

JULIAN. Explain fully. What is the path of freedom?

VOICE. The path of necessity.

JULIAN. And by what power?

VOICE. By *willing*.

JULIAN. What shall I will?

VOICE. What thou *must*.

JULIAN. It grows pale – it is vanishing – ! (*Goes closer.*)
    Speak, speak! What must I do?

VOICE (*moans*). Julian!

*The circle of light fades. The lamps on the table burn
as before.*

MAXIMUS (*looks up*). Gone?

JULIAN. Gone.

MAXIMUS. Do you understand *now*?

JULIAN. Now least of all. I tremble on the brink of an
    abyss, suspended between light and darkness. (*Lies
    down again.*) What is the kingdom?

MAXIMUS. There are three kingdoms.

JULIAN. Three?

MAXIMUS. First there is the kingdom founded on the tree
    of knowledge. Then the kingdom founded on the tree
    of the Cross –

JULIAN. And the third?

MAXIMUS. The third is the kingdom of the great mystery; the kingdom which shall be founded on both the tree of knowledge and the tree of the Cross, because it hates and loves them both, and because its life-spring has its source beneath Adam's grove and Golgotha.

JULIAN. And this kingdom shall come – ?

MAXIMUS. At any hour. I have calculated and calculated –

JULIAN (*interrupts him sharply*). There is the whispering again. Who are my guests?

MAXIMUS. The three corner-stones shaped by the wrath of destiny.

JULIAN. Who, who?

MAXIMUS. The three great helpers through denial.

JULIAN. Name them!

MAXIMUS. I cannot. I do not know them. But I could show them to you –

JULIAN. Then show them to me. At once, Maximus!

MAXIMUS. Beware – !

JULIAN. At once, at once! I will see them. I will speak to them, one by one!

MAXIMUS. On thy head be it. (*Swings his staff and cries.*) Take shape and show thyself, O thou first chosen lamb of sacrifice!

JULIAN. Ah!

MAXIMUS (*keeps his face hidden*). What do you see?

JULIAN (*softly*). There he lies. In the corner – ! He is huge like Hercules. And beautiful – no, not – (*Unwillingly.*) If thou canst, speak to me!

A VOICE. What wouldst thou know?

JULIAN. What was thy task in life?

VOICE. My sin.

JULIAN. Why didst thou sin?

VOICE. Why was I not my brother?

JULIAN. Don't be evasive. Why didst thou sin?

VOICE. Why was I myself?

JULIAN. And what didst thou *will*, being thyself?

VOICE. What I had to.

JULIAN. Why didst thou have to?

VOICE. I was myself.

JULIAN. Thou art scant of speech.

MAXIMUS (*without looking up*). *In vino veritas!*

JULIAN. You are right, Maximus. (*Holds out a full goblet in front of the empty seat.*) Bathe in the fumes of the wine, my pale guest. Comfort thyself. Smell them, smell them! They rise into the air like the smoke of sacrifice.

VOICE. The smoke of sacrifice does not always rise.

JULIAN. Why does the scar on thy brow grow red? No, no – do not cover it with thy hair. What is it?

VOICE. The mark.

JULIAN. Hm. Enough of that. And what fruit did thy sin bear?

VOICE. The most glorious.

JULIAN. What dost thou call the most glorious of fruits?

VOICE. Life.

JULIAN. And whence comes life?

VOICE. From death.

JULIAN. And whence comes death?

VOICE (*fades, as though in a sigh*). Ah, *that* is the riddle.

JULIAN. Gone!

MAXIMUS (*looks up*). Gone?

JULIAN. Yes.

MAXIMUS. Did you recognize him?

JULIAN. Yes.

MAXIMUS. Who was it?

JULIAN. Cain.

MAXIMUS. Ah – that way! Ask no more!

JULIAN (*gestures irritably*). The second, Maximus.

MAXIMUS. No, no, no. I will not.

JULIAN. The second, I say! You swore that certain
   mysteries should be revealed to me. The second,
   Maximus! I must see him. I must know my guests!

MAXIMUS. Thou hast willed it, not I. (*Swings his staff.*)
   Come forth and show thyself, thou willing slave, thou
   who next did help to change the world!

JULIAN (*stares for a moment at the empty room, then
   suddenly stretches out his hand as though to ward off
   something on the seat beside him, and says softly*).
   No closer!

MAXIMUS (*his back turned*). Do you see him?

JULIAN. Yes.

MAXIMUS. What do you see?

JULIAN. A red-bearded man. His clothes are torn and he
   has a rope round his neck. Speak to him, Maximus!

MAXIMUS. You must speak.

JULIAN. What wast thou in life?

A VOICE (*close to him*). The twelfth wheel of the
   world's chariot.

JULIAN. The twelfth? A fifth is usually thought superfluous.

VOICE. Where would the chariot have rolled without me?

JULIAN. Where did it roll with thee?

VOICE. Into glory.

JULIAN. Why didst thou help?

VOICE. Because I *willed*.

JULIAN. What didst thou will?

VOICE. What I *had* to will.

JULIAN. Who chose thee?

VOICE. The master.

JULIAN. Did the master know what would happen when
   He chose thee?

VOICE. Ah, *that* is the riddle.

   A short silence.

MAXIMUS. You are silent?

JULIAN. He isn't here any longer.

MAXIMUS (*looks up*). Did you recognize him?

JULIAN. Yes.

MAXIMUS. What was he called in life?

JULIAN. Judas Iscariot.

MAXIMUS (*leaps up*). The abyss blossoms! The night reveals itself!

JULIAN (*cries to him*). Bring forth the third!

MAXIMUS. He shall come. (*Swings his staff.*) Come forth, thou third cornerstone! Come forth, thou third ordained liberator! (*Throws himself down again on the cushion and averts his face.*) What do you see?

JULIAN. I see nothing.

MAXIMUS. But he is here. (*Swings his staff again.*) By the seal of Solomon, by the eye in the triangle – I charge thee, show thyself! (*Pause.*) What do you see now?

JULIAN. Nothing. Nothing.

MAXIMUS (*swings his staff again*). Come forth, thou – ! (*Breaks off suddenly, utters a cry and leaps up from the table.*) Ah, lightning in the night! I see it! All art is in vain.

JULIAN (*rises*). Why? Speak, speak.

MAXIMUS. The third is not yet among the shades.

JULIAN. He is alive?

MAXIMUS. Yes, he is alive.

JULIAN. And *here*, you say – ?

MAXIMUS. Here, or there, or among the unborn – I do not know –

JULIAN. Then it is you or I. But which?

MAXIMUS. Let go my cloak!

JULIAN. Which of us? Which? I must know.

MAXIMUS. You know more than I. What did the voice in the light proclaim?

JULIAN. The voice in the light? (*Cries.*) The kingdom! The kingdom? To establish the kingdom –

MAXIMUS. The third kingdom!

JULIAN. No! No, no! Get away from me, tempter!
     I renounce you and all your works –
MAXIMUS. Would you renounce destiny?
JULIAN. I defy destiny! I will not be its servant. I am free,
     free, free!

Noise outside. The DANCING GIRLS *and* FLUTE
PLAYERS *flee.*

MAXIMUS. What is that noise? Why are they screaming?
JULIAN. Some men are forcing their way into the house –
MAXIMUS. They are maltreating your servants. They want
     to murder us.
JULIAN. Be calm. No one can hurt us.
EUTHERIUS (*runs in from the courtyard*). My lord, my
     lord! Strangers have surrounded the house. They have
     posted guards at every door. They are breaking in – !
     Here they come, my lord! Here they are!

The QUAESTOR LEONTES *enters right, with a large and
splendid* RETINUE.

LEONTES. A thousand pardons, most gracious lord –
JULIAN (*takes a step back*). What is this?
LEONTES. Your servants tried to prevent me from
     entering, and since my business is most urgent, I –
JULIAN. You here in Ephesus, worthy Leontes?
LEONTES. I have ridden day and night. On the orders of
     the Emperor –
JULIAN (*pales*). To me? What does the Emperor want with
     me? I have committed no crime that I know of. I am
     sick, Leontes. (*Indicates* MAXIMUS.) This man is here
     as my doctor.
LEONTES. Pardon me, gracious lord –
JULIAN. Why have you forced your way into my house?
     What does the Emperor want?
LEONTES (*kneels*). Most mighty lord – praising your good

fortune and my own, I hail you Caesar.

LEONTES' MEN. Long live Caesar Julian!

JULIAN (*recoils with a cry*). Caesar! I beseech you – where is Gallus?

LEONTES (*rises*). Gallus is with his beloved wife.

JULIAN. Dead. Dead! Gallus dead! Dead in the midst of his victories. But when – and where?

GREGOR (*forces his way in past the* GUARDS). I must see him! Let me pass, I say. Julian!

JULIAN. Gregor, my brother. So you came back after all.

GREGOR. In the name of Christ, send away this tempter.

JULIAN. He is the Emperor's envoy, Gregor.

GREGOR. Would you tread on your brother's bloody corpse – ?

JULIAN. Bloody – ?

GREGOR. Don't you know? Caesar Gallus has been murdered in Illyria.

JULIAN (*clasps his hands together*). Murdered – ?

LEONTES. Who is this audacious – ?

JULIAN. Murdered! Murdered! (*To* LEONTES.) Tell me he is lying.

LEONTES. Caesar Gallus is the victim of his own deeds.

JULIAN. Murdered! Who murdered him?

LEONTES. It was a necessity, most noble lord. Caesar Gallus abused his power like a madman in those eastern lands.

JULIAN. I'm not asking you what his crime was. Who killed him?

LEONTES. The tribune Skudilo, who attended him, deemed it advisable to have him executed.

JULIAN (*bows his head*). The Emperor is great and just. So I am the last of our line, Gregor. The Emperor Constantius is great.

LEONTES (*takes a purple cloak from one of his* FOLLOWERS). Most noble Caesar, may it please you to wear this – ?

JULIAN. It is red. Take it away. Is this the cloak he wore
in Illyria – ?

LEONTES. It is newly brought from Sidon. (JULIAN *glances
at* MAXIMUS.) It is sent to you by your kinsman, the
Emperor. He bids me tell you that, being childless, he
hopes that you will remedy this his deepest grief. He
wishes to see you in Rome. Afterwards, it is his will
that you go, as Caesar, to Gaul. The German border
tribes have crossed the Rhine and made a dangerous
incursion into the Empire. He puts his trust in you
and is confident that you will crush the barbarians.
Certain things have been revealed to him in dreams,
and his last word to me as I left was he was sure you
would succeed in establishing the Empire.

JULIAN. In establishing the Empire! The kingdom! The
voice in the light, Maximus!

MAXIMUS. Sign against sign.

GREGOR. Say no, Julian. They want to fasten the wings of
corruption to your shoulders.

LEONTES. Who are you, who dare to defy the Emperor?

GREGOR. My name is Gregor. I am the son of the Bishop
of Nazianz. Do what you will with me.

JULIAN. He is my friend and brother. Let no man
touch him.

A large CROWD *has meanwhile filled the courtyard.*

BASIL (*forces his way through the crowd*). Do not take the
purple, Julian!

JULIAN. You too, my loyal Basil.

BASIL. Do not take it. For God's sake –

JULIAN. Through me the Empire shall be established.

BASIL. The Empire of Christ?

JULIAN. The great and glorious Empire of the Emperor.

BASIL. Was it to establish the Emperor's Empire upon

earth that you left Constantinople? Was it his Empire
  that – ?

JULIAN. Mists, mists. All that lies behind me like a
  wild dream.

BASIL. It were better for you that a millstone should be
  hung around your neck and you be cast into the sea
  than that you should put that dream behind you.
  Don't you see that this is a temptation of the Devil?
  All the glory of the world lies at your feet.

MAXIMUS. Sign against sign, Caesar.

JULIAN. A word, Leontes. (*Takes his hand and draws him
  aside.*) Where are you taking me?

LEONTES. To Rome, my lord.

JULIAN. That isn't what I mean. Where are you taking me;
  to fortune and power, or to the slaughterhouse?

LEONTES. My lord, you mock me. How can you think – ?

JULIAN. Gallus's limbs have scarcely rotted yet.

LEONTES. I can still your doubts. (*Takes out a paper.*)
  This letter from the Emperor – I would have preferred
  to hand it to you in private, but –

JULIAN. A letter? What does he write? (*Opens and reads
  it.*) Helena! Oh, Leontes! Helena – for me!

LEONTES. The Emperor gives her to you, my lord. He
  gives you his beloved sister, for whom Gallus Caesar
  begged in vain.

JULIAN. Helena for me? The unattainable attained! But
  she, Leontes – what does she – ?

LEONTES. As I prepared to leave, he took the princess by
  the hand and led her to me. Her virginal blood rose
  into her fair cheeks, she dropped her eyes and said:
  'Greet my dear kinsman, and tell him that he has
  always been the man who –'

JULIAN. Go on, Leontes.

LEONTES. With those words she fell silent, being most
  pure and virtuous.

JULIAN. The pure woman! All is miraculously fulfilled!
  (*Cries in a loud voice.*) Dress me in the purple robe!
MAXIMUS. You have chosen?
JULIAN. I have chosen, Maximus.
MAXIMUS. Remember – sign against sign.
JULIAN. This is no case of sign against sign. Maximus, oh,
  Maximus, my poor seer, you have been blind. Dress
  me in the purple robe!

The QUAESTOR LEONTES *puts the robe on him.*

BASIL. It is done.
LEONTES. And now to the Governor's house. The people
  wish to acclaim Caesar.
LEONTES' MEN. Make way! Make way for Caesar Julian!

All except MAXIMUS *go out through the courtyard amid
the cheers of the* CROWD.

MAXIMUS (*stretches up his hands and mumbles to himself*).
  To him who has the *will* – victory and light!

Act Four

Lutetia, in Gaul. A hall in CAESAR's *palace, 'The Warm Baths,' outside the town. In the background, an entrance door; to the right, another, smaller door; downstage left, a window with a curtain over it. The* PRINCESS HELENA, *richly bejewelled, with pearls in her hair, is seated in a chair looking out through the window.* MYRRHA, *a slave girl, stands opposite her, holding the curtain aside.*

HELENA (*starts to her feet*). Oh, this agonizing uncertainty! Not to know whether he will come as a conqueror or as a fugitive!

MYRRHA. Don't worry, my lady. Caesar always comes as a conqueror.

HELENA. Ah, Eutherius! Well, what news?

EUTHERIUS (*enters upstage*). Your highness, these are only barbarian auxiliaries entering the town, and they know nothing.

HELENA (*wrings her hands*). Oh, have I deserved this misery? Sweet blessed Christ, have I not prayed to you night and day – ? (*Listens and cries.*) Ah, my Julian! I hear him. Julian, my beloved!

CAESAR JULIAN (*enters quickly upstage, in dusty armour. Embraces her passionately*). Helena! Close all the doors, Eutherius.

HELENA. Defeated! A fugitive!

EUTHERIUS. My lord!

JULIAN. Double guards on the doors! Let no one enter. Wait. Has any messenger come from the Emperor?

EUTHERIUS. No, my lord. But a messenger is expected.

JULIAN. Go, go! (*To* MYRRHA.) Get out.

EUTHERIUS *and* MYRRHA *exeunt upstage.*

HELENA. Then it is all over with us!

JULIAN (*closes the curtain*). Who knows?

HELENA. After such a defeat –

JULIAN. What are you talking about, my love?

HELENA. Haven't the Germans defeated you?

JULIAN. If they had defeated me, you would never have
    seen me alive again.

HELENA (*rises quickly*). In God's name, then, what has
    happened?

JULIAN (*quietly*). The worst, Helena. An unimaginable
    victory.

HELENA. Victory? An unimaginable victory, you say? You
    have won, and yet – ?

JULIAN. Oh, you don't understand my position. You know
    only the gilded exterior of a Caesar's misery –

HELENA. Julian!

JULIAN. Why – what is this? How you've changed –

HELENA. What? How?

JULIAN. How you've changed in these few months!
    Helena, have you been ill?

HELENA. No, no. But tell me – ?

JULIAN. Yes, you have been ill. You still must be – these
    feverish temples, those dark rings round your eyes –

HELENA. Oh, they are nothing, my love. Don't stare at
    me, Julian. I've only been worrying and lying awake
    at night thinking about you. I beg you, don't hide
    anything from me.

JULIAN. Hush! What was that? (*Listens at the door.*) No,
    no – I only thought –

HELENA. But all your friends in the army – ?

JULIAN. My friends in the army? I haven't one, my dearest
    Helena. Yes, one – the Perusian knight, Sallust –

HELENA. Ah, Julian!

JULIAN (*walks up and down*). Every week secret letters
leave the camp for Rome. Everything I do is reported
and misconstrued. No slave in the Empire is fettered
like Caesar. Do you know, Helena, the very menu for
my meals is sent to my cook by the Emperor, and I
may not make a single change in it, remove a dish, or
add one.

HELENA. And you have endured all this in secret – ?

JULIAN. Oh, everyone knows about it except you. They
laugh at Caesar's impotence. I can't stand it any
longer. I won't stand it.

HELENA. But the great battle – ? Tell me – has rumour
exaggerated – ?

JULIAN. Rumour could not exaggerate. King Knodomar
had assembled all his armies before Argentoratum,
with the Rhine at his back. Five kings and ten lesser
princes joined him. But before he had gathered the
boats he needed in case of retreat, I gave the orders to
attack. Oh, Helena, I dare not say this aloud, but I
am sure that either treachery or envy all but robbed
me of the fruits of victory. The Roman cavalry were
beaten back time after time by the barbarians, who
flung themselves to the ground and stabbed our
horses in the belly. Defeat stared me in the face –

HELENA. But the God of battles was with you!

JULIAN. I seized a standard, rallied the Imperial Guard,
and flung myself into where the fight was thickest.

HELENA. Julian! Oh, you do not love me.

JULIAN. At that moment, I had no thought for you. I
wanted to die – there seemed no choice. But our
lances seemed to flash fear into the enemy's hearts.
I saw Knodomar, that fearsome warrior – well,
you've seen him yourself – I saw him flee from the
battle on foot, and with him fled all who had not

fallen by our swords.

HELENA. Oh, I see it, I see it! Blessed Saviour – !

JULIAN. Never have I heard such wailing; never have I
seen such hideous wounds as those we trod in as we
waded through the dead. The river did the rest. The
drowning men fought among themselves until they
rolled over and sank. Most of the princes fell into our
hands alive. Knodomar himself threw down his arms
and surrendered.

HELENA. And after such a victory you do not feel safe?

JULIAN (*unwillingly*). The same evening, something
happened. Something trifling –

HELENA. Tell me.

JULIAN. It was a trifle, I tell you. I commanded that
Knodomar should be led before me in chains in the
presence of the whole army. Before the battle he had
threatened that when he captured me he would have
me flayed alive. Now he walked towards me with
uncertain steps. Broken by adversity, as is the way
with barbarians, he threw himself at my feet, clasped
my knees and begged me to spare his life.

HELENA. Those great limbs trembling with fear! Yes, I can
see him lying there. Did you kill him, my beloved?

JULIAN. I could not kill that man. I granted him his life
and promised to send him as a captive to Rome.

HELENA. Without torturing him?

JULIAN. I thought it wise to treat him mercifully. But
then, God knows why, the barbarian sprang to his
feet, raised his chained hands into the air, and cried
in a loud voice: 'Praised be thou, Julian, O mighty
Emperor!'

HELENA. Ah!

JULIAN. My officers began to laugh. But the barbarian's cry
spread like wildfire through the ranks of the soldiers.
'Long live Emperor Julian!', they shouted, and the cry

spread in ever-widening circles until it was taken up
by those who stood out of sight. It was as though
some Titan had cast a mountain into the ocean.

HELENA. Emperor Julian! Those were his words. 'Emperor
Julian!'

JULIAN. What could that crude German know of
Constantius, whom he had never seen? I was his
conqueror, and therefore the greatest –

HELENA. Yes, yes. But the soldiers – ?

JULIAN. I rebuked them sternly, for I saw at once that
Florentius, Severus and certain others stood silent,
white with fear and anger.

HELENA. Yes, yes. They – but not the soldiers.

JULIAN. Scarcely a night passed before my secret enemies
misconstrued the incident. Caesar, they said had
ordered Knodomar to hail him as Emperor, and in
return he had granted the barbarian king his life. And
thus distorted, the news was borne to Rome.

HELENA. Are you sure?

JULIAN. I have proof, Helena. (*Touches his breast.*) Here I
have some letters which were intercepted on the way
to –

HELENA. Oh, my God!

JULIAN. What is it worth to be Caesar on such conditions?

HELENA. No, you are right, Julian. We cannot continue
like this.

JULIAN. Helena, will you stay with me?

HELENA (*softly*). I shall not leave you.

JULIAN. Then let us give up this thankless toil, and seek
the solitude we have so long desired.

HELENA. Solitude?

JULIAN. With you, my beloved; and with my dear books,
which I have so seldom had the chance to open,
except to while away sleepless nights.

HELENA (*looks him up and down*). Oh. That's what

you want?

JULIAN. What else?

HELENA. What else indeed?

JULIAN. What do you mean?

HELENA (*closer*). Julian, how did this barbarian king address you?

JULIAN (*shrinks*). Helena!

HELENA (*closer still*). What was the word that echoed through the soldiers' ranks?

JULIAN. For God's sake! At any door there may be someone listening –

HELENA. What have you to fear from eavesdroppers? Is not God's hand raised over you? Have you not succeeded in everything you have attempted? I see the Saviour beckoning you on. I see the angel with the fiery sword, who cleared my father's path towards the throne: Constantine the Great.

JULIAN. Would you have me challenge the ruler of the Empire?

HELENA. No, only those who stand between you. Go, go! Strike them with the lightning of your wrath! Gaul is a wilderness. I freeze here, Julian. I want to go home, to the sun, to Rome and Greece. The years are ebbing away. The Empress is dead. Her throne stands empty, beckoning me to honour and glory, while I grow old –

JULIAN. You aren't growing old. You are young and beautiful –

HELENA. No, no, no. Life is ebbing away from me.

JULIAN (*looks at her*). You are beautiful and alluring. You are like a goddess –

HELENA (*clings to him*). Am I, Julian?

JULIAN (*embraces her*). You are the only woman I have ever loved. And the only one who has loved me.

HELENA. I am older than you. I don't want to grow any older. When everything is finished, I –

JULIAN (*tears himself loose*). Be quiet! I won't listen to
  you –
HELENA (*follows him*). Constantius is slowly dying. He
  hangs over his grave by a hair. Oh, my beloved
  Julian, you have the soldiers behind you –
JULIAN. Be quiet, be quiet!
HELENA. There needn't be any bloodshed. Fie, how could
  you think I meant that? The fear will be enough –
JULIAN. Do you forget the invisible hand that protects the
  anointed?
HELENA. Christ is good. Oh, be pious, Julian, and He will
  forgive you. I will help you. Prayers shall be offered
  for you. Have no fear. We will atone for everything
  later. Send the Germans to me. I will send priests
  among them to convert them. They will bow to the
  merciful shadow of the Cross.
JULIAN. The Germans will not bow to that shadow.
HELENA. Then they shall die. Their blood will rise to Him
  like a sweet incense. I myself shall assist at the
  ceremony. Give the German women to me. If they
  refuse to kneel, they shall be sacrificed. And then, my
  Julian, when you see me next, I shall be young again,
  young! Give me the German women, my beloved. It
  isn't murder, and they say it is a medicine that never
  fails – to bathe in young virgins' blood –
JULIAN (*glances towards the door*). Helena!
HELENA. Ah!
EUTHERIUS (*enters upstage*). My lord, an envoy from the
  Emperor –
JULIAN. Who is he?
EUTHERIUS. The tribune Decentius.
HELENA. What? The pious Decentius?
JULIAN. Whom has he spoken to?
EUTHERIUS. No one, my lord. He arrived this moment –
JULIAN. I will see him at once. And wait. One thing more.

Bid my generals and captains attend me here.

EUTHERIUS. Yes, most gracious lord. (*Goes out upstage.*)

JULIAN. Now, my Helena. Now we shall see –

The TRIBUNE DECENTIUS *enters upstage.*

HELENA (*goes to greet him*). Welcome, noble Decentius. A
    Roman face – and above all, this face – oh, it is like a
    ray of sunshine in our freezing Gaul.

DECENTIUS. The Emperor meets your hopes and longings
    halfway, your highness. We dare believe that Gaul
    will not bind you for much longer.

HELENA. The Emperor still thinks lovingly of me, then?

JULIAN. Go, go, my beloved Helena.

HELENA. Give him my dearest thanks, pious Decentius.
    And we thank you too. What rich gifts you have sent
    to herald your arrival! Two shining black Nubians –
    oh, you should see them, Julian! – and pearls. Look, I
    am wearing them already. And fruit, too, sweet and
    exotic, ah! Peaches from Damascus, peaches in golden
    bowls. Oh, how they will refresh me! Fruit, fruit. I
    am almost dying here in Gaul.

JULIAN. Go, my beloved wife.

HELENA. I will go to church – to pray for my brother, and
    for all our hopes. (*Goes out right.*)

JULIAN (*after a moment*). Is your message oral or written?

DECENTIUS. Written, my lord. (*Hands him a roll of paper*).

JULIAN (*reads it, stifles a smile and holds out his hand*).
    And the rest?

DECENTIUS. Noble Caesar, that is all, more or less.

JULIAN. Really? Has the Emperor sent his friend this long
    way simply to – ? (*Laughs shortly, then starts pacing
    up and down.*) Had the German king Knodomar
    reached Rome when you left?

DECENTIUS. Yes, noble Caesar.

JULIAN. And how is he faring in that foreign land,
ignorant as he is of the language? Yes, he is very
ignorant, Decentius. My soldiers could scarcely
refrain from laughing at him. Imagine, he even
confused such simple words as Emperor and Caesar.

DECENTIUS (*shrugs his shoulders*). A barbarian. What can
one expect?

JULIAN. Exactly, What can one expect? But the Emperor
showed him mercy?

DECENTIUS. Knodomar is dead, my lord.

JULIAN. Dead? So? Yes, the air of Rome is insalubrious.

DECENTIUS. The German king died of homesickness, my
lord. When a man loses his family and his freedom,
he –

JULIAN. Wastes away, Decentius. Yes, yes. I know. I
should not have sent him alive to Rome. I ought to
have had him killed here.

DECENTIUS. Caesar is merciful.

JULIAN. Hm. Homesickness? Well, well. Ah, here they are.

GENERAL SEVERUS, GENERAL FLORENTIUS, *Commander of
the Praetorian Guard, and other* COMMANDERS *and* OFFICERS
of CAESAR's *court enter.*

JULIAN (*goes to greet them*). Good morning, my brothers in
arms and friends.

FLORENTIUS. Has something happened, my lord?

JULIAN. Yes, indeed, something has happened. Can you
tell me, now – what was lacking to complete Caesar's
happiness?

FLORENTIUS. What could Caesar lack?

JULIAN. Nothing – now. Rejoice, my gallant fellow-
warriors! Here you see the Tribune Decentius, the

Emperor's trusted friend and counsellor. He came this
morning with gifts and greetings from Rome.

FLORENTIUS. Then indeed Caesar's happiness must be
complete.

SEVERUS (*whispers to* FLORENTIUS). Incredible! Then he is
back in the Emperor's favour.

FLORENTIUS (*whispers back*). Ah, this vacillating Emperor
of ours!

JULIAN. You all seem struck dumb with amazement. They
think the Emperor has shown me too much grace,
Decentius.

FLORENTIUS. How can Caesar think such a thing?

SEVERUS. Too much, noble Caesar? Impossible. The
Emperor surely knows what limits to set to his
favour.

FLORENTIUS. And what has Caesar not accomplished
during these few years in Gaul?

JULIAN. I have accomplished nothing. Nothing, nothing!

FLORENTIUS. You call it nothing? Caesar is too modest.
What was the army when you took it over? An
undisciplined rabble –

SEVERUS. Disorderly, mutinous, leaderless –

JULIAN. Come, Severus, you exaggerate.

FLORENTIUS. And did you not transform this rabble into a
victorious army? Did you not conquer the Germans –
recapture Cologne – ?

JULIAN. No, no, friendship makes you see these things
with a biased eye, my dear Florentius. Or – did these
things happen? Did I drive the barbarians from their
islands in the Rhine?

FLORENTIUS. My lord! Can you doubt that you
accomplished this great deed?

JULIAN. No, in truth, I believe I did. And the battle at
Argentoratum? Was I not present there? I seem to
remember having defeated Knodomar. And after the

victory – Florentius, did I dream this, or did I not
rebuild Trajan's fortress when we marched across the
German frontier?

FLORENTIUS. Noble Caesar, could any man be so mad as
to deny you this honour?

SEVERUS (*to* DECENTIUS). I thank the fate that blessed my
declining years by permitting me to serve so great a
leader.

FLORENTIUS (*to* DECENTIUS). What turn this German
campaign might have taken but for Caesar's courage
and wisdom I scarcely dare to think.

SEVERAL COURTIERS (*press forward*). Yes, my lord, Caesar
is great!

OTHERS (*clap their hands*). Caesar has no equal.

JULIAN (*glances for a moment from* DECENTIUS *to the
others, then gives a short, loud laugh*). You see how
blind friendship is, Decentius! How blind, blind!
(*Turns to the others and strikes the roll of paper which
he is holding.*) There is quite a different version here.
Here it is stated that I have accomplished nothing in
Gaul. Here we have the Emperor's own word for it. It
was under the blessed guidance of the Emperor that
the danger threatening our Empire was averted.

FLORENTIUS. Any success that the Empire enjoys occurs
under the guidance of the Emperor.

JULIAN. Here it is told how it was the Emperor who
fought and conquered on the Rhine. It was the
Emperor who raised up the German king as he flung
himself at his feet and humbly prayed for mercy. I
cannot find my name anywhere in this document –
nor yours, Florentius, nor yours, Severus. And here,
in the account of the battle at Argentoratum – where
is it? – yes, here, here it is – it was the Emperor who
drew up the order of battle. It was the Emperor who,
at the peril of his life, hewed until his sword grew

blunt in the foremost ranks of his army. It was the
Emperor who, by the terror of his presence, routed
the barbarians in headlong flight. Read for yourselves,
read!

SEVERUS. Noble Caesar, your word is enough.

JULIAN. Then why do you indulge in these untruthful
ravings, my friends? What think you, Decentius?
What do you say to all this? You see! Here in my
own camp I must endure sycophants like these who
sometimes in their blindness come not far short of
treason.

FLORENTIUS (*quickly to* DECENTIUS). My words were
indeed much misinterpreted if –

SEVERUS (*to* DECENTIUS). Never could it enter my head
to – !

JULIAN. Just now I asked what was lacking to complete
Caesar's happiness. Well, now you know. What was
lacking was the admission of the truth. So weak is
human nature in time of triumph. I had almost
forgotten the precepts of philosophy. The Emperor
has reminded me. Thank him most humbly,
Decentius. Have you anything further to say to me?

DECENTIUS (*takes out another roll of paper*). This letter
expresses the Emperor's will, noble Caesar.

JULIAN. Let me see, let me see. (*Reads.*) Ah! (*Reads again
slowly, with deep emotion. He glances up.*) So it is the
Emperor's will that – ? Very well, noble Decentius.
Let the Emperor's will be done.

DECENTIUS. It must be done today.

JULIAN. Today? But of course. (*Goes over to the window
and reads the two letters again.*) Today! Let me say
one word, Decentius. I have long prayed to be
relieved of this honour and responsibility.

DECENTIUS. I shall inform the Emperor of that.

JULIAN. I call Heaven to witness that I never – you are

going?

DECENTIUS. I have business to discuss with the generals, noble Caesar.

JULIAN. And I am not to be present?

DECENTIUS. The Emperor commanded that I should not trouble his beloved kinsman –

Goes out upstage, followed by all the OTHERS *except* SINTULA, *Master of the Horse, who remains by the door.*

JULIAN. Sintula! (*Looks at him for a moment.*)

SINTULA. My lord?

JULIAN. Come here. Yes, you look like an honest man. Forgive me. I never thought you could be so devoted to me.

SINTULA. How do you know that I am devoted to you, my lord?

JULIAN (*points to the letter*). It says here that you are to desert me.

SINTULA. I, my lord?

JULIAN. The Emperor is disbanding the army in Gaul, Sintula.

SINTULA. Disbanding – ?

JULIAN. Our Batavian and Aerulian auxiliaries are to march eastwards with all expedition so as to be in Asia by the spring.

SINTULA. But that's impossible, my lord! You swore a solemn oath to our allies that they would never be required to fight beyond the Alps.

JULIAN. Exactly, Sintula. I am to be compelled to break my word, dishonour myself in the eyes of my soldiers, and bring upon my head the unbridled rage of the barbarians, and perhaps their swords also.

SINTULA. Have no fear, my lord. The Roman legions will –

JULIAN. The Roman legions? Oh, my innocent friend!
    Every Roman legion is to be depleted of three
    hundred men, to be sent by the shortest route to join
    the Emperor for his Asian campaign.

SINTULA. My lord, not one of your commanders will allow
    himself to be used for this purpose.

JULIAN. My commanders are not to be exposed to the
    temptation. You are the man.

SINTULA. I, my lord?

JULIAN. The Emperor entrusts to you the task of making
    the necessary arrangements and leading the chosen
    detachments to Rome.

SINTULA. To me?

JULIAN. You have no victories to blot your record, Sintula.

SINTULA. Such an honour – ! And from the Emperor
    himself – ! My lord, may I read the – ?

JULIAN. Why do you want to read it? You have just said
    that you will not allow yourself to be used for that
    purpose.

SINTULA. God forbid that I should disobey the command
    of the Emperor!

JULIAN. Would you disarm your Caesar, Sintula?

SINTULA. My lord, I wish to do my duty. May I know the
    Emperor's instructions?

JULIAN (*hands him one of the letters*). Here are the
    Emperor's instructions. Go, and do your duty.

MYRRHA (*runs in, right*). Oh, merciful Saviour – !

JULIAN. Myrrha! What is it?

MYRRHA. Oh, blessed heaven! My mistress – !

JULIAN. Your mistress? Is anything the matter with her?

MYRRHA. She is sick – or distraught. Help, help!

JULIAN. Helena sick! The doctor! Find Oribases, Sintula!
    Bring him here at once!

SINTULA *goes out upstage.* JULIAN *runs towards the door*

right, but is met in the doorway by the PRINCESS
HELENA, *surrounded by* SLAVE WOMEN. *Her face is wild
and distraught and her hair and clothes are disordered.*

HELENA. Loosen the comb! Loosen the comb, I say! It's
    burning me! My hair is on fire! I'm burning, I'm
    burning!

JULIAN. Helena! For God's sake!

HELENA. Will no one help me? They're driving needles
    into me! They're trying to murder me!

JULIAN. Helena, my dearest! What has happened?

HELENA. Myrrha, Myrrha! Save me from these women,
    Myrrha!

ORIBASES (*enters upstage*). What dreadful news is this? Is
    it true? Ah!

JULIAN. Helena! My love, light of my life – !

HELENA. Get away from me! Oh, sweet Jesus, help me!
    (*Half-collapses among the* SLAVE WOMEN.)

JULIAN. She is distraught. What can it be, Oribases? Look!
    Look at her eyes! How huge they are – !

ORIBASES (*to* MYRRHA). What has the Princess eaten? Or
    drunk?

JULIAN. Ah! You think – ?

ORIBASES. Answer me, women! What have you given the
    Princess?

MYRRHA. We? Nothing, I swear. She took them herself –

ORIBASES. Speak, speak.

MYRRHA. Some fruit – peaches, I think – oh, I don't
    know – !

JULIAN. Fruit? Peaches! The ones that – ?

MYRRHA. Yes – no – yes – I don't know, my lord – it was
    the two Nubians – !

JULIAN. Help, help, Oribases!

ORIBASES. My lord, I fear I –

JULIAN. No, no, no!

ORIBASES. Hush, my lord. She is regaining consciousness.

HELENA (*whispers*). Why has the sun gone down? Oh, blessed, secret darkness!

JULIAN. Helena! Listen – try to remember –

ORIBASES. Noble princess –

JULIAN. It's the doctor, Helena. (*Takes her hand.*) No, here, beside me –

HELENA (*tears herself free*). Ugh! There he is again!

JULIAN. She doesn't see me. Listen, Helena, listen!

HELENA. Repulsive man – he's always creeping around me –

JULIAN. What does she mean?

ORIBASES. Leave her for a moment, gracious lord –

HELENA. Ah, sweet peace! He doesn't suspect – ah, my Gallus!

JULIAN. Gallus?

ORIBASES. Go, noble Caesar. It is not fitting –

HELENA. Your thick, curly hair – how closely it lies around your neck! Oh, that short, strong neck – !

JULIAN. Ah!

ORIBASES. She is becoming delirious –

JULIAN. I note it, I note it. We must note what she says, Oribases.

HELENA (*laughs quietly*). Now he's going to take notes again. Ink on his fingers – the dust of books in his hair – unwashed – fie, fie, how he stinks!

MYRRHA. My lord, should I not – ?

JULIAN. Out of my sight, woman!

HELENA. How could you let yourself be vanquished by him, you beautiful, bronzed barbarian? He can't vanquish women. Oh, how I loathe this virtuous impotence – !

JULIAN. Stand aside, all of you! Not so close, Oribases. I will take care of her highness.

HELENA. Are you angry with me, my Saviour? Gallus is

dead, isn't he? They cut off his head. What a blow
that must have been! Don't be jealous. You were my
first love, and my last. Let Gallus burn in hell fire.
There never was anyone but You, You, You – !

JULIAN. No closer, Oribases!

HELENA. Kill the priest, too. I don't want to see him after
this. You know our precious secret – ! Oh, my day's
longing, my night's delight! It was You Yourself –
disguised as Your servant – in the chapel! Yes, yes,
You were there. It was You – in the darkness, in the
air, in the veiling clouds of incense, that night when a
new Caesar stirred beneath my heart –

JULIAN (*recoils with a cry*). Ah!

HELENA (*stretches out her arms*). My lover and my master!
Mine, mine – !

She falls to the floor. The SLAVE WOMEN *run and
gather round her.*

JULIAN (*stands for a moment motionless; then he raises his
clenched fist in the air and cries*). Galilean!

The SLAVE WOMEN *carry the* PRINCESS *out right. As
they do so,* SALLUST *runs in upstage.*

SALLUST. Has the Princess fainted? Ah, then it's true!

JULIAN (*grasps* ORIBASES *by the arm and leads him aside*).
Tell me the truth. Did you know before today that –
you understand me – did you know anything before
today about – about the Princess's condition – ?

ORIBASES. All of us knew, my lord.

JULIAN. And you said nothing to me, Oribases!

ORIBASES. How do you mean, Caesar?

JULIAN. How could you keep silent about such a thing?

ORIBASES. My lord, there was one thing none of us knew.

JULIAN. What was that?

ORIBASES. That Caesar did not know. (*Turns to go.*)

JULIAN. Where are you going?

ORIBASES. To try what medicines my art can –

JULIAN. I think it would be useless.

ORIBASES. My lord, there is still a chance –

JULIAN. Useless, I say!

ORIBASES (*shrinks a step backwards*). Noble Caesar, it is my duty to disobey you in this matter.

JULIAN. Must I spell out my meaning? Go, go. See what your art can achieve. Save the Emperor's sister. The Emperor would be inconsolable if he should learn that his tender thought had brought ill luck in its train. Surely you understand that this fruit was sent to her by the Emperor?

ORIBASES. Ah!

JULIAN. Go, man, go! See what your art can achieve –

ORIBASES (*bows humbly*). I fear my art will prove useless, my lord. (*Goes out right.*)

JULIAN. Ah, Sallust, is it you? Well, it seems the waves of fate are beginning to engulf my family again.

SALLUST. Oh, but she will be saved. Oribases will –

JULIAN (*curtly, finally*). The Princess will die.

SALLUST. Oh, if I dared to speak. If I dared trace all the secret threads in this web of destruction!

JULIAN. Never mind, my friend. One day every thread will be brought to light. And then –

DECENTIUS (*enters upstage*). How shall I enter Caesar's sight!

JULIAN. And how shall I find words gentle and veiled enough to convey this news to her brother's imperial ears?

DECENTIUS. Dreadful that such a thing should occur so soon after my arrival! And just now! A thunderbolt from a cloudless sky of hope.

JULIAN. Yes, that this storm should arise and engulf us just as our ship seemed about to enter its longed-for

harbour. This, this – ! Grief makes us eloquent,
Decentius; you, like me. But first to business. Those
two Nubians must be arrested and tried.

DECENTIUS. The Nubians, my lord? Can you suppose that
my indignant zeal allowed those villains a moment – ?

JULIAN. You have had them both killed?

DECENTIUS. Did they not deserve death seven times over
for their negligence? They were heathen savages, my
lord. Their testimony would have served no purpose.
I could get nothing out of them but that they had
allowed the fruit to stand unguarded in the ante-
chamber, where anyone could –

JULIAN. Aha. I see, Decentius.

DECENTIUS. I accuse no one. Oh, but beloved Caesar, take
care, I beg you. You are surrounded by disloyal
servants –

SINTULA (*enters upstage*). My lord, you have set me a task
which I cannot carry out.

JULIAN. The Emperor set you that task, Sintula.

SINTULA. Relieve me of it, my lord. It is beyond my
powers.

DECENTIUS. What has happened?

SINTULA. The camp is in an uproar. The legionaries and
the allies are seeking common cause –

DECENTIUS. In defiance of the Emperor's expressed
command – !

SINTULA. The soldiers are shouting that they will hold
Caesar to his promises –

JULIAN. Listen, listen. What is that noise?

SINTULA. They are running towards the palace –

DECENTIUS. Don't let anyone in!

SALLUST (*by the window*). It's too late. The whole
courtyard is filled with soldiers. They're shouting
threats –

DECENTIUS. Caesar's precious life is in danger! Where

is Florentius?

SINTULA. Fled.

DECENTIUS. The miserable braggart! What about Severus?

SINTULA. Severus says he is sick. He has left for his
     country estate.

JULIAN. I will speak to these men.

DECENTIUS. You must not leave the palace, noble Caesar.

JULIAN. What?

DECENTIUS. It is my duty, most gracious lord. The
     Emperor's orders – his precious kinsman's life – !
     Caesar is my prisoner.

SALLUST. Ah!

JULIAN. So it has come to that.

DECENTIUS. The household guard, Sintula. You are to
     convey Caesar safely to Rome.

JULIAN. To Rome!

SINTULA. What say you, my lord?

JULIAN. Like Gallus! (*Shouts through the window.*) Help!
     Help!

SALLUST. Fly, my lord! Fly!

Wild shouts are heard outside. ROMAN LEGIONARIES,
BATAVIAN AUXILIARIES, *and* OTHER FOREIGN TROOPS
climb in through the windows. Simultaneously, OTHER
SOLDIERS *swarm in through the door upstage. Among
the first to enter is the Standard Bearer,* MAUROS.
WOMEN, *some of them with* CHILDREN *in their arms,
accompany the* INTRUDERS.

SOLDIERS (*shout*). Caesar, Caesar!

OTHERS. Caesar, why have you betrayed us?

OTHERS. Down with Caesar, the traitor!

JULIAN (*throws himself with outstretched arms into the
     midst of his* SOLDIERS, *and cries*). Comrades. Brothers
     in arms! Save me from my enemies!

DECENTIUS. Ah, what is this – ?

JULIAN. Form a circle round me! Draw your swords!

MAUROS. They are already drawn!

WOMEN. Kill him, kill him!

JULIAN. Thank God you came! Mauros! My loyal Mauros! Yes, yes. You I can trust.

BATAVIAN SOLDERS. How dare you send us to the ends of the earth? Was that the promise you made us?

OTHER FOREIGN SOLDIERS. Not beyond the Alps! We shall not fight there!

JULIAN. Not to Rome! I shall not go! They will murder me, as they murdered my brother Gallus!

MAUROS. What are you saying, my lord?

DECENTIUS. Don't believe him!

JULIAN. Do not touch the noble Decentius. He is not to blame.

LAIPSO (*a centurion*). That's true. Caesar is the guilty one!

JULIAN. Ah, Laipso, is it you? My gallant friend, is it you? You fought bravely at Argentoratum.

LAIPSO. Does Caesar remember?

VARRO (*another centurion*). He doesn't remember his promises.

JULIAN. Was not that the voice of the fearless Varro? Yes, there you are. Your wound is healed, I see. You have deserved well. To think they would not allow me to make you a captain!

VARRO. Did you want that?

JULIAN. Do not blame the Emperor for rejecting my petition. The Emperor does not know any of you as I know you.

DECENTIUS. Soldiers, listen to me –

MANY VOICES. We've nothing to do with the Emperor!

OTHERS. What's he to us?

OTHERS (*crowd forward threateningly*). Caesar shall answer to us!

JULIAN. What power has your unhappy Caesar, my

friends? They want to take me to Rome. They won't
even allow me to control my personal affairs. They
have commandeered my share of the booty. I had
planned to distribute five pieces of gold and a pound
of silver to every soldier, but –

SOLDIERS. What was that?

JULIAN. It is not the Emperor who forbids this. It is his
evil and envious counsellors. The Emperor is good,
my dear friends! But alas, the Emperor is sick. He
cannot accomplish –

MANY SOLDIERS. Five pieces of gold and a pound of silver!

OTHERS. And they won't let us have it!

OTHERS. Who dares refuse Caesar anything?

MAUROS. That is how they treat Caesar, the father of our
army!

LAIPSO. Caesar, who has been our friend more than our
master! Or hasn't he?

MANY VOICES. Yes, yes, he has!

VARRO. Should not Caesar the conqueror be allowed to
choose his own captains?

MAUROS. Should he not be free to decide what's to be
done with his share of the booty?

LOUD CRIES. Yes, yes, yes!

JULIAN. Alas, what good would it be to you? What will be
the use of earthly goods if you are to be sent to the
ends of the earth to a fate no man can predict – ?

SOLDIERS. We won't go!

JULIAN. Do not look at me. I am ashamed. I can scarcely
forbear to weep when I think that within a few
months you will be exposed to pestilence, hunger and
the spears and arrows of a bloodthirsty foe.

MANY SOLDIERS (*Crowd around him*). Caesar! Noble
Caesar!

JULIAN. And what of your wives and children, whom you
must leave defenceless in their scattered homes? Who

will protect these unhappy widows and orphans when
they are exposed to the merciless vengeance of the
Germans?

WOMEN (*weep*). Caesar, Caesar, have pity on us.

JULIAN (*also weeps*). What is Caesar? What can a fallen
Caesar do?

LAIPSO. Write to the Emperor and tell him –

JULIAN. Alas, what is the Emperor? The Emperor is sick
in mind and body. His solicitude for the welfare of
the Empire has broken his health. Is it not so,
Decentius?

DECENTIUS. That is true; but –

JULIAN. Oh, how it pierced my heart when I learned – !
(*Presses the hands of those nearest to him.*) Pray for his
soul, you who worship the good Christ. Offer
sacrifices for his health, you who have remained
faithful to the gods of your fathers. Do you know that
the Emperor has held a triumph in Rome?

MAUROS. The Emperor?

VARRO. What? After his defeat on the Danube?

JULIAN. After his defeat on the Danube he held a triumph
to celebrate our victories –

DECENTIUS (*warningly*). Noble Caesar, consider –

JULIAN. Yes, the tribune is right! Consider how the
Emperor's mind must be clouded if such a thing can
happen. Oh, my poor kinsman, how sadly thou art
afflicted! When he rode in Rome through the mighty
arch of Constantine, he believed himself so great that
he arched his back and bowed his head to his saddle
bow.

MAUROS. Like a cock in a doorway!

The SOLDIERS *laugh.*

SOME OF THE SOLDIERS. Call *him* an Emperor?

VARRO. Shall we obey such a man?

LAIPSO. Away with him!

MAUROS. Caesar, you take command!

DECENTIUS. This is mutiny – !

MANY VOICES. Seize power, Caesar! Seize the throne!

JULIAN. Are you mad? Is this a way for Romans to speak?
    Would you behave like Barbarians? What was it
    Knodomar cried at Argentoratum? Tell me, my good
    Mauros, what was it he cried?

MAUROS. He cried: 'Long live Emperor Julian!'

JULIAN. Oh, hush! What are you saying?

MAUROS. Long live Emperor Julian!

SOLDIERS AT THE BACK. What's happening?

VARRO. They are acclaiming Caesar Julian Emperor!

LOUD CRY. Long live the Emperor! Long live Emperor
    Julian!

*The shout is taken up outside and spreads. Everyone is
talking or shouting. It is some time before* CAESAR
JULIAN *can make himself heard.*

JULIAN. Oh, I beseech you! Soldiers, friends, comrades in
    arms! Look, I stretch out my trembling arms – ! Have
    no fear, good Decentius. Oh, that I should live to
    experience this! I do not blame you, my loyal
    comrades. Despair has driven you to this. It is your
    will. Very well. I submit to the will of my army.
    Sintula, bid my officers assemble. Tribune, you will
    testify to Constantius that I have acted under
    compulsion. (*Turns to* VARRO.) Go captain, and
    announce this unexpected change of plan to the camp.
    I myself shall write forthwith to Rome –

SALLUST. My lord, the soldiers wish to see you.

MAUROS. A golden circlet about your head, Emperor!

JULIAN. I have never possessed such an ornament!

MAUROS. This will serve. (*Takes off his necklace and coils
    it several times round* JULIAN's *forehead.*)

CRIES FROM OUTSIDE. The Emperor! The Emperor! We
    want to see the Emperor!
SOLDIERS. Lift him on a shield! Up with him! Higher!

    The SOLDIERS *nearest to* JULIAN *lift him on a shield*
    high into the air and show him to the CROWD *outside.*
    Renewed and continuous cheering.

JULIAN. Let the will of the army be done. I bow to the
    inevitable, and renew all the promises I made to
    you –
LEGIONARIES. Five pieces of gold and a pound of silver!
BATAVIANS. Not beyond the Alps!
JULIAN. We will make our headquarters in Vienne. That is
    the strongest city in Gaul, and is richly provisioned. I
    propose to wait there until we see whether my
    unhappy kinsman will agree to the measures we have
    taken here today for the sake of our great Empire –
SALLUST. He won't do that, my lord!
JULIAN (*raises his hands*). May the wisdom of God
    enlighten his darkened soul and show him the path! O
    Fortune, who hast never yet abandoned me, stay with
    me now!
MYRRHA AND THE WOMEN (*wail outside*). Dead, dead,
    dead!

Act Five

*Vienne, in Gaul. A vaulted chamber in the catacombs. On the
left, a passage winds upwards. In the rock-face in the
background a flight of steps has been cut, ending in a closed
door. Downstage right, many steps lead down to the lower
galleries. The chamber is dimly illuminated by a hanging lamp.*
CAESAR JULIAN, *unshaven and in dirty clothes, stands leaning
over the opening on the right. Through the door can be heard
muffled psalm-singing from the church beyond.*

JULIAN (*speaks to someone below*). Still no sign?

A VOICE (*far below*). None.

JULIAN. Neither yes nor no? Neither for nor against?

VOICE. Both.

JULIAN. That is the same as nothing.

VOICE. Wait, wait.

JULIAN. I've waited five days. You only asked for three. I
tell you, I'm not in the mood to – ! (*Listens at the exit
and calls softly down.*) Hush! Don't say anything!

SALLUST (*enters down the passage left*). My lord! My lord!

JULIAN. Is it you, Sallust? What do you want down here?

SALLUST. It's so dark, I can't – ah, there you are.

JULIAN. What do you want?

SALLUST. To serve you, if I could. To lead you up to the
world of the living.

JULIAN. What news from the world?

SALLUST. The soldiers are restless. They're beginning to
lose patience.

JULIAN. I suppose the sun's shining up there now?

SALLUST. Yes, my lord.

JULIAN. The sky arches itself like a sea of glittering light. Perhaps it is high noon. It is hot. The air trembles along the walls of the houses. The river ripples over white flints in its half-dried bed. Beautiful life! Beautiful world!

SALLUST. Come, my lord, come. Your refusal to leave these catacombs is being ill construed.

JULIAN. How is it being construed?

SALLUST. May I speak plainly?

JULIAN. You must.

SALLUST. Many believe that it was not grief but a guilty conscience that drove you to hide underground.

JULIAN. They think I killed her?

SALLUST. The mystery surrounding her highness's death must be their excuse if –

JULIAN. No one killed her, Sallust. She was too pure for this sinful world; so an angel came down every night into her bedchamber and called to her. Well? Don't you know this is the explanation the priests of Lutetia gave of her death? And the priests must know. Has not the progress of her coffin here to Vienne been acclaimed like a triumph? Did not the women of Vienne throng to greet her body at the city gates, welcoming her with green branches in their hands and spreading carpets on the road, singing hymns to the glory of the bride of heaven as she was borne home to her bridegroom's house? What are you laughing at?

SALLUST. I, my lord?

JULIAN. Night and day the air has been filled with bridal songs. Listen, listen! She is being wafted upwards on wings of glory to meet her lover. Oh, yes, she was a truly Christian woman. She obeyed the commandment strictly. She rendered unto Caesar what was Caesar's, and to her other lord she gave –

well, you didn't come here to discuss that, Sallust, you
haven't been initiated into the secrets of the one true
faith. What's the news, I asked you?

SALLUST. The chief news is that the Emperor, when he
heard what had happened in Lutetia, fled in haste
to Antioch.

JULIAN. I know that. Constantius in the fever of his
imagination saw us already at the gates of Rome.

SALLUST. Your friends who threw in their lot with you in
this dangerous game also saw us there, in the fever of
their imagination.

JULIAN. The omens are not favourable, Sallust. Don't you
know that during the games on our last day in
Lutetia my shield broke so that I was left with only
the handle? And when I tried to mount my horse, the
groom on whose folded hands I swung myself up
stumbled.

SALLUST. But you came safely into the saddle, my lord.

JULIAN. But the man fell.

SALLUST. Better men will fall if Caesar hesitates.

JULIAN. The Emperor cannot live much longer.

SALLUST. The Emperor is alive. The letters you wrote
telling him of your proclamation –

JULIAN. The proclamation that was forced on me. They
made me do it. It was not my choice.

SALLUST. The Emperor will not accept that explanation.
As soon as he has gathered an army in the eastern
provinces, he intends to march on Gaul.

JULIAN. How do you know that?

SALLUST. By chance, my lord. But I beg you to believe
me –

JULIAN. Very well. When it happens, I will go to meet
Constantius. Not with a sword, but –

SALLUST. Not? How do you intend to meet him, then?

CAESAR. I will render unto the Emperor what belongs to

the Emperor.

SALLUST. Yield the crown?

JULIAN. The Emperor cannot live long.

SALLUST. Oh, this vain hope – ! (*Kneels.*) Then take my
life, lord!

JULIAN. What?

SALLUST. Take my life, Caesar. I would rather die by your
command than by the Emperor's.

JULIAN. Stand up, my friend.

SALLUST. No. Take the life you will soon have no power
to protect. You say the Emperor cannot live long.
(*Gets up.*) Caesar, I was sworn to silence, but I must
speak. Put no hope in the Emperor's sickness. The
Emperor is taking a new wife.

JULIAN. You must be mad! How can you imagine – ?

SALLUST. The Emperor is taking a new wife, my lord.
(*Hands him some papers.*) Read, noble Caesar, read.
These letters will dispel your doubts.

JULIAN (*seizes the papers and reads*). Yes, by the light and
power of the sun – ! What does it say – young,
scarcely nineteen – a daughter of – ah, a daughter of
that overweening house. A zealous Christian, then.
(*Folds the letter.*) You are right, Sallust. I can put no
hope in his sickness. Sick, or dying, what does it
matter? A young Caesar will be fathered on her, and
then –

SALLUST. To delay will mean disaster.

JULIAN. He must have planned this for a long time,
Sallust, in secret. Well, that answers every riddle.
Helena – yes, it wasn't just her careless tongue that
destroyed her –

SALLUST. No, my lord.

JULIAN. I thought she – I supposed – O merciless and
inexorable justice! Yes, that was why she had to die.
They won't stop at that – there will be two corpses

up there in the sarcophagus. Constantius is taking a
wife. That was why I had to be disarmed.

SALLUST. The future Empress's kinsmen are the men who
surrounded Gallus Caesar during his last hours.

JULIAN. I hadn't forgotten that. Am I to yield to this
bloody Emperor and die at his hands? Am I to spare
the man who for long years has stumbled among the
corpses of my closest kinsmen?

SALLUST. If you spare him, within three months he will be
stumbling among the corpses of your followers.

JULIAN. Yes, yes. You are right. I must oppose him. It is
my duty. Sallust, why didn't you tell me all this
before?

SALLUST. In Rome they made me swear a solemn oath to
hold my tongue.

JULIAN. An oath. I see. By the gods of your ancestors?

SALLUST. Yes, my lord. By Zeus and Apollo.

JULIAN. Yet you have broken that oath?

SALLUST. I want to live.

JULIAN. But the gods?

SALLUST. The gods are far away.

JULIAN. Yes, your gods are far away. They bind no one,
they burden no one. They leave a man free to act.
Oh, that Greek happiness, that sense of freedom! You
said that the Emperor in his greed for revenge would
shed the blood of my comrades. Yes, who can doubt
it? Was Knodomar spared? Did not that unfortunate
captive have to pay with his life for a slip of his
tongue? Then what can we expect? Decentius won't
have minced his words in his report to Rome.

SALLUST. The flight of the court to Antioch is proof of
that.

JULIAN. And am I not the father of the army, Sallust?

SALLUST. You are the father of the soldiers, and the shield
of their wives and children.

JULIAN. And what would be the fate of the Empire if I were to weaken now? An Emperor whose days are numbered, and after him a helpless baby on the throne. Civil strife and rebellion; every man's hand raised against his neighbour. A few nights ago I had a vision. I saw a figure with a circle of light around its head. It gazed wrathfully upon me and said: 'Choose!' I must indeed choose, for disaster threatens the Empire. I am not thinking of my own advantage. But *dare* I shun the choice, Sallust? And is it not my duty to the Emperor to protect my life? Have I the right to stand idle and wait for the murderers whom in his mad fear he has paid to strike me down? Have I the right to allow the unhappy Constantius to add a new debt of blood to his long list of sins? Is it not better, as it stands in the Scriptures, that he should suffer wrong than do wrong? Be this as it may, Sallust, I intend to compose a defence of my actions which will clearly justify me –

SALLUST. Do so, gracious lord; but the soldiers are impatient. They demand to see you and hear their fate from your own mouth.

JULIAN. Go, go and calm them. Tell them Caesar will shortly show himself.

SALLUST. My lord, it is not Caesar they want to see. It is the Emperor.

JULIAN. The lives of thousands against the death of thousands!

SALLUST. Have your enemies the right to live?

JULIAN. You are lucky that your gods are far away. Oh to be *sure*, and strong of will – !

A VOICE (*cries from deep down in the catacombs*). Julian, Julian!

SALLUST. What was that?

JULIAN. Go, my good Sallust. Go quickly.

VOICE. Silence the singing in the church, Julian!

SALLUST. Then it is true!

JULIAN. What is true?

SALLUST. That you live down here with a magician, who comes to you by night.

JULIAN (*laughs*). Do they say that? Go, go!

SALLUST. I beg you, my lord, come with me. Come up into the light.

VOICE (*closer, below*). All our toil is wasted.

JULIAN (*at the entrance to the steps, right*). No sign, my brother?

VOICE. Waste and emptiness!

JULIAN. Oh, Maximus.

SALLUST. Maximus!

JULIAN. Go, I say. If ever I leave this house of corruption, I shall leave as Emperor.

SALLUST. What do you seek down here in the darkness?

JULIAN. Light! Go, go!

SALLUST. If Casear hesitates, I fear he may find his path barred.

He goes out left. A moment later, MAXIMUS THE MYSTIC *climbs up the steps. He wears a white sacrificial band around his forehead and carries a long and bloody knife in his hand.*

JULIAN. Speak, my Maximus.

MAXIMUS. All our toil is wasted, Julian. Why didn't you silence the song in the church? It stopped the tongues of the omens. They wanted to speak. But the words would not come.

JULIAN. Silence, darkness! I cannot wait any longer. What shall I do?

MAXIMUS. Go blindly forward, Emperor Julian. The light will find you.

JULIAN. Yes, yes. I think so, too. I had no need to make you toil so long. Do you know what I have just learned – ?

MAXIMUS. I do not want to know what you have learned.
Take your fate into your own hands.

JULIAN (*paces restlessly up and down*). After all, what is he,
this Constantius? This sinner hunted by Furies, this
crumbling relic of what was once a man?

MAXIMUS. You speak his epitaph, Emperor Julian.

JULIAN. Do I owe him thanks for the life he has hitherto
granted me? Every night I have sweated in the fear
that the day just ended had been my last.

MAXIMUS. Were Constantius and death your greatest fear?
Think again.

JULIAN. The priests – ! My whole youth has been one long
night of fear, of the Emperor and of Christ! Oh, He is
terrible, that riddling, that merciless God-turned-man!
Wherever I wanted to go, He barred my way, mighty
and stern with His implacable commandments.

MAXIMUS. And those commandments – did they come
from within you?

JULIAN. Always from without. 'Thou shalt !' If my spirit
revolted in hatred against the murderer of my
kinsmen, His commandment whispered: 'Love thine
enemy!' When my heart longed for the lost world of
Greece, the Christian gospel held me back, saying:
'One thing only is needed.' When I felt the sweet lust
of the flesh, the Prince of Chastity scared me with
His: 'Let the body suffer that the soul may live!'
Every human instinct became sinful from the day
when that seer from Galilee began to rule the world.
He turned life into death, love and hatred into sin.
But did He transform flesh and blood? Has not man
remained what he always was, earthbound? Our
innermost soul revolts against His commandments –
yet He goes on demanding that we *will* everything
that our soul denies. 'Thou shalt, thou shalt, thou
shalt!'

MAXIMUS. Haven't you conquered that yet? Shame on
    you, man of Athens and of Ephesus!

JULIAN. Ah, Maximus, those times are past. Then it was
    easy to choose. Now the problem lies deeper. Now it
    is a question of action. 'Render unto the Emperor that
    which is the Emperor's.' In Athens I once jested
    about that; but it isn't so easy. You can't understand,
    because you have never lived under the tyranny of
    the God-turned-man. It's more than a dogma He has
    spread across the world. It's a witchcraft that takes the
    senses prisoner. I don't think anyone who has once
    been under Him can ever quite break free of Him.

MAXIMUS. Because you do not *will* it with all your might.

JULIAN. How can I will the impossible?

MAXIMUS. What is the value of willing what is possible?

JULIAN. You can't understand how it is with us. We are
    like vines that have been transplanted to a strange
    and unfamiliar soil. If you replanted us again, we
    should die; but in our new soil, we cannot flourish.

MAXIMUS. We? Whom do you call we?

JULIAN. All who live in fear of the revelation.

MAXIMUS. Fear of shadows!

JULIAN. Perhaps. But don't you see that this paralysing
    fear has tightened into a high wall that protects the
    Emperor? Oh, I see why great Constantine
    made a God of so will-binding a teacher and created
    Him ruler of the Empire! No bodyguard with spear
    and shield ever guarded the Imperial throne as
    securely as this seductive faith, for ever pointing
    beyond our earthly life. Have you ever really looked
    at them, these Christians? Hollow-eyed, pale-cheeked,
    flat-breasted, all of them, like the linen weavers of
    Byssos. No dream of ecstasy ever lightens their gloomy
    existence. The sun shines for them and they do not
    see it. The earth offers them its fullness and they

desire it not. All they want is to deny themselves and
    suffer so that they may die.

MAXIMUS. Then use them as they are; but you must not
    be one of them. Emperor or Galilean; that is the
    choice. Be a slave of fear, or an Emperor in the world
    of day, and light, and joy! You cannot reconcile the
    two; though that is what you want. You want to unite
    two opposites, to reconcile the irreconcilable, and
    that is why you lie here rotting in the dark.

JULIAN. Give me light, if you can!

MAXIMUS. Are you that Achilles whom your mother
    dreamed of bringing into the world? A tender heel
    makes no man an Achilles. Rise up, my lord! Ride
    forth on your fiery steed, confident of victory, and
    crush the Galilean! You must, if you are to win your
    way to the Imperial throne.

JULIAN. Maximus!

MAXIMUS. My beloved Julian, look around you. Those
    Christians you spoke of who long for death are few.
    But what about all the others? Are they not drifting
    away from their master one by one? Answer me, what
    has become of that wonderful gospel of love? Are they
    not divided into sects that fight furiously with one
    another? And the bishops, those gilded lords who style
    themselves the chief shepherds of the church? Do
    even the barons of the court outdo them in greed and
    sycophancy and lust for power?

JULIAN. True, true.

MAXIMUS. You stand alone. Your whole Christian host is
    in flight or lies defeated around you. Sound the call to
    battle, and none of them will hear you. Advance, and
    none will follow. How can you advance a cause that
    has already given up the fight? I tell you, you will be
    defeated. And what will happen to you then? Cast off
    by Constantius, you will be cast off by every power in

the world – and outside the world. Would you fly to
the bosom of the Galilean? What is your relationship
with Him? Haven't you said yourself that it is one of
fear? Do you carry His commandments in your heart?
Do you love your enemy, Constantius, even if you
flinch from challenging him? Do you hate the lust of
the flesh and the temptations of the world, even if
you shrink like a hot swimmer from plunging into the
torrent? Are you willing to renounce the world, even
if you lack the courage to make yourself ruler of it?
And are you certain, in your heart of hearts, that
when you die here you will rise and live again?

JULIAN (*paces to and fro*). What has He done for me, this
God who demands so much? If He really holds the
reins of the chariot of the world in His hands, surely
He could have – ! (*The psalm-singing sounds more
loudly from the church.*) Listen, listen. That is what
they call serving Him. And He accepts it like the
sweet smoke of sacrifice. Psalms to His glory – and
the glory of her who lies in the coffin. If He is
omniscient, how can He – ?

EUTHERIUS (*runs in left*). Caesar! My lord, my lord!
Where are you?

JULIAN. Here, Eutherius. What do you want?

EUTHERIUS. You must come up, my lord! You must see it
with your own eyes. The body of the Princess is
performing miracles!

JULIAN. You're lying!

EUTHERIUS. I am not lying, my lord. I am no adherent of
this foreign religion, but I cannot doubt what I have
seen with my own eyes.

JULIAN. What did you see?

EUTHERIUS. The whole city is in an uproar. They are
carrying the sick and crippled to the Princess's coffin.
The priests let them touch it, and they go away healed.

JULIAN. And you saw this yourself?

EUTHERIUS. Yes, my lord. I saw a woman with epilepsy
walk out of the church cured, praising the God of the
Galileans.

JULIAN. Oh, Maximus, Maximus!

EUTHERIUS. Listen to the Christians rejoicing. Another
miracle is being performed.

ORIBASES (*calls from above, left*).Eutherius, have you
found him? Eutherius, Eutherius, where is Caesar?

JULIAN (*goes towards him*). Here, here. Is this true,
Oribases?

ORIBASES (*enters*). Incredible! Inexplicable! But it is true.
They touch the coffin, the priests read and pray over
them, and they rise, cured. From time to time a voice
proclaims: 'Holy, holy is the pure woman!'

JULIAN. A voice proclaims – ?

ORIBASES. A voice high up under the church roof.

JULIAN (*stands motionless for a moment, then turns
suddenly to* MAXIMUS *and cries*). Life – or the lie?

MAXIMUS. Choose.

ORIBASES. Come, my lord, come! The soldiers are
frightened. They threaten to –

JULIAN. Let them threaten!

ORIBASES. They say that you and I are guilty of the
Princess's death.

JULIAN. I will come; I will calm them –

ORIBASES. There is only one remedy. You must turn their
thoughts elsewhere, my lord. They are wild with
despair at the fate which awaits them if you delay
longer.

MAXIMUS. Go to heaven, Julian. Now you must die for
your Galilean master.

JULIAN (*grasps his arm*). The Emperor's Empire for me!

MAXIMUS. Achilles!

JULIAN. What will dissolve the pact?

MAXIMUS (*hands him the sacrificial knife*). This.

JULIAN. What will wash away the water?

MAXIMUS. The blood of the beast. (*Tears the sacrificial bandage from his brow and fastens it around* CAESAR's)

ORIBASES (*comes closer*). What have you in mind, my lord?

JULIAN. Do not ask.

EUTHERIUS. Listen to the noise they are making! Go up, go up, Caesar!

JULIAN. First, down; then up. (*To* MAXIMUS.) My beloved brother, lead me to the sanctuary.

MAXIMUS. You must go alone. It is directly beneath us, in the second chamber.

ORIBASES. Caesar, Caesar! Where are you going?

MAXIMUS. To freedom!

JULIAN. Through darkness to light. Ah – ! (*Steps down into the catacombs.*)

MAXIMUS (*quietly, staring after him.*) So it has come!

EUTHERIUS. Speak, speak! What is the meaning of these secret arts?

ORIBASES. Now, when every second is precious – !

MAXIMUS (*whispers restlessly as he shifts his position*). These wet, gliding shadows! Ugh! This slime creeping about my feet –

ORIBASES (*listens*). They are shouting louder, Eutherius. It is the soldiers. Listen, listen!

EUTHERIUS. It is the singing from the church –

ORIBASES. No, it is the soldiers. Here they come!

SALLUST *appears at the top of the steps surrounded by a large and angry crowd of* SOLDIERS. MAUROS, *the standard-bearer, is among them.*

SALLUST. Calm yourselves, I beseech you –

SOLDIERS. Caesar has betrayed us! Caesar must die!

SALLUST. Are you mad? What will become of you then?

MAUROS. What then? Caesar's head will buy our pardon –

SOLDIERS. Come up, Caesar! Come up!

SALLUST. Caesar, my Caesar! Where are you?

JULIAN (*down in the catacombs, cries*). Apollo! Apollo!

MAXIMUS. Now thou art liberated!

THE CHOIR (*sings in church*). Our Father Which art in
    Heaven –

SALLUST. Where is he? Eutherius, Oribases, what is
    happening here?

CHOIR. Hallowed be Thy name!

JULIAN (*climbs up the steps. He has blood on his forehead,
    his breast and his hands*). It is accomplished!

SOLDIERS. Caesar!

SALLUST. What is this blood – ? What have you done?

JULIAN. Cloven the mists of fear.

MAXIMUS. Now creation lies in thy hand!

CHOIR. Thy will be done, on earth as it is in Heaven!

The singing continues during the rest of the scene.

JULIAN. Constantius has lost his Saviour now!

MAUROS. What are you saying, my lord?

JULIAN. Oh, my loyal comrades! Up into the daylight! To
    Rome and Greece!

SOLDIERS. Long live Emperor Julian!

JULIAN. We will not look back. All roads lie open to us.
    Up into the daylight! No – through the church! Those
    lies shall be silenced! (*Runs up the steps towards the
    church.*) My army, my treasure, my Imperial throne!

CHOIR. Lead us not into temptation; but deliver us from
    evil –

    CAESAR JULIAN *throws the door wide open. The
    brilliantly illuminated church is revealed. The* PRIEST
    stands at the high altar. Below, groups of WORSHIPPERS
    kneel around the PRINCESS's *coffin.*

JULIAN. Free, free! Mine is the kingdom!

SALLUST (*shouts to him*). And the power and the glory!

CHOIR. Thine is the Kingdom, and the Power, and the
    Glory –

JULIAN (*blinded by the light*). Ah!

MAXIMUS. Victory!

CHOIR. For ever and ever, Amen!

Part Two
Emperor Julian

Characters

This translation of Part 2 was broadcast on BBC Radio 3 on 30 March 1990, and repeated on 15 May 1991. The cast was:

EMPEROR JULIAN	Robert Glenister
NEVITA, *a General*	David King
(CAESARIUS OF NAZIANZ, *court physician*)	
EUNAPIUS, *a barber*	David King
HEKEBOLIUS, *a theologian*	Brett Usher
EUTHERIUS, *the* EMPEROR'S *chamberlain*	Garard Green
(MEDON, *a corn merchant*)	
GREGOR OF NAZIANZ	David Timson
FOKION, *a dyer*	Stephen Garlick
PUBLIA	Margot Boyd
HILARION, *her son*	Ben Onwukwe
AGATHON OF CAPPADOCIA,	Charles Simpson
BISHOP MARIS OF CHALCEDON,	John Moffatt
(AGATHON'S YOUNG BROTHER),	
ORIBASES, *a doctor*	Norman Bird
(FROMENTIUS, *a captain*)	
JOVIAN, *a general*	Nigel Anthony
MAXIMUS THE MYSTIC,	Timothy West
NUMA, *a soothsayer*	Danny Schiller
(TWO OTHER ETRUSCAN SOOTHSAYERS),	
ANATOLUS, *Commander of the Imperial Guard*	Nicholas Gilbrook
PRISKOS, *a philosopher*	John Moffatt
KYTRON, *a philosopher*	James Greene
AMMIAN, *a captain*	Joe Dunlop
BASIL OF CAESAREA	Paul Downing
MAKRINA, *his sister*	Helena Breck
A PERSIAN DESERTER	John Bennett

COURTIERS, STATE OFFICIALS, CITIZENS OF ANTIOCH, PEOPLE TAKING PART IN THE PROCESSION OF DIONYSUS (FLUTE PLAYERS, DANCERS, JUGGLERS *and* WOMEN), PEOPLE TAKING PART IN THE PROCESSION OF APOLLO (PRIESTS, TEMPLE SERVANTS, HARP-PLAYERS *and* CITY WATCHMEN), PROCESSION OF CHRISTIAN PRISONERS, ROMAN, GREEK *and* PERSIAN SOLDIERS

Music by Christos Pittas
Directed by Martin Jenkins

ACT 1. Antioch
ACT 2. In and around the eastern provinces of the Empire, and on the plains beyond the Tigris.
ACT 3. Beyond the Tigris.

The action covers the period from December 361 A.D. to the end of June 363 A.D.

Act One

A great hall in the Imperial Palace at Antioch. Doors upstage and on both sides. On a raised throne downstage sits the EMPEROR JULIAN, surrounded by his COURT and HIGH OFFICIALS. A large, veiled object is protected by GUARDS.

JULIAN gives a sign. SERVANTS unveil the object, which is shown to be a large stone altar, at the foot of which stand a flagon of wine, a jug of oil, a small pile of wood, etc. The CROWD remains silent, but registers considerable emotion as JULIAN goes to the altar and prepares to sacrifice. Leaning against the wall by the entrance is a MAN dressed as a Christian priest; he shields his face with his hands, as though buried in prayer.

JULIAN. Thus to the venerable gods of our forefathers do I restore their ancient rights. But let no man offer insult to the God of the Galileans, nor to that of the Jews. The temples which our pious predecessors built with such cunning art shall rise again in a new glory, with altars and images, each to its special god, so that seemly worship may once more be celebrated in these places. But I will on no account permit any indignities to be offered to the churches of the Christians; neither shall their graveyards be desecrated, nor any of those other places which a strange whim compels them to regard as sacred. We must tolerate the delusions of others. I will only say that I wish joy to those who follow my example, extend my blessing to those who do not, and that I shall try to persuade all men, but shall not compel

any man, to do as I have done. I hereby proclaim
absolute religious freedom for all citizens of the
Empire. (*Pauses expectantly. Feeble applause from
here and there among the* CROWD.) Where are you
going, Caesarius?

CAESARIUS (*the court physician*). To church, most
gracious Emperor. I wish to pray for the soul of my
departed master.

JULIAN. Go, go. Each man is free to do as he chooses.
(CAESARIUS *and several other* OLDER COURTIERS *and*
STATE OFFICIALS *go out left.*) But this liberty which I
grant to the meanest citizen I also claim for myself. I
therefore proclaim to you, Greeks and Romans, that I
am returning with a clear heart and a humble soul to
the teachings and customs which our forefathers held
sacred. (*Before the altar, with upstretched arms.*) I
have offered my thanks to thee, Apollo, King of the
Sun, who bringeth and reneweth the light wherein
our life has its source and its beginning. I have
sacrificed to thee too, Dionysus, God of Ecstasy, who
lifteth the souls of men from their meanness and
raiseth them to commune with nobler spirits. Thus
publicly and in dread humility have I poured out oil
and wine for you, most benevolent gods. (*Rises.*) So
far the gods have helped us. Now our work shall roll
forward like a tidal wave. And now, my friends, if
anyone has any other question to raise –

MEDON (*pushes his way forward from the* CROWD). Most
gracious Emperor, do not let me go unheard.

JULIAN (*sits again*). Certainly not, my friend. Who are you?

MEDON. I am Medon, a corn merchant. O most divine and
exalted majesty, if my great love for thee cannot –

JULIAN. Come to the point, man.

MEDON. I have a neighbour, one Alites, who for years has
injured me in every imaginable way. He, too, deals in

corn, and takes the bread from my mouth most
shamefully –

JULIAN. Oh, my good Medon, you don't look underfed.

MEDON. It isn't that, my lord. Oh, by the venerable gods,
whom every day I learn to love and praise more
dearly, the injuries he does to *me* I could ignore. But
what I cannot endure is that he –

JULIAN. He does not mock the gods?

MEDON. Far worse – or anyway, as bad. He – oh, I
scarcely know if my indignation will let me speak of it
– he mocks you, most gracious majesty!

JULIAN. Indeed? What words did he use?

MEDON. He hasn't used any words – much worse –

JULIAN. Worse? In what way?

MEDON. A purple cloak – !

JULIAN. He wears one? Dear me, what impertinence.

MEDON. And I have to see this coxcomb flaunting his pride
every day! Oh, most gracious majesty, punish this
presumptuous man. Let him be banished from the city –

JULIAN. Tell me, my good Medon, what clothes does
Alites wear apart from his purple cloak?

MEDON. I can't actually recall, my lord. Ordinary ones,
I think. I've only noticed the purple cloak.

JULIAN. A purple cloak with untanned sandals?

MEDON. Yes, my lord. It looks as ludicrous as it is brazen.

JULIAN. We must do something about this, Medon.

MEDON (*joyfully*). Oh, most gracious majesty – !

JULIAN. Come to the palace tomorrow morning –

MEDON (*even more joyfully*). I shall come as soon as the
day dawns, most gracious majesty.

JULIAN. Ask for my Chamberlain –

MEDON. Yes, yes, most noble and gracious majesty.

JULIAN. From him you will receive a pair of slippers,
embroidered with gold –

MEDON. Oh, most munificent majesty – !

JULIAN. These slippers you will take to Alites. You will
 hand them to him and tell him that he must wear
 them every time he feels the inclination to parade in
 his purple cloak upon the public streets in daylight –
MEDON. Oh!
JULIAN. And when you have done this, you can tell him
 from me that he is a fool if he supposes that the
 imperial cloak ennobles one who does not possess the
 imperial power. Go; and come back for the slippers
 tomorrow.

 MEDON *goes out, crestfallen, amid the laughter of the*
 CITIZENS. *The* COURTIERS, ORATORS, POETS, *etc,*
 applaud the EMPEROR *and cry: 'Bravo!'.*

JULIAN. And now, if no one else has any matter to raise –
THE PRIEST AT THE DOOR (*draws himself up*). In the name
 of God the Father!
JULIAN. Who speaks there?
PRIEST. One who serves God and the Emperor.
JULIAN. Come closer. What do you want?
PRIEST. To speak to your heart, and your conscience.
JULIAN (*springs up*). Whose voice is that? Who are you?
 Beneath that beard and cloak – ? Gregor!
PRIEST. Yes, gracious majesty.
JULIAN. Gregor! Gregor of Nazianz!
GREGOR. Yes, my lord.
JULIAN (*steps down from the dais, seizes his hands and*
 gazes long at him). A little older; more bronzed;
 heavier. No, only at first glance. You're the same
 as ever.
GREGOR. Would it were so with you, my lord.
JULIAN. Athens – ! No man has been so close to my heart
 as you.
GREGOR. Your heart? Oh, Emperor, you have torn from
 your heart a better friend than me.

JULIAN. You mean Basil?

GREGOR. I mean One greater than Basil.

JULIAN (*frowns*). Oh, I see. That's what you've come to tell me. And wearing this –

GREGOR. I did not choose this dress, my lord.

JULIAN. You didn't? Who did, then?

GREGOR. He Who is greater than the Emperor

JULIAN. I know these Galilean sophistries. For the sake of our friendship, let's have done with them.

GREGOR. Then let me begin by telling you why you see me here as an ordained priest of the Church which you persecute.

JULIAN (*gives him a sharp look*). Persecute! (*Returns to the dais and resumes his throne.*) Proceed.

GREGOR. You know how I felt about theological matters during our happy days together in Athens. But I had no thought then of forsaking the pleasures of this world. Those petty bickerings within our Church troubled me deeply. But I took no part in them. I served my countrymen in worldly matters only. Then news came from Constantinople that Constantius, overcome with terror at your exploits, had died, naming you as his successor. Acclaimed as more than mortal, and with the fame of your victories flying ahead of you, you ascended the throne of Constantine without needing to strike a blow. The world lay at your feet. Then further tidings reached us. The lord of earth was girding himself to do battle against the Lord of Heaven –

JULIAN. Gregor, are you presuming to – ?

GREGOR. The ruler of our bodies was preparing to wage war against the Ruler of our souls. I stand here before you in bodily fear and trembling. But I dare not lie. Do you wish to hear the truth, or shall I keep silent?

JULIAN. Speak, Gregor.

GREGOR. What have my fellow-believers not already been
    compelled to suffer in these few months? How many
    death sentences have not been pronounced, and
    executed with fearful cruelty?

JULIAN. You don't understand these things.

GREGOR. Most mighty Emperor, you owe me no account
    of your actions. I wished only to tell you that all these
    tidings smote the people of Caesarea and Nazianz and
    the other cities of Cappadocia like so many
    thunderbolts. How shall I describe their effect? Our
    internal bickerings were silenced by our common
    danger. Many of the weaker limbs of the Church fell
    away. But in many lukewarm hearts the light of God
    was kindled with a new brightness hitherto unimagined.
    Affliction had descended on God's people. The
    heathens – yes, my lord, I call them heathens – began
    to threaten us, to maltreat and persecute us –

JULIAN. Retribution! Retribution, Gregor!

GREGOR. Far be it from me to defend all that my fellow-
    believers may have done through misplaced zeal. But
    the persecution now being inflicted on all who bear
    the name of Galilean has already resulted in more
    than one apostasy. My lord, this is a rape of souls
    from the Kingdom of God!

JULIAN. Oh, my wise Gregor –

GREGOR. My lord, can you wonder if my brothers
    believed this persecution to be God's judgement on
    them for having allowed unbelief to flourish openly in
    their midst? They demanded that the city fathers
    should render proof of their loyalty to Christ by
    ordering the destruction of every evidence that
    heathendom had once held sway in Caesarea.

JULIAN. You don't mean that – ?

GREGOR. In the terrible earthquake that smote Caesarea
    two years ago, all the temples save one were destroyed.

JULIAN. Yes, yes. The temple of Fortuna.

GREGOR. The city fathers summoned a meeting at which
the people vowed to consummate the judgement of
God as proof that they would henceforth bind
themselves to Him alone, and would no longer allow
the abomination of heresy to flourish in their midst.

JULIAN. Gregor, you were once my friend. Do you value
your life?

GREGOR. I could not bring myself to support this
resolution. But it was agreed to almost unanimously.
Therefore, my lord, I stand humbly before you here
to inform you that we Christians in Caesarea have
resolved that the temple wherein the heathens
worshipped a false god called Fortuna shall be torn
down and levelled with the earth.

JULIAN (*springs to his feet*). Gregor, I command you to
return to Caesarea and tell the citizens that I forbid
them to take this presumptuous step.

GREGOR. Impossible, my lord. Things have reached the
point where we must choose between our fear of
human wrath and our duty to God. We cannot yield.

JULIAN. Oh, you Galileans, you count on my tolerance.
Don't be too sure. I tell you —

Noise at the door. The barber EUNAPIUS *runs in,
followed by several* CITIZENS.

JULIAN. What is this? Eunapius, what has happened
to you?

EUNAPIUS. See, most gracious majesty! I come before you
bloody and beaten —

JULIAN. Speak, man. Who has beaten you?

EUNAPIUS. Permit me, my lord, to present my complaint.
This morning I went outside the city to visit the little
temple of Venus which you lately rebuilt. When I got
there, I was met by the sound of flutes and song.

Women were dancing before the entrance, and the
whole space was filled with jubilant worshippers,
while the priests offered sacrifices before the altar in
obedience to your commands.

JULIAN. Yes, yes. Well?

EUNAPIUS. Then a crowd of young men rushed into the
temple –

JULIAN. Not Galileans?

EUNAPIUS. Yes, my lord – Galileans.

JULIAN. Ah!

EUNAPIUS. They fell upon us, assaulted us, and abused us
most shamefully.

JULIAN (*steps down from the dais*). Wait, wait!

EUNAPIUS. But the ruffians went further. The altar has
been torn down, the statue of the goddess smashed to
pieces, the entrails of the sacrifices thrown outside to
be eaten by dogs –

JULIAN (*paces up and down*). Wait, wait, wait!

GREGOR. My lord, this man's word alone is not sufficient –

JULIAN. Silence! (*To* EUNAPIUS.) Do you know any of the
men who committed this sacrilege?

EUNAPIUS. No, my lord. But these good citizens recognized
some of them.

JULIAN. Take soldiers and seize as many of the guilty as
you can lay hands on. Throw them into prison. They
shall be made to name their accomplices. And once I
have them all in my power –

GREGOR. What then, my lord?

JULIAN. The executioner will give you details. You and
your fellow citizens of Caesarea shall learn what to
expect if you continue in your Galilean stubbornness.

He goes out left in a violent rage. EUNAPIUS *and
his* WITNESSES *go out with* SOLDIERS. *The*
CROWD *disperses.*

*A market-place in Antioch. Downstage right a street leads into
it. Upstage left can be seen the entrance to a narrow, curved
alley. A great* CROWD *fills the market-place. An* OLD WOMAN,
*distraught, her hair dishevelled, pushes her way through,
surrounded by* OTHER WOMEN *vainly trying to
hold her back.*

OLD WOMAN. Let me go! He's my only son, the prop of
my old age. Let me go, let me go! Will no one tell me
where I can find the Emperor?

FOKION (*the dyer*). What do you want with the Emperor,
mother?

OLD WOMAN. I want my son back! Help me. My son,
Hilarion! They took him from me. They broke into
our house, and then they took him.

CITIZEN (*to* FOKION). Who is this woman?

FOKION. What? Don't you know the widow Publia? The
psalm singer?

CITIZEN. Ah, yes, yes, yes.

PUBLIA. Hilarion! My boy! What will they do to him? Ah,
Fokion, it's you. Thank God! A Christian brother –

FOKION. Ssh, quiet! Don't shout so loud. The Emperor's
coming.

PUBLIA. Ah, the ungodly Emperor! The Lord of Wrath is
punishing us for his sins. Famine is ravaging the land.
The earth quakes beneath our feet!

A detachment of SOLDIERS *enters from the street right.*

CENTURION. Move aside. Make way there!

PUBLIA. Come, good Fokion! Help me in the name of our
friendship and the brotherhood of –

FOKION. Are you mad, woman? I don't know you.

PUBLIA. What? Not know me? Aren't you Fokion the
dyer? Aren't you the son of – ?

FOKION. I'm not the son of anyone. Get away from me,

woman. I don't know you. I've never seen you before.
(*Hurries off among the* CROWD.)

OFFICER (*enters right with* SOLDIERS). Make way there!

The SOLDIERS *force the* CROWD *back against the
houses.* PUBLIA *collapses in the arms of* WOMEN, *left.
Everyone stares expectantly up the street.*

FOKION (*in the* CROWD *behind the* GUARDS, *right*). Yes,
by Apollo, isn't that him coming now, our blessed
Emperor?

A SOLDIER. Stop pushing, there.

FOKION. Can you see him? The man with the white fillet
round his brow – that's the Emperor.

The EMPEROR JULIAN *enters in the garb of a high
priest, surrounded by* SACRIFICIAL PRIESTS *and*
SERVANTS OF THE TEMPLE. COURTIERS *and*
SCHOLARS, *including the theologian* HEKEBOLIUS, *have
joined the procession, together with a number of*
CITIZENS. *In the front of the* EMPEROR *walk*
MUSICIANS *playing flutes and harps.* SOLDIERS *and*
STATE OFFICERS *with long staves clear the way in
front and on either side.*

CROWD IN THE MARKET-PLACE (*applauds*). Long live the
Emperor! Praised be Julian, hero and bringer of luck!

FOKION. Welcome to Julian and the Sun King! Hail
to Apollo!

CITIZENS (*downstage right*). Emperor, Emperor, stay long
among us!

JULIAN *makes a sign with his hand. The* PROCESSION
halts.

PUBLIA. My lord, give me back Hilarion!

FOKION. All good citizens entreat your favour upon our
city!

JULIAN. Seek to win the gods' favour, and you shall have
    mine. When I feel this fillet around my brow, when I
    look down at this robe, dearer to me than the purple
    cloak, I tremble at the sacred presence of the god.
    See, see, the light quivers about us in glory. Feel, feel,
    the air is pregnant with the fresh scent of garlands. O
    beautiful earth, thou home of light and life, home of
    joy, of beauty and happiness – what thou wert, thou
    shalt again become. Into the bosom of the Sun King!
    Mithra, Mithra! Forward on our victorious march!

The PROCESSION *begins to move again, amid applause
from the* CROWD, *but as those in front reach the
entrance to the narrow alley they are forced to stop by
another* PROCESSION *entering the market-place.*

SONG (*in the distance*).
    O blest are those who suffer,
    And blest are those who die
    For Christ. Their names in glory
    Shall live eternally.
FOKION. The Galileans, my lord! They have caught them!
PUBLIA. Hilarion!
FOKION. They've got them!
JULIAN. Proceed past them.
EUNAPIUS (*forces his way eagerly through the* CROWD). My
    lord, we have succeeded beyond all expectation!
JULIAN. I do not wish to see them. Proceed, I say!
SONG OF THE PRISONERS (*nearer*).
    Blessed to meet the glorious saints of old!
    Blessed to receive the crown of martyrdom!
JULIAN. The madmen! Not so close! Guards, guards!

The two PROCESSIONS *have meanwhile met and
become intermingled. The* PROCESSION OF APOLLO *is
forced to halt while that of the* PRISONERS, *who are*

fettered, surrounded by SOLDIERS *and accompanied by
a large* CROWD *of people, moves past.*

PUBLIA. My son! Hilarion!

HILARION (*among the* PRISONERS). Rejoice, mother!

JULIAN. You poor, deluded fools. When I hear such
madness from your lips, I almost wonder whether I
have the right to punish you.

ANOTHER VOICE FROM AMONG THE PRISONERS. Do not
take our crown of thorns from us!

JULIAN. Whose voice is that?

CAPTAIN OF THE GUARD. This man, my lord.

He pushes forward one of the PRISONERS, *a* YOUNG
MAN *who is holding a half-grown* YOUTH *by the hand.*

JULIAN (*cries*). Agathon!

(*The* PRISONER *looks at him and is silent.*)

JULIAN. Agathon, Agathon! Answer me. Are you
not Agathon?

PRISONER. Yes.

JULIAN. You here among these – ? Speak to me!

AGATHON. I do not know you.

JULIAN. You don't know me? You don't know who I am?

AGATHON. I know you are the lord of the earth. Therefore
I do not know you.

JULIAN. And this child – ? Is this your young brother? (*To
the* CAPTAIN.) This man must be innocent.

EUNAPIUS. My lord, this man is the ringleader. He has
confessed. He even boasts of his deed.

JULIAN. It is strange how hunger, sickness and misfortune
can blind a man. (*To the* PRISONERS.) Say one word
of regret for what you have done, and no harm shall
befall you.

PUBLIA (*cries*). Don't say it, Hilarion!

AGATHON. Be strong, dear brother.

PUBLIA. Go, go, to what awaits you, my only son!

JULIAN. Listen, the rest of you! Consider – !

AGATHON (*to the* PRISONERS.) Choose between Christ and the Emperor!

PRISONERS. Praised be the Lord on high!

JULIAN. They must be broken. Proceed past them. They are abominable to us. They darken the sun. (*To the* MUSICIANS.) Men and women, sing. Sing – sing your praises to life, and light, and joy!

APOLLO PROCESSION (*sings*).
Blessed to be cooled by a garland of roses!
Blessed to be warmed by the light of the sun!

PRISONERS.
Blessed to die in a blood-filled grave!
Blessed to enter the gardens of heaven!

APOLLO PROCESSION. Blessed to be drugged by the sweet fumes of incense!

PRISONERS. Blessed to be drowned in rivers of blood!

(*The two* PROCESSIONS *pass each other, singing. The* CROWD *in the market-place watches in dull silence.*)

The sacred grove of Apollo's temple. The entrance, raised on pillars and with a broad flight of steps leading up to it, can be seen through the trees upstage left. The PROCESSION OF APOLLO *enters through the grove from the right and forms a semi-circle in front of the temple to the music of flutes and harps.*

JULIAN (*faces the temple with upraised hands*). I accept the omen! Never have I felt such close kinship with the immortal gods. The Lord of the Bow is among us. The earth booms beneath his heel. But it is not on us that he turns his angry eye, but on those unfortunate

souls who hate him and his shining kingdom. Where
are the Galileans now? Some in the hangman's hands,
others fleeing through the narrow streets, ashen with
fear, their eyes starting from their heads, shrieking
through half-clenched teeth, their hair erect with
terror or wrenched out in despair. And where are we?
Here, in the fair grove of Daphne, where the sweet
breath of Dryads cools our foreheads, before the
glorious temple of the King of Glory, lulled by the
sound of flute and lyre – here, in light and joy and
peace, the god himself apparent among us. Where is
the Galileans' god? Where is the Jew, that crucified
carpenter's son? Let him reveal himself. He forbears
to. It is therefore meet that we throng Apollo's
sanctuary. Here with my own hands I shall perform
the task which, so far from seeming to me lowly and
unbecoming, is one that I set above all others.

He walks to the head of the PROCESSION *and leads it
through the* CROWD *of onlookers to the temple.*

VOICE (*amid cries from the* CROWD). Stop, ungodly man!
JULIAN. Have we a Galilean among us?
VOICE. Go no further, blasphemer!
JULIAN. Who is that who speaks?
OTHERS. A Galilean priest! An old blind man! Here he is!
DIFFERENT VOICES. Away with him! Away with the
    villain!

An OLD BLIND MAN, *in priest's attire, supported by two*
YOUNG MEN *similarly clothed, is helped forward until
he stands below the temple steps in front of the*
EMPEROR.

JULIAN. Why, what is this? Tell me, old man, are you not
    Bishop Maris of Chalcedon?
OLD MAN. Yes, I am that most unworthy servant of

our Church.

JULIAN. I remember you as a timorous man who cared for nothing but the Emperor's favour. Yet now you stand before me and throw insults in my face.

BISHOP MARIS. Now I fear you no longer. For now I belong to Christ, and to Him alone. In our time of travail, His light and glory have been revealed to me. All the blood you spill, all the violent injustices you perpetrate, cry aloud to Heaven, and echo so loud that they ring even in my deaf ears and show me, in the dark night of my blindness, which way I must go.

JULIAN. Go home, old man.

BISHOP MARIS. Not until you have sworn to cease these satanic practices. What are you trying to do? Can dust rebel against the Spirit? Can the lord of earth prevail against the Lord of Heaven? Do you not see that as a result of your sins the Day of Wrath is upon us? The wells have dried up, like eyes that have no more tears to weep. The clouds, that should pour down the manna of fertility, pass over our heads and will not release their treasure. The very earth, cursed since the morning of time, trembles and quakes beneath the weight of your blood-guilt.

JULIAN. What reward do you expect from your god for this foolish zeal, old man? Do you hope your Galilean master will start working miracles again and give you back your sight?

BISHOP MARIS. It was He who laid the temple of Jerusalem in ruins.

JULIAN. If so, then the churches of the Galileans shall be closed and his priests shall be forced by the lash to rebuild that temple in all its former glory.

BISHOP MARIS. Try, impotent man! Who has the power to raise the temple of Jerusalem when the Prince of Golgotha has pronounced its destruction?

JULIAN. I have the power! The Emperor has the power!
  Your god shall be proved a liar. Stone by stone I shall
  raise that temple of Jerusalem until it stands in all the
  pomp and glory it possessed in the days of Solomon.

BISHOP MARIS. Not one stone shall you set upon another;
  for the place has been cursed by God.

JULIAN. Wait, wait. You would see – if you had eyes
  to see, instead of standing there abandoned and
  helpless, groping in the dark, not knowing where to
  set your foot.

BISHOP MARIS. My eyes shall see the lightning that shall
  one day strike you and all who believe like you! I
  have all the sight I need; and I thank the Lord that
  He closed my earthly eyes, and spared me from seeing
  the man who walks in a more terrible night than mine.

JULIAN. Stand aside.

BISHOP MARIS. Where are you going?

JULIAN. Into the house of the Sun King.

BISHOP MARIS. You shall not enter it! I forbid you in the
  name of the One True God!

JULIAN. You stupid old fool! Away with him!

BISHOP MARIS. Yes, lay your hand on me! The hand of
  him who dares to touch me shall be withered! The
  Lord of Wrath shall reveal Himself in His might – !

JULIAN. Your god is not a mighty god. I shall show you
  that the Emperor is mightier than he – !

BISHOP MARIS. Art thou lost? Then in the name of
  Heaven I curse thee, apostate!

HEKEBOLIUS (*pale*). My lord and Emperor, do not let this
  thing happen!

BISHOP MARIS (*cries in a loud voice*). Cursed be thou,
  Julian Apostata! Cursed be thou, Emperor Julian! The
  Lord God hath spat thee from His mouth! Cursed be
  thine eyes and thine hands! Cursed be thy head and
  all thy work! Woe, woe, woe to the Apostate! Woe,

woe, woe – !

A hollow, rumbling sound is heard. The roof and columns of the temple buckle and crumple with a thunderous crash. The whole building is enveloped in a cloud of dust. The CROWD *utters a cry of terror; many flee, others fall to the ground. For a moment there is a breathless silence. Gradually the cloud of dust disperses, and the temple of Apollo is revealed in ruins.* BISHOP MARIS's *two* ATTENDANTS *have fled, leaving him alone.*

BISHOP MARIS (*in a hushed voice*). God spoke!
JULIAN (*pale, whispers*). Apollo spoke!

The road outside Antioch. JULIAN *alone. Night is falling. After a few moments,* GENERAL JOVIAN, *his clothes besmirched with dust, hurries in right with some* ATTENDANTS.

JOVIAN. Most gracious Emperor, pardon your servant for disturbing you here.
JULIAN (*joyfully*). Jovian! Most welcome messenger!
JOVIAN. I have just arrived from Judaea. They told me at the palace that you were here –
JULIAN. O ye blessed gods! That lie about the temple of Jerusalem shall be exposed before the sun sets. How far has the rebuilding progressed? Speak, my dear Jovian. Tell me everything.
JOVIAN. My lord – I arrived in Jerusalem with the masons and soldiers, and the two thousand workmen. We began at once to clear the ground. Large parts of the temple walls were still standing. They fell before our pickaxes and crowbars, so easily that it seemed as though some invisible power was helping us to destroy them –
JULIAN. You see, you see!
JOVIAN. While this was going on, huge piles of mortar

were being gathered for the rebuilding. Then without
any warning a whirlwind arose and scattered the
mortar in a cloud over the whole area.

JULIAN. Go on. Go on.

JOVIAN. That same night the earth quaked repeatedly.

JULIAN. Go on, I said.

JOVIAN. We did not allow this strange event to daunt us.
But when we dug deeper into the ground and exposed
the vaults, and the stonebreakers descended into them
to work by torchlight –

JULIAN. Jovian – what happened then?

JOVIAN. My lord, a huge and terrible torrent of fire issued
from the caverns. A noise as of thunder shook the
whole city. The vaults exploded, hundreds of men
were buried alive, and the few who escaped did so
with fearful injuries.

JULIAN. You saw this?

JOVIAN. I was there myself. We started afresh. My lord, in
the sight of many thousands of people – some
terrified, some jubilant, many kneeling and praying –
the same miracle was repeated twice.

JULIAN (*pale and trembling*). Well? Speak, man! In a word,
what has the Emperor accomplished in Jerusalem?

JOVIAN. The Emperor has fulfilled the prophecy made by
the Galilean.

JULIAN. Fulfilled the – ?

JOVIAN. Through you the prophecy is acomplished: 'Not
one stone shall remain upon another.'

*On a mound. A moonlit night. Before the ruined temple of
Apollo. The* EMPEROR JULIAN *and* MAXIMUS THE MYSTIC,
*both dressed in long robes, enter from the rear through the
fallen pillars.*

MAXIMUS. Whither, my brother?

JULIAN. To where it is loneliest.

MAXIMUS. But here – where the abomination took place?
Among these rubbish-heaps – ?

JULIAN. Is not the whole world a rubbish-heap?

MAXIMUS. Yet you have proved that what has been cast
down can be raised again.

JULIAN. You mock me.

MAXIMUS. Does not everything happen piecemeal? What is
entity but the sum of various pieces?

JULIAN. A poor wisdom! (*Kicks the head of the statue of
Apollo.*) Strange, Maximus, that strength can come
from delusion. Look at the Galileans. And look at me,
who thought it might be possible to bring back the
lost world of beauty.

MAXIMUS. My friend, if you can't live without illusions,
go back to the Galileans. They'll welcome you with
open arms.

JULIAN. You know that's impossible. Emperor and
Galilean! How can those two opposites ever be
reconciled? Yes, this Jesus Christ is the greatest rebel
who ever lived. What was Brutus, what was Cassius,
compared to Him? They only murdered Julius
Caesar, but He murders Caesar, Augustus and all of
us. And yet – could the Galilean and the Emperor be
reconciled? Is there room for both of them in this
world? 'Render unto the Emperor what belongs to the
Emperor, and unto God the things that are God's.'
A more cunning remark was never uttered. What,
and how much, is the Emperor's due? That saying
is a sword, forged to strike the crown from the
Emperor's head!

MAXIMUS. But Constantine the Great found a way
to come to terms with the Galilean – and so did
your predecessor.

JULIAN. Yes, if one could be contented as easily as they.

But do you call that ruling the kingdom of earth? I
can't be content to be Emperor just in name. No, no,
I can't compromise in this. But – to be forced to
yield! Oh, Maximus, after this defeat I can't go on
being Emperor – but I can't give it up either.
Maximus, you can interpret omens whose meaning is
hidden from other men – you can read the eternal
book of the stars. Can you tell me how this contest
will end?

MAXIMUS. Yes, my brother. I can tell you how it will end –

JULIAN. You can? Tell me, then! Who will conquer,
Emperor or Galilean?

MAXIMUS. Both Emperor and Galilean will be destroyed.

JULIAN. Destroyed? Both of us?

MAXIMUS. Both. Whether in our time or in a thousand
years, I do not know. But happen it must, when the
right one appears.

JULIAN. And who is the right one?

MAXIMUS. He who will comprise both Emperor and
Galilean.

JULIAN. You answer the riddle with a yet obscurer riddle.

MAXIMUS. Is not the child destroyed by the youth, and the
youth again by the man? But neither the child nor the
youth dies. O my beloved pupil, have you forgotten
our dialogue in Ephesus concerning the three kingdoms?

JULIAN. Oh, Maximus, that was years ago! Speak!

MAXIMUS. You know I have never approved of your policy
as Emperor. You have sought to turn the youth back
into a child. The kingdom of the flesh has been
absorbed by the kingdom of the spirit. But the
kingdom of the spirit is not the ultimate kingdom, any
more than the youth is the ultimate form of the body.
You wanted to stop the youth from growing, stop him
from becoming a man. You are mad to draw your
sword against the future – against the third kingdom,

in which he who is two-in-one shall rule.

JULIAN. He who is two-in-one?

MAXIMUS. The Jews have a name for him. They call him the Messiah, and await his coming.

JULIAN (*slowly, thoughtfully*.) The Messiah? Neither Emperor nor Redeemer?

MAXIMUS. Both in One and One in Both.

JULIAN. Emperor-God; God-Emperor. Emperor in the kingdom of the spirit – and God in the kingdom of the flesh.

MAXIMUS. *That* is the third kingdom, Julian.

JULIAN. Yes, Maximus, that is the third kingdom.

MAXIMUS. In *that* kingdom, the uncertain voice of rebellion shall become truth.

JULIAN. 'Render unto the Emperor that which is the Emperor's and unto God that which is God's.' Yes, yes – then the Emperor will be in God and God in the Emperor. Ah, dreams, dreams! Who will break the power of the Galilean?

MAXIMUS. Wherein lies the power of the Galilean?

JULIAN. I have asked myself that but found no answer.

MAXIMUS. It is written somewhere: 'Thou shalt have no other gods but me.'

JULIAN. Yes – yes – yes!

MAXIMUS. The seer of Nazareth did not name this god or that. He said: 'God is me; I am God!'

JULIAN. The third kingdom? The Messiah? Not the Messiah of the Jews, but of the kingdom of the spirit and the kingdom of the world – ? Maximus, how will he reveal himself?

MAXIMUS. He will reveal himself in the man who wills himself to be Him. Put an end to this divided authority! But don't imagine you will be able to crush the rebels if you come to them as a general sent by a ruler whom they do not recognize. You must come in

your own name, Julian. Did Jesus of Nazareth come
as the emissary of another? Did he not say that he
was the One who had sent him? I tell you, in you is
time fulfilled, and you do not see it. Do not all signs
and portents point with an unwavering finger towards
you? Must I remind you of your mother's dream – ?

JULIAN. She dreamed she had given birth to Achilles.

MAXIMUS. Must I remind you that fortune has borne you
safely through danger and adversity as though on
charmed wings? Who are you, my lord? Are you the
new Alexander, not as then unready, but mature and
equipped to accomplish your task?

JULIAN. Maximus!

MAXIMUS. There is One who reappears at intervals in
the history of the human race. He is like a rider who
has to tame a wild horse in an arena. Each time the
horse throws him. In a moment he is back in the
saddle, always more assured and skilful than before;
but in whatever guise he has appeared, he has always
been rejected – until now. He was rejected as the first
man, created by God in Eden. He was rejected as he
who founded the kingdom of earth. And he was
rejected again as the Prince of the Kingdom of the
Spirit. Who knows how many times he may have
wandered among us without anyone knowing him?
Who knows, Julian, if you yourself may not have lived
in Him whom you now persecute – ?

JULIAN (*stares unseeingly*). O unfathomable riddle – !

MAXIMUS. Must I remind you of that ancient prophecy
which is once again on all men's lips? It has been
foretold that for as many years as the year has days,
so long shall the kingdom of the Galilean survive. In
two years it will be three hundred and sixty-five years
since that man was born in Bethlehem.

JULIAN. Do you believe in that prophecy?

MAXIMUS. I believe in him who will come.

JULIAN. Always riddles!

MAXIMUS. I believe in freedom within the orbit
of necessity.

JULIAN. That's even more obscure.

MAXIMUS. Listen, Julian. When Chaos ruled the vast
emptiness of space, and Jehovah was alone – on that
day when, according to the ancient Jewish scriptures,
He flung out His hand and divided light from
darkness, land from sea – then the great Lord of
Creation stood at the pinnacle of His power. But with
man was created will. Men and beasts and trees and
flowers reproduced their like according to eternal
laws; and according to eternal laws the stars circle in
the heavens. Did Jehovah repent of creation? The
ancient lore of every race tells of a penitent Creator.
But when He created He embodied the law of
perpetuity. It was too late to repent! The things He
created willed that they should be perpetuated – and
so, they were perpetuated. But the two unreconciled
kingdoms war on each other. Where is he, where is
he, the King of Peace, the Double King who shall
reconcile them?

JULIAN (*to himself*). Two years! All the gods sleep – ! No
fickle power lurking to thwart my plans – ! Two
years? In two years I can conquer the earth!

MAXIMUS. You spoke, my Julian. What did you say?

JULIAN. My beloved teacher, I must leave you.

MAXIMUS. Where are you going?

JULIAN. To the city. The King of Persia has sent me an
offer of peace, which I impetuously accepted. My
envoys are already on their way. I must send after
them and call them back.

MAXIMUS. You want to declare war on King Sapores
again?

JULIAN. I want to do what Cyrus dreamed of, and
   Alexander attempted – !

He waves farewell and runs out. MAXIMUS *looks after
him thoughtfully.*

Act Two

On the eastern frontiers of the Empire. Wild and mountainous country. A deep valley separates the high foreground from the mountains behind. EMPEROR JULIAN, *in battle dress, stands on a protruding crag looking down into the ravine. A short distance from him on the left stand the* GENERALS, NEVITA *and* JOVIAN, *and several other high-ranking* OFFICERS. *On the right, beside a roughly constructed stone altar, lie the* SOOTHSAYER NUMA *and two other* ETRUSCAN SOOTHSAYERS, *busy removing omens from the entrails of an animal that has been sacrificed. Downstage of them,* MAXIMUS *is seated on a stone, surrounded by* PRISKOS, KYTRON *and other* PHILOSOPHERS. *Small detachments of lightly-armed* MEN *pass at intervals across the stage from left to right.*

JULIAN (*points down into the ravine*). Look! Look at those legions winding through the ravine. Like a mailed serpent! Who are those men in sheepskin coats?

NEVITA. Those are the Scythians, my lord.

JULIAN. What's that terrible howling?

NEVITA. Their usual song, my lord.

JULIAN. More like howling than singing.

NEVITA. Here come the Armenians. Arsaces himself is leading them.

JULIAN. Our own legions must already have reached the plain. All the local tribes are hastening to offer their submission. (*Turns to his* COMMANDERS.) On the Euphrates lie twelve hundred ships with all our supplies and munitions. I have now received assurance that the fleet will be able to sail up into the Tigris through the old canal. The whole army will

travel by ship. Then we will march along the eastern
bank as quickly as the adverse current will allow the
fleet to keep pace with us. (*Goes over to the*
SOOTHSAYERS.) Well, Numa, what are the omens for
our campaign this morning?

NUMA. The omens warn you not to overstep the frontiers
of your Empire this year.

JULIAN. Hm! How do you interpret this omen, Maximus?

MAXIMUS. I interpret it thus. The omens counsel you to
conquer every region through which you pass. Thus
you will never overstep the frontiers of your Empire.

JULIAN. That must be the answer. We must study these
miraculous revelations carefully, for there is usually a
double meaning in them. It sometimes seems as
though strange powers delight in leading men astray,
especially when great enterprises are afoot.

JOVIAN. Most gracious majesty, here comes a captain from
our advance guard.

AMMIAN (*a Captain, enters right*). My lord, you
commanded me to inform you if anything unusual
occurred on the march.

JULIAN. Yes, well? Has something happened this morning?

AMMIAN. Yes, my lord. A double portent –

JULIAN. What? Tell us.

AMMIAN. First, my lord, soon after we had passed the
town of Zaita, a lion of monstrous size broke from the
undergrowth and charged at our soldiers, who killed it
with a volley of arrows.

JULIAN. Ah!

PHILOSOPHERS. A most fortunate omen!

NEVITA. King Sapores calls himself the lion of the world.

NUMA (*busy at the altar*). Turn back! Turn back,
Emperor Julian!

MAXIMUS. March boldly on, thou chosen conqueror!

JULIAN. Turn back – now? Like the lion at Zaita, so shall

the lion of the world fall to our arrows. (*To* AMMIAN.)
But the second portent? You spoke of two –

AMMIAN. The other is more doubtful, my lord. Your
charger Babylonius was, as you commanded, saddled
and led forward to await your descent from the
mountain. But while this was being done, a
detachment of Galilean conscripts happened to pass.
Since they were heavily-laden, and not over-zealous,
we had to use the whip on them. In spite of this they
raised their arms as though in joy and sang loudly in
praise of their god. This sudden noise frightened
Babylonius, who reared in terror, and fell over
backwards. And while he rolled on the ground your
golden harness was splashed and bespattered with
mud from the road.

NUMA (*at the altar*). Emperor Julian – turn back,
turn back!

JULIAN. The Galileans have done this out of spite. Yet
thereby, against their will, they have given us an
omen, which I joyfully accept. Yes, just as Babylonius
fell, so shall Babylon fall, stripped of her splendour
and glory.

PRISKOS. How wise an interpretation!

KYTRON. By the gods, that must be it.

OTHER PHILOSOPHERS. It is the only possible explanation.

JULIAN (*to* NEVITA). The army will proceed. But this
evening, for still greater certainty, I shall offer further
sacrifices and see what the omens must confirm. But
as for you, Etruscan charlatans, whom I brought here
at such expense, I shall no longer tolerate your
presence in the camp, for you do nothing but alarm
and discourage the soldiers. I tell you, you understand
nothing of the difficult art you have presumed
to follow. Your audacity and impudence are
overweening. Away with them! I do not wish to see

them again.

Some of the GUARDS *drive out the* SOOTHSAYERS, *left.*

Babylonius fell. The lion was killed by my soldiers.
But these signs do not tell us on what invisible aid we
dare rely. The gods, whose nature is obscure to us,
sometimes appear to slumber, or at any rate to take
little hand in human affairs. So, my dear friends, I
fear it seems now. We have even seen that certain
gods have disdained to support measures undertaken
to increase their honour. But we must not let this
lead us to false conclusions. It may be that the
immortals who rule the world sometimes delegate
their power into mortal hands – whereby the gods in
no wise demean themselves, for it is thanks to them
that so blest a mortal – if he exists – is permitted to
appear on earth.

PRISKOS. O matchless Emperor, do not your own deeds
bear witness to this?

JULIAN. I don't know, Priskos, whether I dare rate my
exploits so highly. That the Galileans regard the Jew,
Jesus of Nazareth, as such a chosen being, I need not
mention. They are mistaken, as I shall conclusively
prove in a pamphlet I am writing to confound them.
But I may name Prometheus of ancient times, that
excellent hero who obtained for men greater blessings
even than those which the gods had granted them;
wherefore he too had to suffer greatly, enduring both
pain and scorn, until at length he was taken up into
the company of the gods, where he had always really
belonged. And may not the same be said of both
Heracles and Achilles and, finally, of Alexander the
Macedonian, in whose deeds some have found a
parallel to what I have accomplished in Gaul and,
more particularly, to what I intend to accomplish on

this campaign?

NEVITA. My lord, the rearguard is now beneath us. Is it
not perhaps time to – ?

JULIAN. Soon, Nevita. But first I wish to tell you of a
strange dream I had last night. I dreamed I saw a
child being pursued by a rich man, who owned
countless herds but thought it beneath him to worship
the gods. This evil man killed all the child's kinsmen.
But Zeus himself took pity on the child and stretched
his hand over him. Then I saw this child grow into a
youth, under the protection of Athene and Apollo.
And I dreamed that the youth fell asleep on a stone
under the broad sky. Then Hermes descended to
earth in the guise of a young man and said: 'Come, I
will show you the path that leads to the house of the
god of gods.' And he led the youth to the foot of a
very steep mountain, and there he left him. Then the
youth began to weep and complain, and cried in a
loud voice to Zeus. And behold, Athene and the Sun
King, who rules on earth, descended and lifted him
up to the top of the mountain, and pointed, and
showed him the inheritance of his race. This
inheritance was the whole round earth from sea to
sea, and beyond the seas. They told the youth that all
this would belong to him. And they commanded three
things: that he should not sleep, as his kinsmen had
done; that he should not listen to the counsel of
hypocrites; and, finally, that he should honour as gods
those who resemble the gods. Do not forget, they said
as they left him, that you have an immortal soul, and
that that soul is of divine origin. If you follow our
counsel, you shall see our father, and become a god
like us.

PRISKOS. What are signs and omens compared with this!

KYTRON. I do not think it is an exaggeration to say that

even the Fates may have to think twice if their plans
do not coincide with your majesty's.

JULIAN. We dare not build with certainty on such an
exception. But I find this dream remarkable, although
my brother Maximus, to judge from his silence, seems
surprisingly to delight neither in it nor in the
interpretation I have placed on it. But we must bear
with him. (*Takes out a roll of parchment.*) Look,
Jovian. Early this morning, in my tent, I wrote down
my dream. Take it, and have copies made, and let it
be read to every legion in the army. I hold it
important, on so vital a campaign, that the soldiers,
amid all their dangers and hardships, should
confidently repose their destinies in the hands of their
commander, believing him infallible in those things
which determine the outcome of wars.

JOVIAN. I beg you, my lord, to excuse me from this task.

JULIAN. What do you mean?

JOVIAN. I dare not lend my hand to something that is
against the truth. O my Emperor and most noble
master, hear me! Does one of your soldiers doubt that
he is safe in your hands?

JULIAN. Well? And yet – ?

JOVIAN. And yet, my lord, you are but a mortal. But by
telling the army of your dream you seek to suggest
that you are a god – and in this I dare not be your
accomplice.

JULIAN. What say you, my friends, to this speech?

KYTRON. Its ignorance is matched only by its audacity.

JULIAN. In your passion for the truth, my dear Jovian, you
seem to have forgotten that the Emperor Antoninus,
whom men called the Pious, had a special temple
erected to him in the forum in Rome, in which he
was worshipped as an immortal god. And not only he,
but other Emperors before and after him.

JOVIAN. I know, my lord, But our ancestors did not always walk in the light of truth.

JULIAN (*gives him a long look*). Galilean!

JOVIAN. My lord, you yourself sent me to Jerusalem, and I witnessed all that happened there. I have pondered much since then, and have concluded that the Galilean's teaching is the divine truth.

JULIAN. Is it possible? Is this really possible? You see how this infectious lunacy spreads! My closest advisers, my own commanders desert me – !

JOVIAN. Set me in the front rank against your enemies, my lord, and you shall see that I will most gladly render unto the Emperor that which is the Emperor's.

JULIAN. How much – ?

JOVIAN. My life and blood.

JULIAN. Life and blood are not enough. He who would rule must rule men's minds and wills. That is where this Jesus of Nazareth defies me and challenges my power. Don't think I'm going to punish you, Jovian. You Galileans long to suffer, as other men long for happiness. Then they call you martyrs. Am I not right? Have they not thus glorified the men I had to punish for their stubbornness? Go and join the vanguard. I don't want to see you any more. Oh, this treachery, these sophistries about divided duty and divided kingdoms! Things must be different henceforth. Other Kings besides Sapores shall feel my foot upon their necks. To the vanguard, Jovian!

JOVIAN. I shall do my duty, my lord. (*Goes out right.*)

JULIAN. We do not wish this morning of joyful omens to be darkened. We shall accept this, and other such vexations, philosophically. But my dream shall be made known to the whole army. You, Kytron, and you, my dear Priskos, and you, my other friends, will see that it is done fittingly.

PHILOSOPHERS. Gladly, my lord, most gladly. (*They take the roll of parchment and go out right.*)

JULIAN. Go. And you, too, Nevita, and the rest of you, to your duties. I will join you when the army is drawn up on the plain.

A wooded mountainside, with a stream flowing among the trees. On the peak is a small farm. It is towards sundown. Detachments of SOLDIERS *cross from left to right down the slope.* BASIL OF CAESAREA *and his sister,* MAKRINA, *both dressed as hermits, are standing by the side of the road, offering water and fruit to the exhausted* SOLDIERS.

MAKRINA. Oh, Basil, look. How pale and tired they are!

BASIL. And see how many of our Christian brothers are among them. Woe to Emperor Julian! It is not against the King of Persia that he leads his armies but against Christ.

MAKRINA. You believe that?

BASIL. Yes, Makrina. More and more I realize that it is upon us that the blow will fall.

A DETACHMENT *passes. One of them, a* YOUNG SOLDIER, *collapses exhausted on the road.*

AN OFFICER (*strikes him with his stick*). Get up, you lazy dog!

MAKRINA (*runs down to them*). Oh, don't hit him!

THE SOLDIER. Let them hit me. I don't mind.

AMMIAN (*enters*). What's this? Oh, him. Can he really go no further?

OFFICER. I don't know what to say, sir. He falls down every minute.

MAKRINA. Ah, be patient! Who is this poor man? Here, suck the juice of this fruit. Who is he, my lord?

AMMIAN. A Cappadocian. One of the madmen who defiled

the temple of Venus at Antioch.

MAKRINA. Oh – one of those martyrs – !

AMMIAN. Try to get up, Agathon. I feel sorry for this man. They beat him more than he could bear. He's been off his head ever since.

AGATHON (*gets up*). I can bear it. And I'm in my right mind. Beat me, beat me – it doesn't hurt me.

AMMIAN (*to the* OFFICER). March on. No use wasting time here.

OFFICER (*to the* SOLDIERS). March on, march on.

AGATHON. Babylonius fell. Soon the whoremonger of Babylon shall fall! The lion of Zaita was destroyed. The crowned lion of the world shall be destroyed likewise!

The SOLDIERS *are driven out right.*

BASIL (*points left*). Oh, look! There he is.

MAKRINA. The Emperor? Is that the Emperor?

BASIL. Yes, that's him.

The EMPEROR JULIAN, *with several of his* GENERALS, *enters left, attended by a detachment of the* IMPERIAL BODYGUARD *under the command of* ANATOLUS.

JULIAN (*to his* SUITE). What do you mean, tired? Am I to stop because a horse has fallen? It is an Emperor's duty to set an example of endurance – ah! By the great light of heaven, are you not Basil of Caesarea?

BASIL (*makes a deep bow*). Your humble servant, most mighty lord.

JULIAN. And this woman – she must be your sister Makrina?

BASIL. She is, my lord.

JULIAN. You are a beautiful woman, and still young. Yet they tell me you have renounced life.

MAKRINA. My lord, I have renounced life that I may truly

learn to live.

JULIAN. Oh, I know these delusions you people cling to. If
my information is correct, Basil, your sister has
gathered around her a group of young women whom
she is teaching to follow her example. And I hear
that you yourself have conscripted twelve disciples,
like your Galilean master. What do you plan to do
with them?

BASIL. To send them out into the world to strengthen our
brethren in the fight.

JULIAN. I see! Equipped with all the weaponry of
eloquence, you will send this army to oppose me?

BASIL. Yes, my lord. You conquer lands and make yourself
master over peoples whose languages you do not
understand and of whose customs you are ignorant. It
is your right to do this. But this same right which you
have in the visible world, He whom you call the
Galilean possesses in the invisible world –

JULIAN. Why do you smile, woman? What are you
laughing at?

MAKRINA. I wondered, my lord, why you rage so furiously
against One whom you call dead.

JULIAN. Oh, I see. You mean that proves he is alive?

MAKRINA. I mean, O mighty lord, that it proves you feel
in your heart of hearts that He is alive.

JULIAN. I? What do you mean? *I* feel – ?

MAKRINA. What is it that you hate and persecute? Not
Him but your belief in Him. Does He not live in your
hatred and persecution just as He lives in our love?

JULIAN. Are you mad? *I* feel that that crucified Jew lives?
Oh, what a degenerate age that can accept such
nonsense! But I tell you, the end has not yet come.
You will be amazed. You will see how all the forces
that are at present scattered will gather and unite.
You'll see. That cross on which you rest your hopes

I shall re-carpenter into a ladder for him whom you
do not acknowledge.

MAKRINA. And I tell you, Emperor, that you are nothing
but a scourge in the hand of God, a scourge ordained
to punish us for our sins. Woe on us, that this should
have to be! Woe on us that, divided and poor in love,
we strayed from the true path! There was no King
left in Israel, and therefore the Lord afflicted you with
madness that you might chastise us. He clouded a
noble spirit that it might rage against us, and stripped
a flowering tree of its branches to make a rod for our
guilty shoulders. Omens warned you and you heeded
them not. Voices called you and you heard them not.
Hands wrote their messages of fire upon your walls,
and you rubbed it out without seeking to decipher it.

JULIAN. Basil. I wish I had known this woman before today.

BASIL. Come, Makrina.

MAKRINA. Oh, God! Why didst Thou let me see those
shining eyes? Angel and serpent united in one; the
apostate's passion and the tempter's guile! Oh, how
have our brothers and sisters managed to stay
confident of victory in the face of such an adversary?
A Greater One dwells in him. Oh, Basil, don't you
see? Through him the Lord God will smite us even
unto death!

JULIAN. The words were thine, woman.

MAKRINA. No! They were not mine!

JULIAN. My first-won soul!

MAKRINA. Go away from me!

BASIL. Come – come!

JULIAN. Stay here. Anatolus, set a guard on them. It is my
will that you shall both accompany the army – you
and your disciples – the women and children also.

BASIL. My lord, you cannot want this!

JULIAN. It is not prudent to leave fortresses in one's rear.

BASIL. No, no, my lord! Surely you will not compel us – !
MAKRINA. Oh, Basil! Here or elsewhere – all is finished!
JULIAN. Is it not written that you shall render unto
    the Emperor that which is the Emperor's? I need
    everyone I can lay hands on for this campaign. You
    can tend my sick and wounded. That way you will be
    serving the Galilean too; and if you still feel that is
    your duty, I advise you to make good use of your
    time. His days are numbered.

Some SOLDIERS *have surrounded* BASIL *and* MAKRINA.
OTHERS *run through the trees up towards the house.*

MAKRINA. The sun is setting behind our home. The hope
    and the light of the world are setting too. Oh, Basil,
    that we should live to see the night!
BASIL. It is still day.
JULIAN. The day is about to dawn. Turn your backs on
    the sunset, Galileans. Raise your eyes to the east, to
    the east where Apollo dreams! I promise you, you
    shall see the Sun King rule this earth.

He goes out right. They all follow him.

*Beyond the Euphrates and the Tigris. A broad plain; the
Imperial camp. To the left and rear, trees hide the curves of
the Tigris. Above the treetops, ships' masts can be seen in a
long row stretching as far as the eye can see. It is a cloudy
evening.* SOLDIERS *and* CAMP PERSONNEL *of all kinds are
busy pitching camp on the plain. All manner of stores are being
carried ashore from the ships. In the distance can be seen the
light of camp fires.* GENERALS NEVITA *and* JOVIAN, *and other
high-ranking* OFFICERS, *come from the direction of the fleet.*

NEVITA. Was not the Emperor's decision wise? Here we
    stand on enemy soil without having had to strike a
    blow. No one contested our crossing of the river.

There isn't a single Persian horseman in sight.

JOVIAN. No, my lord, the enemy certainly wasn't expecting us to come this way.

NEVITA. You say that as though you still thought it was unwise to choose this route.

JOVIAN. Yes, my lord. I still believe we would have done better to have followed a more northerly route. That way we would have had our left flank covered by Armenia, which is friendly to us, and we could have got all the provisions we needed from that fertile countryside. But here? Our progress hampered by these heavy cargo-ships, a bare plain all around us, almost a desert – ! Ah, here comes the Emperor. I'll go. I'm not in his favour these days.

He goes out right. As he does so, EMPEROR JULIAN *comes from the ships with some* ATTENDANTS. *The doctor,* ORIBASES, *appears from among the tents on the right with the philosophers,* PRISKOS *and* KYTRON, *and several other* PEOPLE. *They advance to greet the* EMPEROR.

JULIAN. Thus we see our Empire grow. Every step I take eastwards extends the Imperial frontier. (*Stamps on the ground.*) This earth is mine! I stand in the Empire, not outside it. Well, Priskos – ?

PRISKOS. Incomparable majesty, your orders have been carried out. Your miraculous dream has been read to all sections of the army.

JULIAN. Good, good. And what effect did the news of my dream have on the soldiers?

KYTRON. Some praised you with joyful voices, and called you a god. Others, however –

PRISKOS. But those were Galileans, Kytron.

KYTRON. Yes, yes, most of them were Galileans. They beat their breasts and wailed aloud.

JULIAN. I do not intend to stop there. The busts of myself
which I have had cast, to be erected in the cities I shall
conquer, shall be set up in the camp by every table
from which the treasurers distribute the soldiers' pay.
Lamps shall be lit on either side of the busts, braziers
with sweet-smelling incense shall burn before them,
and every soldier shall cast a few grains of incense
into the fire as he goes forward to receive his wages.

ORIBASES. Most gracious majesty, forgive me, but – is
this wise?

JULIAN. Wise? My dear Oribases, you astound me. Has
not Plato declared that only a god can rule over men?
What did he mean by that? Answer me – what did he
mean? Far be it from me to assert that Plato had in
mind any particular man, even the mightiest – ! But
enough of that. I have already ordered that the busts
shall be set up throughout the camp.

JOVIAN, *accompanied by an unarmed* MAN *in Persian
dress, comes from the camp.*

JOVIAN. Forgive me, my lord, for entering your presence.
This man –

JULIAN. A Persian warrior!

PERSIAN (*throws himself on the ground*). No warrior, most
mighty one!

JOVIAN. He galloped across the plain unarmed and
surrendered to our advance posts.

JULIAN. So your countrymen are near?

PERSIAN. No, no.

JULIAN. Then where have you come from?

PERSIAN (*pulls aside his clothes*). See these arms, O ruler
of the world! They bleed from rusty chains. Feel this
flayed back – wound upon wound! I come from the
torture chamber, my lord.

JULIAN. Ah! You have fled from King Sapores?

PERSIAN. Yes, mighty one, who knowest all things. I stood
high in King Sapores' favour until, driven by fear at
your approach, I dared to prophesy that this war
would cause his downfall. Do you know, my lord,
how he rewarded me? My wife he gave as a prize to
his archers from the mountains. My children he sold
as slaves. All my possessions he gave to his servants
to divide out among themselves. And me he tortured
for nine days. Then he bade me ride out and die like
a beast upon the plain.

JULIAN. And what do you want with me?

PERSIAN. What do I want with you? After this? I want to
help you to destroy my persecutor.

JULIAN. Why, my poor man, how can you help me?

PERSIAN. I can fasten wings to the feet of your soldiers.

JULIAN. What do you mean? Stand up, and tell me what
you mean.

PERSIAN (*gets up*). No one in Ctesiphon imagined you
would take this route –

JULIAN. I know that.

PERSIAN. Now it is no longer a secret.

JULIAN. You're lying, man. No Persian knows of my plans.

PERSIAN. My lord, whose wisdom comes from the fire and
the sun, you know full well that my countrymen now
know of your plans. You have crossed the river in
your ships. These ships, more than a thousand in
number, and loaded with everything that your army
requires, are to be drawn up the Tigris with your
army marching alongside –

JULIAN. How in heaven's name – ?

PERSIAN. When the ships have come as near as possible to
Ctesiphon – that is, two days journey from the city –
you will march on it, surround it, and force King
Sapores to capitulate.

JULIAN (*looks around*). Who has betrayed us?

PERSIAN. But you can no longer carry out this plan. My
    countrymen have built stone dams across the river,
    and your ships will run aground on them.

JULIAN. Do you know, creature, what this will cost you if
    you are lying to me?

PERSIAN. My body is in your power, O mighty one! If I
    am not speaking the truth, what is to prevent you
    from burning me alive?

JULIAN (to NEVITA). The river blocked! It will take weeks
    to make it navigable again.

NEVITA. If we can do it, my lord. We have no equipment –

JULIAN. That this should happen to us now! Now, when
    we have not an hour to lose.

PERSIAN. Master of the world, I told you I could give your
    army wings.

JULIAN. You know a shorter way?

PERSIAN. If you swear to me that after your victory you
    will give me back the property that was stolen from
    me, and procure me a new wife of noble birth, I can –

JULIAN. You shall have everything, I swear. Only
    speak, speak!

PERSIAN. If you march straight across the plain, within
    four days you can stand outside the walls
    of Ctesiphon.

JULIAN. You forget the mountains beyond the plain.

PERSIAN. My lord, have you never heard tell of a secret
    pass across those mountains?

JULIAN. Yes, yes. A ravine. Ariman's Way, they call it.
    Does it really exist?

PERSIAN. I rode along Ariman's Way two days ago.

JULIAN. Nevita!

NEVITA. Indeed, my lord, if this is true –

JULIAN. A miracle! When we most need it!

PERSIAN. But if you take this road, O mighty one, there is
    no time to lose. The Persian army has been recalled

from the northern provinces to close the passes.

JULIAN. You are sure?

PERSIAN. If you hesitate, you will find that it is true.

JULIAN. How many days will it take your countrymen to get there?

PERSIAN. Four days, my lord.

JULIAN. Nevita, we must be through that pass within three days.

NEVITA (*to the* PERSIAN). Can we get there in three days?

PERSIAN Yes, great warrior. You can, if you march tonight.

JULIAN. Break camp! No sleep; no rest now. In four days, five at the most, I must be at the gates of Ctesiphon. Why do you hesitate? Ah. Yes, I know.

NEVITA. The fleet, my lord.

JULIAN. Yes, yes, yes. The fleet –

NEVITA. If the Persian army reaches the pass the day after us, and if it cannot damage you in any other way, it will turn west against your fleet –

JULIAN. With them and their contents they could prolong the war for months –

NEVITA. If we could leave twenty thousand men to guard the ships, their safety would be assured –

JULIAN. Are you mad? Twenty thousand? That's almost a third of our entire armed strength. Where would my victorious army be then? Scattered and divided. I can't spare a single man for such a purpose. No, no, Nevita. But there's a third way –

NEVITA (*recoils*). My lord – !

JULIAN. The fleet must not fall into the Persians' hands. Nor must it be allowed to sap our strength. There is a third way, I tell you. Well, why do you hesitate? Why don't you say it?

NEVITA (*to the* PERSIAN). Do you know if the people of Ctesiphon are supplied with corn and oil?

PERSIAN. In Ctesiphon there are rich supplies of
    everything.

JULIAN. And once we have the city, all the riches of Persia
    are ours for the picking.

PERSIAN The citizens will open their gates to you, my
    lord! I am not the only Persian who hates King
    Sapores. They will rise against him and fall before
    your feet if you come upon them unexpectedly in the
    terror of your glory and your assembled might.

JULIAN. Yes. Yes.

PERSIAN. Burn the ships, my lord!

NEVITA. Ah!

JULIAN. His hatred sees, Nevita, while your loyalty gropes
    in darkness.

NEVITA. My loyalty saw, my lord. But it shrank from
    what it saw.

JULIAN. Are these ships not as a chain about our foot? We
    have provisions in the camp for four full days. It is
    good that the soldiers will not be overburdened. And
    what use are the ships to us now? We have no more
    rivers to cross –

NEVITA. My lord, if it is really your will that we –

JULIAN. My will – my will? Look at the storm clouds
    there! Why can't the lightning strike down and – !

MAXIMUS (*hurries in, left*). O chosen son of Apollo!
    Listen – listen!

JULIAN. Not now, my Maximus.

MAXIMUS. Nothing can be more important than this. You
    must listen.

JULIAN. In the name of joy and wisdom, then speak,
    my brother.

MAXIMUS (*draws him aside and whispers*). You know I
    have searched continuously in books and among
    omens to find what will be the outcome of this
    campaign –

JULIAN. I know you haven't been able to give me any prediction.

MAXIMUS. The omens spoke and the writings agreed with them. But the answer they always gave was so strange that I could only suppose I had miscalculated.

JULIAN. But now – ?

MAXIMUS. When we left Antioch I wrote to Rome to consult the Sibylline Books –

JULIAN. Yes, yes!

MAXIMUS. An hour ago I received the answer. A courier has arrived with it from the Governor of Antioch.

JULIAN. Ah, Maximus! Well?

MAXIMUS. It confirms all that the books and the omens have told me. And now I dare to interpret it. Rejoice, my brother. On this campaign, you are invulnerable.

JULIAN. The oracle – the oracle!

MAXIMUS. The Sibylline Books say: 'Let Julian beware of the place called Phrygia.'

JULIAN (*recoils*). Phrygia – ? Oh, Maximus!

MAXIMUS. Why do you turn pale, my brother?

JULIAN. Tell me, dearest teacher, how do you interpret this reply?

MAXIMUS. Is more than one interpretation possible? The place called Phrygia? What have you to do with Phrygia? Phrygia is a country that lies wide of your path and far behind you. You will never need to set foot in that land. No danger threatens you, blessed one. That is what the oracle means.

JULIAN. This riddling answer has a double meaning. No danger threatens me in battle – but from that far country – ! Nevita, Nevita!

NEVITA. My lord?

JULIAN. Phrygia, then? Alexandros writes that strange things are afoot in Phrygia. It was prophesied once that the Galilean should return, and – ! Burn the ships, Nevita!

NEVITA. My lord, is it your fixed resolve – ?

JULIAN. Burn them! Now, at once! Secret dangers threaten
us from our rear. (*To a* CAPTAIN). Take good care of
this barbarian. He shall be our guide. Give him food
and drink, and let him rest well.

JOVIAN. My lord, I entreat you, do not risk all your hopes
on the word of a deserter.

JULIAN. Ah, you seem frightened, my Galilean counsellor.
This new development seems not to please you.
Perhaps you know more than you care to admit. Go,
Nevita, and burn the ships.

NEVITA *bows and goes out left. The* CAPTAIN *leads the*
PERSIAN *out through the tents.*

JULIAN. Traitors in my own camp! Wait, wait. I shall
unmask their cunning plots. Order the army to break
camp! Go, Jovian, and see that the vanguard is ready
to march within the hour. The Persian knows the
way. Go!

JOVIAN. I shall do as you command, most noble Emperor.
(*Goes out right.*)

MAXIMUS. You are burning the fleet? You must have great
things in mind.

JULIAN. I wonder if Alexander of Macedon would have
dared to do this?

MAXIMUS. Did Alexander know whence danger threatened?

JULIAN. True, true. But I know. All the powers of victory
are on my side. Signs and portents reveal their secret
knowledge to bring my kingdom nearer. Do not they
say of the Galilean that spirits came and served him?
Whom do the spirits serve now? What would the
Galilean say if he were invisibly among us?

MAXIMUS. He would say: 'The third kingdom is at hand.'

JULIAN. The third kingdom has come, Maximus! I feel

that the Messiah of the world is alive in me. The
spirit is made flesh, and the flesh spirit. All creation
lies within my power, at the mercy of my will. Look,
look! There are the first sparks drifting in the air. The
flames are licking the riggings and the crowded masts!
(*Shouts towards the fire*). Burn! Burn!

MAXIMUS. The wind senses your will. It is rising, that it
may serve you.

JULIAN (*clenches his fist imperiously*). Blow faster! To the
west! I command it!

*As he speaks, a brilliant light flares up. Flames rise into
the air from the ships.*

OFFICERS and MEN (*in terror*). The fleet is burning!

JULIAN. Yes, the fleet is burning! And more than the fleet.
On this red and flaming pyre the crucified Galilean is
being burned to ashes! And the Emperor of the world
is burning with the Galilean! But out of the ashes
shall arise, like a miraculous bird, the God of Earth
and the Emperor of the Spirit, united in One, in One,
in One!

NEVITA (*enters left*). It is done, my lord.

JOVIAN (*runs in from the camp*). Put out the fire! Quench
it, quench it!

JULIAN. Burn, burn!

AMMIAN (*from the camp*). My lord, you have been
betrayed! The Persian deserter was a traitor – !

JULIAN. You're lying, man. Where is he?

AMMIAN. Fled.

JOVIAN. Vanished like a shadow –

NEVITA. Fled!

JOVIAN. His escorts say he seemed to vanish out of
their hands –

AMMIAN. His horse is gone too. The barbarian must have
fled across the plain.

JULIAN. Put out the fire. Nevita.

NEVITA. Impossible, my lord!

JULIAN. Put it out, put it out! It must be possible!

NEVITA. Nothing could be more impossible. All the
    riggings have been cut. The whole fleet is drifting
    down upon the flaming wrecks.

AGATHON. Antichrist, Antichrist, bid the wind be silent!
    Command the flames to die!

JULIAN. The wind is rising. The fire is like a raging sea –

MAXIMUS (*whispers*). Beware of Phrygia!

JULIAN (*cries to the* ARMY). Let the fleet burn! In seven
    days you shall burn Ctesiphon!

Act Three

A barren, stony plain without trees or grass. On the right stands the EMPEROR'S *tent. It is afternoon. Exhausted* SOLDIERS *lie in groups on the ground. Now and then* DETACHMENTS OF MEN *pass from left to right. Outside the tent, the philosophers* PRISKOS *and* KYTRON, *together with several others of the* EMPEROR'S RETINUE, *pace up and down uneasily.* ANATOLUS, *the Commander of the Guard, stands with some of his* MEN *in front of the doorway of the tent.*

KYTRON. How on earth can they take so long to decide?

PRISKOS. Yes, you'd think they have only one choice.
    Either to go on, or turn back.

KYTRON. Ridiculous. Tell me, good Anatolus, why in the
    name of the gods don't we go on?

PRISKOS. Yes, why have we halted here, in the middle of
    the desert?

ANATOLUS. Do you see that haze quivering on the
    horizon, north, east and south?

KYTRON. Yes, yes. That's only the heat –

ANATOLUS. It is the plain burning.

PRISKOS. What? Is the plain on fire?

ANATOLUS. Out there where the desert ends, the Persians
    have set fire to the grass. We can't go anywhere until
    the earth has cooled.

PRISKOS. But then we have no choice. Without food
    and water –

KYTRON. Ah, here comes Nevita. Now we'll find out –

    NEVITA *comes out of the tent. In the doorway he turns
    and makes a sign to someone within. A few moments
    later,* ORIBASES *comes out.*

NEVITA (*draws the doctor aside*). Tell me the truth,
    Oribases. Is there something wrong with the
    Emperor's mind?

ORIBASES. What makes you ask that, my lord?

NEVITA. How else can one explain his conduct?

ORIBASES. Oh, my beloved Emperor – !

NEVITA. Oribases, you mustn't hide anything from me.

KYTRON (*approaches them*). Most gallant general, pardon
    my interrupting –

NEVITA. Later, later.

ORIBASES (*to* NEVITA). Don't worry, my lord. No accident
    will happen. Eutherius and I have undertaken to keep
    an eye on him.

NEVITA. You surely don't mean – ?

ORIBASES. Last night he was close to killing himself.
    Luckily Eutherius happened to go in – don't tell
    anyone about this –

NEVITA. Don't let him out of your sight.

PRISKOS (*approaches*). It would be of great comfort to us
    to learn what the council of war has –

NEVITA. Forgive me, I've important things to do.

He goes out behind the tent. As he does so, JOVIAN
comes out of it.

JOVIAN (*speaks back into the tent*). It shall be done,
    your majesty.

KYTRON. Ah, the noble Jovian! Well? Have we decided
    to retreat?

JOVIAN. I wouldn't advise anyone to call it a retreat.

He goes out behind the tent. The EMPEROR JULIAN
comes out; he is pale and haggard. The Chamberlain
EUTHERIUS *follows, together with several high-ranking*
OFFICERS. *These at once go out right, into the plain.*

JULIAN (*to the* PHILOSOPHERS). Be of good cheer, my

friends. Everything will soon be all right now.

KYTRON. Ah, my good lord, have you hit on a way out?

JULIAN. There are several ways out, Kytron. It is just a question of choosing the best one. We are making a slight alteration to the army's line of advance –

PRISKOS. Oh, praised be the Emperor's wisdom!

JULIAN. This eastward march – that isn't going to lead us anywhere.

KYTRON. No, no, of course not.

JULIAN. We are going to march northwards, Kytron.

KYTRON. Northwards, my lord?

PRISKOS. Not westwards?

JULIAN. Not westwards. Certainly not westwards. That would be difficult because of the rivers. And Ctesiphon we must leave till later. Without ships we cannot hope to take the city. It's the Galileans' fault, they burned them; I've been keeping my eyes open. Who dares call it a retreat, that I turn northwards? What do you know of my plans? The Persian army lies somewhere to our north – we're fairly sure of that now. When I have defeated Sapores – and one battle will suffice for that – we shall find all the supplies we need in the Persian camp. When I lead the King of Persia in chains through Antioch and those other cities, then we'll see whether those people won't prostrate themselves at my feet.

CHRISTIAN SOLDIERS (*pass across the plain, singing*).
The axe is set to the root of the tree;
The cedar of the world shall fall.
On Golgotha from the blood of Christ
Rises the palm tree that shall never age.
(*They go out right.*)

JULIAN (*watches them go*). The Galileans are always singing. Songs about death and wounds and pain. Those women I brought along to help the wounded,

they've done us more harm than good. They've taught
the soldiers strange songs I haven't heard before.
However, I don't intend to punish anyone. It'll only
lead to greater madness. Do you know, Priskos, what
happened with those rebels who refused just now to
treat the imperial busts with due respect?

PRISKOS. *Just now*, my lord?

JULIAN. When, to inculcate a wholesome fear, I proclaimed
that some of them were to be executed, the oldest
man among them stepped forward and begged, amid
loud cries of ecstasy, to be allowed to die first. Well,
Priskos, when I learned that yesterday –

PRISKOS. Yesterday? Oh, my lord, you are mistaken. That
happened forty days ago.

JULIAN. So long? Yes, yes, yes. The Hebrews had to
wander forty years in the wilderness. All the old
people had to die. A new generation had to arise. But
they – mark this – *they* entered into the land which
had been promised to them all.

EUTHERIUS. It is late, my lord. Will you not sup?

JULIAN. Not yet, Eutherius. A little mortification of the
flesh is good for us all. Yes, I tell you, we must waste
no time. We must *become* a new generation. I can't do
anything with you as you are now. If you want to
escape from this desert, you must start a new life.
Look at the Galileans. There are things we could
learn from those people. They never allow any of
their number to want. They love each other like
brothers and sisters – especially now, when their
stubbornness has forced me to chastise them. These
Galileans, I tell you, have something in their hearts
which I wish you would seek to emulate. Is there
one of you who would go joyfully to his death for
Plato's sake? Would you, my dear Priskos, offer your
left hand for Socrates? Would Kytron allow his ear to

be chopped off for Diogenes? Indeed you would not. I
know you, hypocrites. Get out of my sight, I have no
use for you!

The PHILOSOPHERS *retire, crestfallen. The* OTHERS *move
away, whispering uneasily. Only* ORIBASES *and* EUTHERIUS
remain with the EMPEROR, *although* ANATOLUS *and his*
MEN *stay outside the tent.*

JULIAN. How strange! Isn't it incredible, when you think
    of it? Oribases, can you explain this riddle to me?
ORIBASES. What riddle, my lord?
JULIAN. With twelve poor men, fishermen, ignorant
    people, he started all this.
ORIBASES. Oh my lord, these musings sap your strength.
JULIAN. And who have kept it alive all these years?
    Women and quite simple people, mostly –.
ORIBASES. Yes, yes, my lord. But soon the fortunes of our
    expedition will change, and –
JULIAN. Very true, Oribases. Once our luck changes, all
    will be well. The kingdom of the carpenter's son will
    soon fall. We know that. For as many years as the
    year has days, so long shall he reign. And now we
    have only –
EUTHERIUS. My beloved master, would it not refresh you
    to bathe?
JULIAN. You think so? You can go, Eutherius. Go, go! I
    have something to discuss with Oribases.

    EUTHERIUS *goes out behind the tent. The* EMPEROR
    draws ORIBASES *over to the other side.*

JULIAN. Did Eutherius say anything to you this morning?
ORIBASES. No, my lord.
JULIAN. He didn't say anything about last night – ?

ORIBASES. No, my lord. Nothing at all. Eutherius is most discreet –

JULIAN. If he should tell you anything, you mustn't believe it. It didn't happen the way he says. It is he who seeks my life.

ORIBASES. He? Your old and faithful servant – ?

JULIAN. I'm going to keep my eye on him.

ORIBASES. I will too, my lord.

JULIAN. We will both keep our eye on him.

ORIBASES. My lord, I fear you slept ill last night.

JULIAN. Yes. (ORIBASES *is about to speak, but thinks better of it.*) Do you know why I couldn't sleep?

ORIBASES. No, my lord.

JULIAN. The victor of the Mulvian Bridge was with me.

ORIBASES. Constantine the Great?

JULIAN. Yes. These last nights his ghost has given me no peace. He comes soon after midnight, and does not leave until just before dawn.

ORIBASES. My lord, it is full moon, and that has always strangely swayed your mind.

JULIAN. According to the ancients, such visions are wont to – where is Maximus? But their meaning cannot be trusted. We know how often, and how greatly, they have led men astray. We cannot even unreservedly accept everything they say about the gods. Nor about ghosts, and those other powers that rule human existence. What do we know about these powers? We know nothing, Oribases – except that they are fickle and untrustworthy – of that we have proof enough. I wish Maximus would come – ! (*To himself.*) Here? But it isn't here the storm will break. That was to be in a place called Phrygia –

ORIBASES. What place, my lord – and what storm – ?

JULIAN. Oh, nothing. Nothing.

NEVITA (*enters right*). My lord, the army is on the march –

JULIAN. Northwards?

NEVITA (*starts*). Of course, my lord!

JULIAN. We should have waited for Maximus –

NEVITA. What would be the use of that, your majesty?
There is nothing to wait for here. We have no food.
Persian outriders have already been sighted to the
east and south –

JULIAN. Yes, yes. We *must* march – northwards. Maximus
will come soon. I have ordered the Etruscan
soothsayers to be brought to me from the rearguard.
They must try once more to see if ... I have also
found some Magi who seem well versed in the
Chaldean mysteries. Our own priests are consulting
the omens in nine different places –

NEVITA. My lord, whatever the omens say, I tell you we
must march. The soldiers are growing restive. They
know our only hope is to reach the mountains of
Armenia.

JULIAN. We shall make that our objective, Nevita –
whatever the omens say. But it is a great consolation
to know that one is acting in accord with the wishes
of those unfathomable powers who can, when thus
inclined, so potently influence our destinies.

NEVITA (*turns from him and says curtly and commandingly*).
Anatolus, strike the Emperor's tent. (*He whispers a
few words to* ANATOLUS *and goes out right.*)

JULIAN. These forty days the omens have been unlucky.
And that shows one should believe in them; for in all
this time our cause has advanced but little. But, listen
now, my good Oribases – now I have a new plan – !
Ah, Maximus!

MAXIMUS (*enters from the plain*). The army is on the
march, my lord. Mount your horse.

JULIAN. The omens – the omens.

MAXIMUS. The omens! Do not ask about them.

JULIAN. Speak! I must know what answer they have given.

MAXIMUS. All the omens are silent.

JULIAN. Silent?

MAXIMUS. I went to the priests. The entrails of the victims gave no sign. I went to the Etruscan charlatans. The flight and cries of birds had told them nothing. I went to the Magi too. Their scriptures had no answer for us. And I myself –

JULIAN. You yourself, my dear Maximus?

MAXIMUS. I can tell you now. Last night I studied the position of the stars. They told me nothing, Julian.

JULIAN. Nothing. Silence – silence, as though the sun itself were about to pass into eclipse. Alone. No bridge between me and the spirits any longer. Where are you now, white fleet of shining sails which came and went in the sunlight and bore messages between earth and heaven? The fleet is burned. That fleet too is burned. Oh, all my shining ships! Tell me, Maximus, what do you believe will happen?

MAXIMUS. I believe in you.

JULIAN. Yes, yes. Do that.

MAXIMUS. The world-will has placed its power in your hand. That is why it is silent.

JULIAN. We shall interpret it thus. And we shall act accordingly – although we could have wished that –! This silence. To stand so alone. But there are others, too, who may be said to stand almost alone. The Galileans. They have only one god. And one god is almost the same as no god. Yet how is it that every day we see these people – ?

ANATOLUS (*who has meanwhile been supervising the striking of the tent*). My lord, you must mount your horse. I dare not let you stay here any longer.

JULIAN. Yes. Now I shall mount my horse. Where is my good Babylonius? Thus, now. Sword in hand – !

Come, my dear friends.

They all go out right.

Marshy, wooded country. A dark, still lake among the trees.
Watchfires in the distance. A moonlit night, with drifting
clouds. Some SOLDIERS *stand on guard in the foreground.*

MAKRINA *and* WOMEN (*sing offstage left*).

> Alas! Alas!
> God's wrath is come
> Upon our race.
> Ah! Death is nigh.

FIRST SOLDIER (*listens*). Hush! Do you hear? It's the
    Galilean women singing.

SECOND SOLDIER. Sounds like owls and crows.

THIRD SOLDIER. I'd like to be with them all the same. It's
    safer among the Galileans than here. The Galileans'
    god is stronger than ours.

FIRST SOLDIER. The Emperor has offended the gods, that's
    the root of it. How did he get that idea of setting
    himself up in their place?

THIRD SOLDIER. What's worse is that he's offended the
    Galileans' god. Haven't you heard, a few nights ago
    he and his magician opened the belly of a pregnant
    woman to take omens from her entrails.

FIRST SOLDIER. Oh, I don't believe that. Couldn't have
    been a Greek woman, anyway. Must have been a
    barbarian woman.

THIRD SOLDIER. They say the Galileans' god takes care of
    the barbarians too. If that's so, it'll go ill with us.

SECOND SOLDIER. Oh, nonsense. The Emperor's a great
    general.

FIRST SOLDIER. So is King Sapores.

SECOND SOLDIER. Do you think it's the *whole* Persian army we've got facing us?

FIRST SOLDIER. Some say it's just the advance guard. No one knows for sure.

THIRD SOLDIER. I wish I was over there among the Galileans.

FIRST SOLDIER. Are you going to defect to them too?

THIRD SOLDIER. Plenty of others have. These last few days there's been –

FIRST SOLDIER. Halt! Halt! Who goes there?

VOICE. Friends.

Some SOLDIERS *enter through the trees with the Cappadocian,* AGATHON, *among them.*

SECOND SOLDIER (*laughs*). Here's someone who's tried to run away.

FOURTH SOLDIER. No, he's off his head.

AGATHON. I'm not mad. Oh, in the name of merciful God, let me go!

FIFTH SOLDIER. He says he wants to kill a beast with seven heads.

AGATHON. Yes, yes, I shall! Oh, let me go! You see this spear? Do you know what spear it is? With this spear I shall kill the beast with the seven heads and so win back my soul again. Christ himself has promised me. He visited me last night.

FIRST SOLDIER. Poor devil's tired out and starving. He's lost his wits.

FOURTH SOLDIER. Take him to the camp, so he can get some sleep.

AGATHON. Oh, let me go! If only you understood what this spear is to accomplish – !

The SOLDIERS *take him out downstage right.*

THIRD SOLDIER. What did he mean by all that about the beast?

FIRST SOLDIER. Some Galilean superstition. They've got so many.

EUTHERIUS and ORIBASES hurry in right, as though searching for someone.

EUTHERIUS. Can't you see him anywhere?

ORIBASES. No. Ah, soldiers! Tell me, good friends, has anyone passed this way?

FIRST SOLDIER. Some spearmen.

ORIBASES. Good, good. But no one else? No high-ranking officer? None of the generals?

SOLDIERS. No, no one.

ORIBASES. He's not here, then. Oh, Eutherius, how could you – ?

EUTHERIUS. What could I do? What could I? My old eyes haven't closed for three nights –

ORIBASES (*to the* SOLDIERS). You must help us to find him. I demand it in the General's own name. Spread out among the trees. If you find any of our leaders, report it at the watchfire over there.

SOLDIERS. We will, my lord.

They all go out left, in various directions. A few moments later, EMPEROR JULIAN *appears from behind a tree, right. He listens, looks round, then beckons to someone behind him.*

JULIAN. Hush! Come out, Maximus. They didn't see us.

MAXIMUS (*comes out*). Oribases was among them.

JULIAN. Yes, yes. Eutherius and he are keeping a watch on me. They seem to think I might – did neither of them say anything to you?

MAXIMUS. No, my Julian. But why did you wake me? And

what do you want here in the middle of the night?

JULIAN. I want to be alone with you for the last time, my
beloved teacher.

MAXIMUS. Not for the last time, Julian.

JULIAN. Look at this black water. Do you think – if I
vanished from the earth without trace, and my body
was never found, and no one knew what had
happened to me – do you think the legend would
grow that Hermes had descended and carried me
away, and that I had been taken up into the company
of the gods?

MAXIMUS. The time is at hand when mortals will not need
to die to live as gods upon the earth.

JULIAN. Oh, Maximus! How I long to go home! Home to
the light and the sun and all the stars!

MAXIMUS. I beg you, do not let your mind dwell on such
thoughts. The Persian army is almost upon us.
Tomorrow there will be a battle. You will win, and –

JULIAN. I – win? You don't know who was with me an
hour ago.

MAXIMUS. Who was with you?

JULIAN. I had fallen asleep on my bed in the tent. Then I
was woken by a strong reddish light which seemed to
pierce my closed eyelids. I looked up and saw a figure
standing there in the tent. Over its head it wore a
long cowl which fell down on both sides leaving the
face free.

MAXIMUS. Did you know this figure?

JULIAN. It was the same face that I saw that night in
Ephesus many years ago. That night when we held
the symposium with the two others.

MAXIMUS. The spirit of the kingdom.

JULIAN. It appeared to me again in Gaul. On an occasion
I dare not think of.

MAXIMUS. Did it speak?

JULIAN. No. It seemed to want to speak; but it said
     nothing. It stood motionless, looking at me. Its face
     was pale and haggard. Suddenly with both hands it
     pulled the cowl about its head, veiling its face, and
     went out through the wall of the tent.

MAXIMUS. The decisive moment is at hand.

JULIAN. Yes, it is indeed at hand.

MAXIMUS. You have not been forsaken, Julian. He who
     has the will shall conquer.

JULIAN. And what will the conqueror win? Will the victory
     be worth the toil? What did Alexander of Macedon,
     what did Julius Caesar win? Greeks and Romans
     speak of their deeds with cold admiration – while the
     other, the Galilean, the carpenter's son, reigns as the
     King of Love in warm and trusting human hearts.
     Where is He now? Has He been active elsewhere
     since that thing happened at Golgotha? (*Pause.*) The
     other night I dreamed about Him. I dreamed I had
     conquered the whole world. I commanded that the
     memory of the Galilean should be wiped from the
     earth; and it was wiped out. Then the spirits came
     and ministered unto me, and tied wings to my
     shoulders, and I flew out into the great emptiness of
     space, until at last I set foot upon another world.
     There *was* another world than mine. Its horizon was
     broader, its sunshine more golden, and several moons
     revolved about it. Then I looked down at my own
     world, the Emperor's world, which I had liberated
     from the Galilean, and I saw that all that I had done
     was exceeding good. But listen, Maximus. Then a
     procession walked past me on this alien world on
     which I now stood. There were soldiers and judges
     and executioners at its head, and weeping women
     followed it. And behold, there in the middle of this
     great slow procession walked the Galilean, alive, and

bearing a cross on His back. Then I called to Him
and said: 'Whither goest Thou, Galilean?' And He
turned His face to me, smiled, nodded slowly, and
said: 'To the Place of the Skull.' (*Pause.*) Where is
He now? Was that business at Golgotha outside
Jerusalem just a provincial episode, something done as
it were in passing, during a spare moment? Does He
walk perpetually, and suffer and die and conquer
anew in one world after another? Oh, if I could lay
the earth waste! Maximus, is there no poison, no
consuming fire, that could render all creation as waste
as it was on that day when the Spirit hovered alone
above the waters?

MAXIMUS. The watchposts are sounding the alarm. Come,
Julian.

JULIAN. To think that century must follow century, and
that in every one of them people will live who will
know that it was I who yielded and He who won!
I won't yield! I'm young! I am invulnerable! The third
kingdom is at hand! (*With a loud cry.*) There He is!

MAXIMUS. Who? Where?

JULIAN. Don't you see Him? Over there among the trees.
Wearing a crown and a purple cloak –

MAXIMUS. It is the moonlight playing on the water. Come
– come, my Julian.

JULIAN (*goes threateningly towards the vision*). Go away
from me! You're dead. Your kingdom is finished. Off
with your magician's cloak, carpenter's son! What are
you doing? What's that you're hammering? Ah!

EUTHERIUS (*from the left*). The gods be praised!
Oribases! Here.

JULIAN. Where has He gone?

ORIBASES (*from the left*). Is he there?

EUTHERIUS. Yes. Oh, my beloved Emperor!

JULIAN. Who was that who said: 'I am carpentering the

Emperor's coffin'?

ORIBASES. What do you mean, my lord?

JULIAN. Who spoke, I say! Who was that who said: 'I am carpentering the Emperor's coffin'?

ORIBASES. Come with me to your tent, I beseech you.

Noises and cries are heard in the distance.

MAXIMUS. War-cries! The Persians are upon us!

EUTHERIUS. They have attacked the outposts!

ORIBASES. The enemy is in the camp! Oh, my lord, you are unarmed –

JULIAN. I shall sacrifice to the gods.

MAXIMUS. What gods, fool? Where are they – and what are they?

JULIAN. I will sacrifice to some god. I will sacrifice to many. One of them must hear me. I shall call upon the power that lies outside me and above me –

ORIBASES. There isn't a moment to waste –

JULIAN. Ah! Did you see that burning torch behind the cloud? It flamed and was quenched in the same moment. A message from the spirits! A shining ship between heaven and earth! My shield! My sword! (*Runs out right.* ORIBASES *and* EUTHERIUS *follow him.*)

MAXIMUS (*cries*). Emperor! Emperor! Do not fight tonight! (*Goes out right.*)

The open plain, with a village in the distance. A grey and misty dawn. Noise of battle. Cries and the clang of swords are heard from the plain. In the foreground, ROMAN SPEARMEN *led by* AMMIAN *are fighting with* PERSIAN BOWMEN. *The latter are gradually driven back towards the left.*

AMMIAN. That's the way, lads! Follow them! Cut them down! Don't give them time to shoot!

NEVITA (*enters right with* SOLDIERS). Well fought, Ammian!

AMMIAN. Oh, my lord, why don't the horsemen come to our aid?

NEVITA. Impossible. The Persians have elephants in their van. The mere smell of them strikes the horses with terror. Thrust, thrust! Upwards, friends! Under their breastplates!

KYTRON (*enters right in his nightclothes, weighed down with books and rolls of paper*). Oh, why did I ever get mixed up in this dreadful business?

NEVITA. Have you seen the Emperor, friend?

KYTRON. Yes, but he pays no attention to me. Oh, I pray you, my lord, let me have a few soldiers to protect me.

NEVITA (*to his* MEN). They're falling back! Shield-bearers forward!

KYTRON. You don't hear me, my lord. It is most important that nothing should happen to me. My pamphlet 'On the Importance of Remaining Calm in Adversity' is not yet completed –

NEVITA (*as before*). The Persians have reinforced their right wing! They're advancing again!

KYTRON. Are they advancing? Oh, this dreadful lust for blood! An arrow! It nearly hit me! How carelessly they're shooting! No respect for life and limb! (*Runs out downstage left*).

NEVITA. The armies are locked. Neither side advances. (*To* FROMENTIUS, *who enters with more* SOLDIERS *from the right*.) Captain! Have you seen the Emperor?

FROMENTIUS. Yes, my lord. He is fighting at the head of the white cavalry.

NEVITA. Not wounded?

FROMENTIUS. He seems invulnerable. Arrows and spears swerve away from him wherever he shows himself.

AMMIAN (*shouts back from the thick of the fighting*). Help, help! We can't hold out any longer!

NEVITA. On, on, my brave Fromentius!

FROMENTIUS (*to his* MEN). Close your ranks, Greeks, and
    charge! (*Runs to* AMMIAN'*s aid. The battle recedes
    slightly.*)
ANATOLUS (*enters with more* SOLDIERS, *right*). Isn't the
    Emperor here?
NEVITA. The Emperor? Aren't you responsible for the
    Emperor's safety?
ANATOLUS. His horse was shot under him – a great crowd
    gathered round – it was impossible to get through to
    him –
NEVITA. Ah! Do you think he's hurt?
ANATOLUS. No, I don't think so. The cry went up that he
    was unwounded, but –
SEVERAL OF NEVITA'S FOLLOWERS. There he is! There
    he is!

> *The* EMPEROR JULIAN, *bearing no armour nor helmet
> but only his sword and shield, enters right, accompanied
> by* MEN OF THE IMPERIAL GUARD.

JULIAN. Oh, thank the gods I have found you, Nevita!
NEVITA. My lord! But – no armour – ? How rash of you – ?
JULIAN. No weapon can harm me here. Go, Nevita. Take
    command of the battle. My horse was shot beneath
    me, and –
NEVITA. My lord! Then you are wounded?
JULIAN. No. Just a blow on the head. I'm a little dazed.
    Go, go – ! What's this? Who are all these strange
    figures crowding among us – ?
NEVITA (*whispers*). Anatolus, take care of the Emperor.
ANATOLUS. Never fear, my lord.

> NEVITA *goes out right with his* STAFF. EMPEROR
> JULIAN, ANATOLUS, *and some of the* IMPERIAL GUARD
> *remain. The battle on the plain recedes further and
> further into the distance.*

JULIAN. How many of our men are dead, do you
　　think, Anatolus?

ANATOLUS. No small number, my lord. But I'm sure the
　　Persians have lost more.

JULIAN. Yes, yes. But many of ours have fallen, both
　　Greeks and Romans. Don't you think so?

ANATOLUS. My lord, you are not well. Your face is ashen –

JULIAN. Do you see those men lying there – some on their
　　backs, some on their stomachs, with their arms
　　outstretched? They're all dead, aren't they?

ANATOLUS. Yes, my lord. No doubt of that.

JULIAN. They're dead, yes. Then they know nothing about
　　my defeat at Jerusalem, or the other defeats – ! Many
　　more Greeks will fall in this battle. Don't you think
　　so, Anatolus?

ANATOLUS. My lord, let us hope that the bloodiest work
　　is over.

JULIAN. Many, many more will fall, I tell you. But it's of
　　no avail. What does it help if thousands fall? Others
　　will be born – ! Tell me, Anatolus, that sword that
　　the Emperor Caligula envisaged – what do you
　　suppose it was like?

ANATOLUS. What sword, my lord?

JULIAN. You know. He wanted to have a sword with
　　which, in a single blow, he could –

ANATOLUS. Listen to the battle-cries, my lord! I'm sure
　　the Persians are retreating now.

JULIAN (listens). What is that song in the air?

ANATOLUS. My lord, permit me to send for Oribases. Or,
　　better still – come, come, you are sick –

JULIAN. There is a song in the air. Can't you hear it?

ANATOLUS. If there is, it must be the Galileans –

JULIAN. Yes, of course it's the Galileans. (Roars with
　　laughter.) They're fighting in our ranks, and don't see
　　who's standing on the other side. Oh, you fools, all of

you! Where is Nevita? Why is he attacking the
Persians? Can't he see it isn't the Persians we have to
fear? You're all betraying me!

ANATOLUS (*whispers to a* GUARD). Run to the camp.
Fetch the Emperor's doctor.

The GUARD *goes out right.*

JULIAN. There are thousands of them. Do you think
they've seen us, Anatolus?

ANATOLUS. Who, my lord? Where?

JULIAN. Can't you see them? Hush! High above us – and
far away! You're lying! You can see them clearly!

ANATOLUS. By the immortal gods, those are only the
morning clouds. The day is breaking.

JULIAN. They are the Galilean's armies, I tell you. Look,
look! Those ones in the robes edged with red, they're
the ones who died in martyrdom. Women stand
around them singing, and spinning bowstrings from
their long hair torn from their heads. And they've
children with them, twining slings from the entrails
that have been wound out of them. Burning
torches – ! How many they are – thousands – they're
innumerable! They're coming here. They're all
looking at me! They're all coming towards me!

ANATOLUS. It's the Persians, my lord. Our ranks are
breaking –!

JULIAN. They mustn't break! They mustn't! Stand fast,
Greeks! Stand, Romans, stand! Today we shall set
free the world!

The battle has meanwhile swept back across the plain.
JULIAN *throws himself with drawn sword into the
thickest part of the fight. General confusion.*

ANATOLUS (*shouts, right*). Help! The Emperor is in danger!

JULIAN (*fighting*). I see him! I see him! A longer sword!

Who will lend me a longer sword?

SOLDIERS (*fighting their way forward, right*). With Christ
for the Emperor!

AGATHON (*among them*). With Christ for Christ!

He throws his spear. It grazes the EMPEROR's *arm and
pierces his side.*

JULIAN. Ah!

*He grasps the blade of the spear to pull it out, but cuts
his hand, utters a loud cry and falls.*

AGATHON (*cries from the thick of the battle*). The Roman's
spear from Golgotha!

He throws himself unarmed into the midst of the
PERSIANS, *and is cut down.*

CONFUSED CRIES. The Emperor! Is the Emperor wounded?

JULIAN (*tries to rise, but falls back and cries*). Oh,
Galilean! You've won!

MANY VOICES. The Emperor has fallen!

ANATOLUS. The Emperor is wounded! Protect him –
protect him, in the name of the gods!

He launches himself desperately against the advancing
PERSIANS. *The* EMPEROR *is carried out, unconscious.
At the same time,* JOVIAN *enters with fresh* TROOPS.

JOVIAN. On, on, my Christian brothers! Render unto the
Emperor that which is the Emperor's!

RETREATING SOLDIERS (*shout to him*). He has fallen! The
Emperor has fallen!

JOVIAN. Fallen? Oh, Lord of Vengeance! On, on! The
Lord wills that His people shall live! I see the heavens
open! I see the angels with their flaming swords – !

SOLDIERS (*storm forward*). Christ is among us!

AMMIAN'S MEN. The God of the Galileans is among us!

Follow him! He is the strongest!

Wild fighting. JOVIAN *fights his way into the enemy ranks. The sun rises. The* PERSIANS *flee on all sides.*

The EMPEROR's *tent, with a curtained doorway in the background. Broad day. The* EMPEROR JULIAN *is lying unconscious on his bed. The wounds in his right side, arm and hand are bandaged. Close to him stand* ORIBASES, MAKRINA *and* EUTHERIUS. *Further back stand* BASIL OF CAESAREA *and* PRISKOS. *At the foot of the bed stands* MAXIMUS THE MYSTIC.

MAKRINA. He's bleeding again. I must tie the
    bandage tighter.
ORIBASES. Thank you, gentle lady. Your careful hands
    have served us well.
EUTHERIUS. Is he really alive?
ORIBASES. Of course he is alive.
EUTHERIUS. But he isn't breathing.
ORIBASES. He is breathing.

AMMIAN *comes quietly in with the* EMPEROR's *sword
and shield. He puts them down and remains standing
by the curtained doorway.*

PRISKOS. Ah, my good Captain, how goes the battle
    outside?
AMMIAN. Better than in here. Is he – ?
PRISKOS. No, no – not yet. But is it true that we have
    forced the Persians to retire?
AMMIAN. Yes, they are in full flight. Thanks to Jovian.
    Three noble emissaries from King Sapores have come
    to the camp to seek an armistice.
PRISKOS. Do you think Nevita will agree to that?
AMMIAN. Nevita has handed the command over to Jovian.
    Everyone is flocking to Jovian. They see him as our
    only saviour –

ORIBASES. Speak quietly. He's moving.

AMMIAN. Moving? You mean he may regain consciousness?
Oh, that he should live to experience this!

EUTHERIUS. What, Ammian?

AMMIAN. The officers and legionaries are voting to elect a
new Emperor.

PRISKOS. What?

EUTHERIUS. What shameless impatience!

AMMIAN. The danger of our situation partly excuses it.
And yet –

MAKRINA. He's waking. He's opening his eyes –

The EMPEROR JULIAN *lies silent for a moment, looking
gently at those standing around him.*

ORIBASES. My lord, do you know me?

JULIAN. Of course, my dear Oribases.

ORIBASES. You must lie quiet.

JULIAN. Lie quiet? What do you mean? I must get up.

ORIBASES. Impossible, my lord – I entreat you –

JULIAN. I must get up, I tell you. How can I lie quiet
now? I must beat King Sapores.

EUTHERIUS. King Sapores is beaten, my lord. He has sent
emissaries to the camp to seek an armistice.

JULIAN. Has he really? That is good news. Then I beat
him, anyway. But – no armistice. I shall beat him to
his knees. Oh, where is my shield? Did I lose my
shield?

AMMIAN. No, your majesty. Here is your shield, and
your sword.

JULIAN. I hold it very dear. My good shield. I would
not wish it to fall into the barbarians' hands. Put it
on my arm –

MAKRINA. Oh, my lord, it is too heavy for you now.

JULIAN. Ah – you? Yes, my pious Makrina, you are right.
It is a little too heavy. Put it in front of me, so that I

can see it. What? Is that you Ammian? Are *you*
keeping watch on me? Where is Anatolus?

AMMIAN. He is in heaven, my lord.

JULIAN. Dead? The loyal Anatolus dead, for me? In
heaven, did you say? Hm! One friend the less. Alas,
my Maximus! I shall not receive the Persian king's
emissaries today. They are only hoping to gain time.
But I shan't agree to any treaty. I shall follow up my
victory with the utmost despatch. The army will turn
and march again on Ctesiphon.

ORIBASES. Impossible, my lord. Think of your wound.

JULIAN. My wound will soon be healed. Won't it,
Oribases? Won't you promise me that?

ORIBASES. You must rest, my lord.

JULIAN. What an untimely accident! Just now, when I
have so many important things to do. I can't leave
these things to Nevita. They're too important to
entrust to him, or the others. I must do all this
myself. I do feel a little tired. Most vexatious! Tell
me, Ammian, what was that accursed place called?

AMMIAN. What place, your majesty?

JULIAN. The place where the Persian spear hit me.

AMMIAN. It is called Phrygia, my lord.

MAXIMUS. Ah!

JULIAN. What? What do you say the place is called?

AMMIAN. My lord, the village there is called Phrygia.

JULIAN. Ah, Maximus! Maximus!

MAXIMUS. Betrayed!

*He covers his face and sinks down at the foot of
the bed.*

ORIBASES. My lord, what makes you so distressed?

JULIAN. Nothing, nothing. Phrygia? I see. Then Nevita
and the others had better take charge of things. Go
and tell them –

AMMIAN. My lord, they have already, on your behalf –

JULIAN. Have they? Yes, well, that's good. The world-will
    has tricked me, Maximus.

MAKRINA. Your wound is opening, my lord.

JULIAN. Oh, Oribases, why did you try to hide it from me?

ORIBASES. Hide what, my lord?

JULIAN. I've got to die. Why didn't you tell me before?

ORIBASES. Oh, my Emperor!

BASIL. Julian, Julian!

He throws himself weeping by the bed.

JULIAN. Basil – my friend and brother – we two have
    known happy days together. You mustn't weep
    because I'm leaving you so young. It isn't always a
    sign that the gods are displeased with a man if they
    take him away before he grows old. What is death? Is
    it anything but paying one's debt to the ever-changing
    kingdom of dust? No tears! Do we not all love
    wisdom? And does not wisdom teach us that the
    highest happiness belongs to the life of the soul and
    not that of the flesh? Thus far the Galileans are right,
    although – but we won't talk of that. Had the powers
    of life and death granted me time to complete a
    certain pamphlet, I think I might have –

ORIBASES. Oh, my lord, does it not tire you to talk
    so much?

JULIAN. No, no, no. I feel strangely light and free.

BASIL. Julian, my beloved brother – have you nothing you
    wish to recant?

JULIAN. What should I?

BASIL. Is there nothing you regret, Julian?

JULIAN. I have nothing to regret. The power which
    circumstances placed in my hands, and which is an
    expression of the divine spirit, I used as best I knew.
    I never wished to do any man wrong. I had good and

valid cause for embarking on this campaign; and
although some might feel that I have not achieved all
I might have, they should remember that there is a
mysterious power outside and above us which to an
essential degree determines the outcome of human
enterprises.

MAKRINA (*whispers to* ORIBASES). Oh, listen. How heavily
he's breathing!

ORIBASES. His voice will soon fail him.

JULIAN. As regards the choice of my successor, I shall not
presume to advise you. Eutherius, you will divide my
possessions among those who have been closest to me.
I shall not leave much; for I have always believed that
a true disciple of wisdom – What is this? Is the sun going
down already?

ORIBASES. No, my lord. It is still broad day.

JULIAN. Strange. I thought it seemed to grow so dark
before my eyes. Yes, wisdom, wisdom – ! Cling to
wisdom, my good Priskos! But keep yourself always
armed against that which lies beyond wisdom –
the unknown and unknowable that – has Maximus
left me?

MAXIMUS. No, my brother.

JULIAN. My throat is burning. Can't you cool it?

MAKRINA. Drink this water, my lord. (*She holds a cup to
his lips.*)

ORIBASES (*whispers to* MAKRINA). His wound is bleeding
inwardly.

JULIAN. Don't weep. No Greek must weep for me. I am
ascending to the stars. Beautiful temples – ! Visions – !
But so far away.

MAKRINA. What is he talking about?

ORIBASES. I don't know. I think he's delirious.

JULIAN (*his eyes closed*). It was granted to Alexander to
ride in triumph into Babylon. I would like to do that

too. Beautiful youths with vine-leaves in their hair –
dancing maidens – but so far away! Beautiful earth –
beautiful life on earth – ! (*Opens his eyes wide.*) Oh,
Sun, Sun! Why did you betray me? (*Dies.*)

ORIBASES (*after a moment's silence*). That was death.

OTHERS. Dead – dead!

ORIBASES. Yes, now he is dead.

> BASIL *and* MAKRINA *kneel in prayer*. EUTHERIUS *covers
> his head. The sound of trumpets and drums is heard in
> the distance.*

A CRY FROM THE CAMP. Long live Emperor Jovian!

ORIBASES. Ah! Did you hear that cry?

AMMIAN. General Jovian has been proclaimed Emperor.

MAXIMUS (*laughs*). Jovian – the Galilean! Yes – yes – yes!

ORIBASES. They lost no time. They didn't even wait to
know if he was –

PRISKOS. Jovian! The victorious hero who saved us all!
Emperor Jovian is certainly worth a panegyric. I hope
that artful Kytron hasn't already – ! (*Hurries out.*)

BASIL. Forgotten, even before your hand grew cold. And
for this fleeting glory you sold your immortal soul.

MAXIMUS (*gets up*). The world-will shall answer for
Emperor Julian's soul.

MAKRINA. Do not blaspheme. I know you loved him. But –

MAXIMUS (*goes closer to the body*). Loved him – and
tricked him. No, not *I*! Tricked like Cain! Tricked like
Judas! Your God is a wasteful God, Galileans! He
demands many souls. Were you not the right one
either, poor victim on the altar of necessity? What is
life worth? Everything is a game, a hazard. To *will* is
to be forced to *will*! Oh, my beloved, all the signs
betrayed me, all the omens spoke with two tongues,
so that I saw in you the One who would reconcile the
two kingdoms. But the third kingdom shall come! The

spirit of man shall enter into its inheritance – and then shall offerings of atonement be lit for you and for your two guests at the symposium. (*He goes.*)

MAKRINA (*gets up, pale*). Basil – did you understand what the pagan was saying?

BASIL. No. But I realize now that here before us lies a glorious and broken instrument of God.

MAKRINA. Yes. A precious instrument, and one for which a terrible price was paid.

BASIL. O Christ, Christ, where were Thy people that they did not hearken unto Thy voice? Emperor Julian was a rod to scourge us. Not unto death, but unto resurrection.

MAKRINA. His ways are mysterious and terrible. How shall we understand them?

BASIL. Is it not written: 'Some vessels are created for dishonour, and some for glory'?

MAKRINA. Oh, my brother, let us not seek to fathom that abyss. (*She bends over the corpse and covers its face.*) Deluded soul – if you were forced into delusion, it shall surely be forgiven you on the latter day when the Mighty One shall descend upon a cloud to judge the living who are dead and the dead who are alive.